THE BEST SHORT PLAYS *1968*

BOOKS AND PLAYS *by Stanley Richards*

BOOKS:

Best Short Plays of the World Theatre: 1958–1967
Canada on Stage

PLAYS:

Through A Glass, Darkly
August Heat
Sun Deck
Tunnel of Love
Journey To Bahia
O Distant Land
Mood Piece
Mr. Bell's Creation
The Proud Age
Once To Every Boy
Half-Hour, Please
Know Your Neighbor
Gin and Bitterness
The Hills of Bataan
District of Columbia

Chilton Book Company
PHILADELPHIA / NEW YORK / LONDON

THE BEST SHORT PLAYS *1968*

The Margaret Mayorga Series

edited by STANLEY RICHARDS

First Edition

Published in Philadelphia by Chilton Book Company
and simultaneously in Ontario, Canada,
by Thomas Nelson & Sons Ltd.

Library of Congress Catalog Card Number 38-8006
Designed by Adrienne Onderdonk Dudden
Manufactured in the United States of America by
Vail-Ballou Press, Inc., Binghamton, New York

to Margaret Mayorga

"When my cue comes,
call me,
and I will answer."

S. R.

CONTENTS

INTRODUCTION

One of the many pleasant aspects of being an editor and anthologist is that moment or two when he is permitted alone on stage to offer his introductory comments. An introduction to a collection is as de rigueur as an aperitif is to a well-planned dinner party. Without either, there is a seeming air of inhospitality. At least tradition promulgates this theory and practice and while, personally, I contend that plays in a collection ought to possess enough stamina and voice to stand up and speak out for themselves, nonetheless, I am most pleased to have this opportunity to share the spotlight, at least momentarily, with the fifteen outstanding dramatists who dominate these pages.

To begin with, one of the most difficult of all human predicaments is to be next in line of succession. Almost any prominent scion, protege, politician or theatrical cast replacement will corroborate this for until the shadow of his immediate predecessor fully has retired into the wings, he stands not firmly but rather one footed in the soil of comparison.

As a former contributing playwright to Margaret Mayorga's noted annuals, *The Best Short Plays,* I now find myself in this prestigious yet singular position. To literally replace Miss Mayorga is impossible for, as shall be noted in a moment, she is irreplaceable. Consequently, the most a new editor of her long-established series must do is make a concerted effort to fully and significantly complement her pioneer and distinguished accomplishments in the field of the short play.

While the history of the one-act play, now more fashionably described as the "short" play, goes back through the centuries, it didn't stir the consciousness of American audiences until 1915, the year that the Washington Square Players (later to become the nucleus of the Theatre Guild) commenced its career with a program of one-act plays at the Bandbox Theatre, New York. During their three-year existence, this enterprising group presented more than sixty one act plays, many of them outstanding and some which now are regarded as modern classics. Among the authors who contributed to their noteworthy repertoire were: Susan Glaspell, Zona Gale, Theodore Dreiser, Ben Hecht, Edward Goodman, Philip Moëller, George Cram Cook, Elmer Rice, Lawrence Langner and Zoë Akins.

In 1916, the one-act play took an even more significant step forward with the Provincetown Players' staging of Eugene O'Neill's first produced play, *Bound East for Cardiff.*

A firm exponent of the principle that "the roots of drama have to be in life," O'Neill's short plays of the sea (four of which eventually were collected under the title of *S. S. Glencairn*) were drawn from his own personal knowledge and experience as a seaman. They also reflected a brilliant insight into the human heart and condition and succeeded in elevating the American one act play to new artistic levels as well as unprecedented critical acceptance of the form.

As Miss Mayorga previously has noted, it was O'Neill's early short plays that also aroused public awareness to the new social development in American drama. Until his emergence, the short play field, by and large, was brimming with works of inconsequential nature and often, creaky craftsmanship. Most examples of the genre dealt with a single, frequently contrived incident rather than with themes of import and full-bodied characterizations. And most were performed within the limitations of a conventional, inflexible setting. This stringent compliancy largely was due to the profitable amateur market that had sprung from the one-actor's popularity in vaudeville where such dazzling stage luminaries as Sarah Bernhardt, Ethel Barrymore, Mrs. Patrick Campbell, Mrs. Leslie Carter and others played the two-a-day circuits in specially written playlets or truncated versions of their international successes. Spurred on by the wide public acceptance of one-act plays in the variety houses—at the time, the nation's most popular form of entertainment—the sprouting little theatres converged upon play publishers in pursuit of suitable material for their own minuscule stages and these, in the interest of luring family audiences to their premises, had to be rather simple and utterly harmless pieces of entertainment. Production-wise, they also had to be as uncomplicated as possible for in the amateur theatre of the period, ambition frequently had to be subordinated to restrictive talent availabilities and technical facilities.

Such artistic restraints are a deterrent to creative progress, of course, and this is where Margaret Mayorga, an intrepid and spirited woman, began to assert herself. As an early and dauntless crusader for the elevation of the short play to a respected art form, she resented the contrivances that were passing for "native drama" in the nation's widespread little theatre movement. Propelled by the accomplishments of the Washington Square Players and the achievements of Eugene O'Neill, Miss Mayorga determined that the propitious moment had arrived to introduce a collection of outstanding short plays of serious caliber and professionalism to the American public. Thus, in 1919, she published the first anthology of short plays to be compiled in this country: *Representative One-Act Plays by American Authors.*

The volume was hailed in the press by many of the era's leading drama authorities including Kenneth Macgowan, who was associated with O'Neill and Robert Edmond Jones at the Provincetown Playhouse. In reviewing the book, he wrote: "The significance of this becomes considerable when one considers that, except for a few short farces, no one-act plays of any merit were in existence half a century ago."

Miss Mayorga foresaw a steady progression for the modern short play now that American dramatists (to a large extent, influenced by Continental authors) had discovered that "plays might be unified about a single dramatic idea, that they could round out a social or domestic theme instead of sprawling through a romantic or melodramatic narrative."

It is axiomatic that no dramatic work can endure if its thesis is not rooted in the inner truths of life. A play in its highest estate must reveal man's deepest insight and dramatically explore and express those values by which he lives. Without these basic elements of truth and humanity, the theatre is left with nothing more than shallow contrivances.

It was not only the growth of the centralized idea in drama and the exploration of the human condition that stimulated the development of the one act play; there also were the burgeoning "art theatres" of post-World War I which encouraged experimentation and provocative ideas on their stages. The short play provided a resourceful area for such experimentation. Concordantly, within the shorter length and stricter technical demands of the one act play, the dramatist found an admirable and receptive means for learning and perfecting his craft.

(It is a misconception to believe that an effective short play is comparatively simple to write. As the late John van Druten noted: "The one-act play seems to me quite extraordinarily difficult of achievement, needing enormous compression, and a high degree of technical facility.")

When, in 1937, Miss Mayorga published the second enlarged edition of her *Representative One-Act Plays by American Authors* the verdict of the press was: "This substantial volume has served its purpose valiantly. A wise and illuminating picture of what the one-act play has meant in the American theatre."

Instead of idly basking in the light of such recognition, Miss Mayorga decided to press on and in that same year, 1937, she launched her annuals, *The Best Short Plays,* and for the next twenty-five years (and until her retirement in 1962) she remained a salient force in establishing the short play as a vivid and esteemed branch of American drama. She was also instrumental in elevating a number of erstwhile "new" dramatists to the vanguard of eminent modern playwrights. During her tenure as editor of this influential series, among those whose works she published for the first time or whose plays initially appeared in her collections are: Tennessee Williams, William Inge, William Saroyan, Arthur Miller, Edward Albee, Lynn Riggs, Arthur Laurents, Tad Mosel, Betty Smith, Robert Ardrey, Paul Green, Archibald MacLeish, N. Richard Nash, Norman Rosten, Arnold Perl, Horton Foote and dozens of others.

As Shakespeare's Antipholus of Syracuse observed in *The Comedy of Errors,* "there's a time for all things" and, surely, providence could not have proffered a more auspicious moment for a new editor to assume the reins of *The Best Short Plays* for within the past few years there has been an extraordinary and unparalleled recrudescence of the short play throughout the world. Even hardened, commercially-minded Broadway witnessed this phenomenon during the recent 1966–67 season. As this book was being prepared, three of its prevailing successes were productions of short plays: Robert Anderson's *You Know I Can't Hear You When the Water's Running;* Peter Shaffer's *Black Comedy;* and the Sheldon Harnick–Jerry Bock musical triad, *The Apple Tree.* And to gild the lily, there was (off-Broadway) Jean-Claude van Itallie's devastating three-part sampler of contemporary Americana: *America Hurrah.*

Having four enormously successful presentations of short plays running *concurrently* on the New York stage was unprecedented in the modern professional theatre. And to stretch the significance a bit further, Otis L. Guernsey Jr., editor of the theatre yearbook, honored all *four* of the aforementioned presentations as among the "ten best plays of the New York theatre season, 1966–1967."

As this introduction is being written, the current seems to be sustaining: Broadway's outstanding success of the incumbent season is Neil Simon's trio of short comedies, *Plaza Suite,* while off-Broadway's number one dramatic venture is Israel Horovitz's double bill headed by *The Indian Wants the Bronx.*

Elsewhere in the world, authors of international stature also have proven that the short play form indeed can be an effective and rewarding area for dramatic expression and interpretation. To cite some: Peter Weiss, Jean Anouilh, Nöel Coward, Max Frisch, John Osborne, Friedrich Dürrenmatt, Harold Pinter, Jean Genet, Samuel Beckett, Peter Shaffer, Frank Marcus, Terence Rattigan, David Mercer, Brigid Brophy, Karl Wittlinger, Norman Ginsbury and Günter Grass.

In less than a decade, the short play has emerged from the ranks of largely amateur theatre to a noble place in the international professional theatre. While it may be true that commercial success does not always assure merit and distinction, nonetheless, one can not dispute the salient fact that commercial success *is* a barometrical measure of public acceptance and pleasure. And the wide acceptance of the short play in the United States and abroad in recent years as a staple of the modern stage has been and will continue to be an exciting development of the twentieth century theatre.

When Miss Mayorga first began to publish her collections, the production market was comparatively limited. In the sixties, however, it is limitless. Burgeoning urban cultural centers and regional theatres, the growth of off-Broadway and its progeny off-off-Broadway, the expansion of academic drama departments, the popularity of television drama and anthological motion pictures, international drama festivals and cultural exchange programs all have provided a mighty stimuli to the constantly increasing presentations of short plays.

As the new editor of *The Best Short Plays,* I intend to carry through with Miss Mayorga's policy of introducing outstanding young dramatists juxtaposed with important new works by established authors. And since the world has cast off isolation and time and distance have been lessened by our jet age, I also intend to give the annuals an international flavor. Foreign authors will find as much hospitality in these collections as their North American colleagues. Finally, in an admitted split with tradition, rather than including the customary ten plays in each volume, I have increased the number to fifteen.

The primary function of the theatre is, was, and forever will be entertainment. Even the most sublime of poetry, the most noble thoughts, could not exist on stage without a concomitant quota of entertainment: without the latter, we are left with little more than disembodied speeches, dull propaganda or impersonal dialectics.

When J. B. Priestley was asked to comment upon "problem plays as against entertainments," he pointedly replied: "All plays should be entertaining. Good plays are entertaining on a high level of thought and feeling. They also bring new life, new characters, new situations, new attitudes of mind, into the theatre. The trouble with poor plays is not that they have no problems—often they have—but that they handle routine characters, routine situations, in a routine manner."

Thus, I hope to include plays that are both entertaining and dramatically stimulating. Plays that restore a sense of reality, immediacy, dramatic excitement and personal involvement to the theatre. Plays that convey the author's sense of life to us, for a work of art is a direct extension of the personality of the artist. Plays that offer pertinent commentary and dramatically striking ideas, spoken in original and articulate voices.

In short, a tall order but we are living in a mettlesome and challenging world. The challenge generally is half the excitement of the doing and now, as the new editor of *The Best Short Plays,* I accept the challenge of maintaining Margaret Mayorga's high standards and dedication to the continuing development of the short play and, in the process, I sincerely hope to add a sprinkling of my own principles and experience in a field of dramatic art that I, personally, have found amply rewarding.

STANLEY RICHARDS
New York, New York
March, 1968

THE BEST SHORT PLAYS *1968*

Karl Wittlinger

THE NIGHT NURSE

Karl Wittlinger

Karl Wittlinger was born in May, 1922, in Karlsruhe, Germany, the only child of a cabinetmaker. After completing his secondary school education, he was drafted into the military service, was wounded and taken prisoner. In 1946, he was released and, shortly after, made his first contact with the American theatre by assisting in a U.S. Army production of Thornton Wilder's *Our Town*. More than all else, this experience kindled his determination to dedicate himself solely to the theater. Yet, to support himself, he worked at intervals as a male nurse (where he absorbed much of the background and technical knowledge for *The Night Nurse*), roofer, night watchman, and interpreter. During this period, he also managed to complete his formal education and earned a Ph.D. in philosophy.

His first professional play, *The Heaven of the Defeated,* was given its premiere in Berlin in September, 1956. This was followed by a comedy, *Young Love on a Visit,* but it was his third entry, *Do You Know the Milky Way?,* that "caught fire" and established him as one of the leading dramatists of the postwar European theatre. Initially presented in Cologne, the two-character comedy soon became an international success, totaling more than 7,000 performances throughout the world. Described by a European critic as "an atomic shock-treatment for a world going mad," the play has had a number of productions in the United States, including a Broadway presentation (1961) with Hal Holbrook and George Voskovec. (It may be of interest to note that Mr. Wittlinger originally wrote *Do You Know the Milky Way?* for twenty characters and in fourteen scenes, but after reappraising the manuscript realized that he could express his thoughts more clearly and effectively by confronting his protagonist with just *one* other man, who would represent *all* the other characters in the hero's tragicomic life.)

Responding to the critical and public success of *Do You Know the Milky Way?,* Mr. Wittlinger buckled down and completed three plays in a row: *Lazarus, Children of the Shadows,* and *Two to the Right and Two to the Left.* In 1964, he received the Prize Italia (the award for best European television play of the year) for his drama, *Migration of Souls.*

Karl Wittlinger's latest stage works, *Two Men for Breakfast* and *Corinne and the Old Salt,* currently are being performed throughout Europe. The latter, another two-character comedy, has been translated into English for production in the United States and Great Britain.

The author lives with his family in an isolated house near one of the largest Swiss lakes and the time he does not devote to his writing is absorbed in woodcutting and gardening.

The publication of *The Night Nurse* in *The Best Short Plays 1968* represents Karl Wittlinger's initial appearance in book form in this country.

Characters

DR. SILENT
MR. STILL, *the patient*
GRISELDA, *the night nurse*

Scene:

A private room in a hospital

Time:

Tonight

The hospital room contains regulation varnished furniture. A couch opposite the bed. A chair. A reading lamp. Telephone. The hospital table at the end of the bed is still empty. The overhead light, fluorescent, is lit.

Dr. Silent, middle-aged, overworked and nervous, holds the pulse of the still-unconscious patient, Mr. Still. The latter is approximately the same age as the doctor—and exhausted and resigned. Griselda, the night nurse, is somewhere—or anywhere—between twenty and forty, with a never-failing, cheerful, gossipy voice.

As the lights come up, Dr. Silent is dictating to Nurse Griselda.

DR. SILENT: Do you have that—?

GRISELDA: (*Reading from her notes*) Narcotic poisoning—Phanodorm. That was about 12:50—?

DR. SILENT: Yes. (*Continuing*) The stomach was pumped—flushing interrupted because of respiration difficulties. Then, Eukraton, 100 cc.'s in thirty minutes—no reaction. (*Glancing at his watch*) 1:55—pulse 110, strong. (*He places the arm of the patient back on the bed*) Well. . .

GRISELDA: This would be the *fourth* one this year that we didn't save.

DR. SILENT: (*Sighing*) It's a mystery to me. . .

GRISELDA: This time, I'm absolutely certain. . .

DR. SILENT: We were certain about the other three, too.

GRISELDA: And each time it had to be the two of us. Fate!

DR. SILENT: Nonsense!

GRISELDA: Now, I'm prepared. When Dr. Silent has the service and I'm on night duty—then, it's time for another suicide attempt. A successful one.

DR. SILENT: Are you superstitious—?

GRISELDA: Heavens, no. And no one else in my family is either. Oh, my aunt perhaps. Just a little. She tells fortunes with cards. But that's about the extent of it. No, no, it's just our own personal bad luck, Doctor. But—how shall I put it?—tragedies like this bring two people closer together, somehow. Don't you think—?

DR. SILENT: No!

GRISELDA: Naturally, men aren't expected to have very strong feelings about such things. And just as well. After all, the differences between. . .

DR. SILENT: (*Interrupting*) Who is the other night nurse?

GRISELDA: Nurse Waltraud. Oh, dear! I still must notify her that I'm remaining on duty here. It's that first half-hour after the patient regains consciousness—that's the most crucial period. It always seems to happen then. . .

DR. SILENT: Don't talk to the patient too much. And above all, don't ask him any personal questions!

GRISELDA: Really, Doctor! When I planned to study psychology—and believe me, I would have, too, except for—but, oh, Lord, that's a long story. . .

DR. SILENT: Please! Keep it to yourself.

GRISELDA: Of course, with a patient like this it's naturally difficult. I mean: unless you really *know* a person, something about his background and. . .

DR. SILENT: He registered at the hotel as a salesman. I can't tell you any more than that.

GRISELDA: Salesman—? We never had one before—as a suicide. Surprises me, really, when you consider that. . .Though, personally, I am always exceptionally pleasant to salesmen, even when I don't intend to make a purchase.

DR. SILENT: Good! Now, notify Nurse Waltraud. . .

GRISELDA: (*Crosses to the door*) I shall be as quick as lightning. . .

DR. SILENT: One more point. . .(*Griselda stops*) On no account are you to mention his *wife* to him.

GRISELDA: (*Returning*) Oh—? Then you *do* know more than you admitted—?

DR. SILENT: Only that his wife tried to phone him.

GRISELDA: And—?

DR. SILENT: Instead of picking up the receiver, he picked up the Phanodorm.

GRISELDA: Well! That's really half a detective story right there!

DR. SILENT: Exactly. And it doesn't concern us! (*Mr. Still begins to stir*) Go on! And hurry back.

(*Griselda hastens out of the room. Mr. Still rubs his eyes*)

DR. SILENT: Is the light too bright for you?

(*Without waiting for a reply, he turns on the reading lamp and turns off the overhead light. Mr. Still takes his hand away from his face*)

MR. STILL: Thank you. What time is it?

DR. SILENT: (*Glances at his watch*) Almost two.

MR. STILL: Hm. Then it hasn't been even an hour and a half. How come they found me right away? I did lock the door—?

DR. SILENT: They broke in.

MR. STILL: At the request of my wife?

DR. SILENT: Probably.

MR. STILL: (*Miserably*) She won't let me live and she won't let me die! May I have a cigarette—?

DR. SILENT: That wouldn't be good for you just now.

MR. STILL: Why not? My heart is in miserable shape. Last year, I had an attack. A cigarette might even finish me off.

DR. SILENT: I don't attach the slightest importance to that.

MR. STILL: If you were married to my wife, even for one day—or, if you were a salesman—and I'm both. . .

DR. SILENT: You should try to sleep.

MR. STILL: I tried that. Four times already. But you insist

upon waking me: Eukraton—hm? Anyway, as far as I'm concerned, you don't need to stay here.

DR. SILENT: Nurse Griselda will relieve me in a few moments. A regulation—sorry.

MR. STILL: I won't jump out the window. That would be too unappetizing for me.

DR. SILENT: I'm glad that you're reacting so sensibly. . .

MR. STILL: And I'm glad that you're not asking any stupid questions.

DR. SILENT: (*Shrugs his shoulders*) For that, we have psychiatrists.

MR. STILL: Just because you're so astonishingly normal for a doctor, it would interest me to know what you think of it?

DR. SILENT: Of what?

MR. STILL: Of a man who attempts to kill himself because his wife talks too much. Do you find that ridiculous?

DR. SILENT: On the contrary. To me that is really the only defensible motive for suicide. That's why I'm still a bachelor! But I'm confronted with this problem every day, anyway. I had my heart attack last year, too.

MR. STILL: You appeal to me more and more, Dr.—?

DR. SILENT: Silent.

MR. STILL: Dr. Silent! And if you could give me some advice. . .

DR. SILENT: Get a divorce!

MR. STILL: She won't agree to one.

DR. SILENT: Give her a—good reason.

MR. STILL: Even adultery is no reason to her. Just another topic for conversation. I've tried everything.

DR. SILENT: Still, your business makes you relatively independent. . . ?

MR. STILL: Yes, but—I'm not even a good salesman. Especially Orientofix. You are bound by professional secrecy?

DR. SILENT: Naturally!

MR. STILL: Orientofix is the most worthless appliance that ever was created. The death of any carpet. Beats the dirt in and sucks the wool out at the same time. The dry cleaning attachment makes the colors fade. The only positive thing about the whole damned apparatus: its manufacture is so incredibly shoddy that the thing falls apart, at the latest, three days after the guaranty runs out.

DR. SILENT: Then, why do you work for such a company?

MR. STILL: The company itself is first class: organization, publicity, commission—everything ideal! Only the appliance isn't any good. But that has little or no influence on sales. Orientofix sells splendidly.

DR. SILENT: But still, wouldn't you prefer to represent an article about whose quality you were convinced—?

MR. STILL: No, that would be too discouraging.

DR. SILENT: Why—?

MR. STILL: Don't you see—our business is one constant series of disappointments. You're refused at nineteen out of twenty doors. For me, each rebuff is bearable only because of the knowledge that the customer was lucky.

DR. SILENT: And the unlucky ones at whose doors you meet with success—?

MR. STILL: I have a perfectly clear conscience. I never complete a sale without first giving the customer the true facts about Orientofix.

DR. SILENT: And, in spite of that—they buy?

MR. STILL: Naturally, sometimes after my sudden admission, I'm thrown right out. But the reaction of most women—and my customers are almost exclusively women—generally is exactly the opposite: first, the shock—speechlessness. And then they sign.

DR. SILENT: The contract?

MR. STILL: Yes. Most of them, simply because they find it quite touching that such examples of decency still exist in this world.

DR. SILENT: And the others—?

MR. STILL: Because they suspect personal reasons. And they're not too wrong, for I find this kind of sympathy rather touching, too. Really, the nicest women are always those who react just this way. But even in those cases where I'm spared anything worse, at the very least, a condition of confidence is created. And when a woman has once grabbed hold of a confidence—well, she suddenly erupts like a volcano. Two, three, as much as six hours, I sit in this hell of the most intimate disclosures, or still worse—under the rain of ashes of absolute trivia. Oh, Doctor—why didn't you let me die?

DR. SILENT: (*Sighs understandingly*) I'm not permitted to.

MR. STILL: But you do understand me now?

DR. SILENT: Oh, yes! Even at this moment, there's a patient waiting for me in the private wing. She comes now and then just to talk herself out with the only person in whom she has faith—and *I* am that person. It will be a long night for me!

MR. STILL: Then you're familiar with that, too.

DR. SILENT: I enjoy the confidence of about a half dozen women patients, several nurses, two lady doctors, one laboratory assistant, and a midwife.

MR. STILL: At least, you can rest up in between. But with me, it continues without pause. When I return to the hotel in the evening, wherever I happen to be, my wife's call is always waiting for me. And these conversations last—well, to give you an idea: our telephone bills average between four and five hundred dollars a month. Three-fourths of my earnings!

(*The telephone rings. Dr. Silent answers it*)

DR. SILENT: Dr. Silent. . . .Mrs. K.? No, no, you aren't disturbing me. Just that I *am* in the middle of a very difficult operation. But we're all hurrying as much as possible. . . .Where is it cracking? In the knee? That's very serious indeed— Just a minute, please! (*As an aside*) Doctor, we'll have to interrupt this operation. Mrs. K. needs me rather urgently! (*Into the telephone*) What was that—? No, no. . .spectators are *not* permitted. Perhaps if you were to ask the Director. . .Unfortunately, Mrs. K., I'm not in a position to do it. (*Aside*) Now, close up the abdominal wall temporarily. Use the large needle. And tomorrow, we'll continue. Until then, gentlemen! (*Into the telephone*) Well, that's taken care of! I'll be with you in a moment or two—yes, just long enough to remove my gloves and wash my hands! (*He hangs up the receiver*)

MR. STILL: I see you don't have it very easy either.

DR. SILENT: Sometimes I think of Phanodorm, too.

(*Nurse Griselda returns. She carries her knitting and a book*)

DR. SILENT: (*To Griselda*) I must see Mrs. K. at once. . .

GRISELDA: Oh, is she here again?

DR. SILENT: Have you told Nurse Waltraud where you are—?

GRISELDA: Yes. She wanted to lie down for a bit—but on the other hand, she has a stack of letters to write. . .so she says. But I'd like to know *who to!*

DR. SILENT: Yes, yes—all right. (*Introducing her to Mr. Still*) This is Nurse Griselda.

GRISELDA: (*Shakes hands with him*) Without a doubt, you are in the best of hands now. If you think about it, tomorrow morning you'll clutch your head and say: "How could I have!"

DR. SILENT: Mr. Still is still very tired. . .

GRISELDA: I'm not surprised, after such goings on. . .

DR. SILENT: . . .and would like to sleep.

GRISELDA: Exactly. And so I brought along something to knit. And a book. Oh, but I can't show that to him; it's really too silly! (*She shows the book to Mr. Still*) *The Night With His Friend*—of course, that could mean all sorts of things, but I haven't gotten that far yet.

DR. SILENT: Listen, Nurse! Mr. Still has only one single wish right now!

GRISELDA: Immediately granted!

DR. SILENT: He doesn't want to talk!

GRISELDA: Now, really, Doctor, who could he talk with? There won't be a soul in here, except me.

DR. SILENT: Not with you either!

GRISELDA: After all, he doesn't even know me yet.

DR. SILENT: At the moment, he doesn't want to get to know *anyone.*

GRISELDA: In other words. . .

DR. SILENT: Yes. Keep your mouth shut! Otherwise, I'll have to ask you to take over the ward, and assign Nurse Waltraud. . .

GRISELDA: Nurse Waltraud!! Now I've got to laugh—hahaha!—or, am I not allowed to *laugh* anymore?

MR. STILL: (*Dismally*) Oh, Doctor, why didn't you let me die?

DR. SILENT: (*To Griselda*) Did you hear that?

GRISELDA: Naturally, although. . .(*To Mr. Still*). . .if you ask *me*. . .

MR. STILL: (*Softly*) I'm not asking you!

DR. SILENT: (*To Griselda*) Will you promise me then. . . ?

GRISELDA: (*Nodding vigorously*) You see, I'm just nodding my head. I'm not even saying "yes" at all.

DR. SILENT: Let us hope that you keep it up.

GRISELDA: You can rely on. . .(*Horrified, she claps her hand to her mouth*) Forgive me!

DR. SILENT: (*Shakes hands with Mr. Still*) Sleep well!

MR. STILL: Thanks.

DR. SILENT: I should thank you, too.

MR. STILL: Perhaps we could stay in touch.

DR. SILENT: Call me when you're nearby.

MR. STILL: I'll be back again next Tuesday.

DR. SILENT: Well, then—goodbye.

MR. STILL: Goodbye.

(*Dr. Silent leaves. Nurse Griselda closes the door behind him, then sits down on a chair and glances over at Mr. Still*)

GRISELDA: (*Finally*) I'm sorry! I'm not allowed to turn off the light. (*Pause*) I hope you're able to sleep with that horrible glare. (*Pause*) Not everybody can. . .

MR. STILL: I just need complete quiet.

GRISELDA: You shall have that—with me. (*Pause*) Except if I read, when I turn the pages they may rustle a bit. Even with the best of intentions, you can't help that sometimes. Hear—? (*She rustles the pages*) Or if I knit, the needles click, of course—like this. . .(*She clicks her needles*) Or I may whisper to myself—unintentionally, as I count the stitches. . . .(*She counts stitches and whispers*) Two-four-six-eight-ten-twelve. . .But I shall try to keep it under control! (*Whispering again*) Fourteen-sixteen-eighteen-twenty-twenty-two. . .It doesn't matter to you, does it, if I read or knit?

MR. STILL: I would rather you read until I've fallen asleep.

GRISELDA: Of course, as you wish! (*Putting her knitting aside*) But *why—?*

MR. STILL: Because you can't read and talk at the same time.

GRISELDA: Ridiculous! If you read aloud, you can read and talk at the same time. Shall I read aloud to you?

MR. STILL: No!

GRISELDA: Then, you'd rather have me knit?

MR. STILL: (*Resignedly*) It's all the same to me.

GRISELDA: A second ago you indicated that it *wasn't* all the same to you.

MR. STILL: Please. . .

GRISELDA: It's only to be expected that you'd be confused, after what you've been through! And, believe me, no one can sympathize with you more than I. . .(*Resumes counting*) Twenty-four-twenty-six-twenty-eight-thirty. Oh, now there I go! Counting aloud to myself again! That's a dreadful habit, don't you agree?

MR. STILL: (*Weakly*) Would you be so kind and open the window for a minute?

GRISELDA: (*Rising; eagerly*) I would have done that long ago, but I kept thinking you wanted absolute silence—but that's the way you delude yourself! (*Opening the window*) Generally, it's pretty quiet up here—compared to downstairs. But every now and again, you still hear *some* noise! Just pay attention for a second. . .(*She listens. Pause*) You see, that's the way it always is: if you wait for a noise, then it doesn't come! (*Suddenly, almost gleefully*) There! Did you hear that!

MR. STILL: (*Sighs*) No.

GRISELDA: Oh, I did! I have ears like a lynx! Even as a child. Once, at my aunt's house—that is, she was my uncle's second wife, so she wasn't a real aunt. Or, was she—? Anyway, Uncle Erwin is Papa's brother and for the second time. . .(*Sound of a distant automobile horn*) Surely you heard that now!

MR. STILL: (*Miserably*) Yes. . .

GRISELDA: It's very difficult to differentiate whether that was a private car or a commercial truck. From up here, they all sound alike. Now, you take the lower floors. . .(*Closing the window*) I believe I'll close it again. Street noises are poison for unstable people. They affect me the same way. (*She sits down again and knits*) Day before yesterday, directly in front of the Women's Clinic, a truck full of rocks—oh, I don't know *how many* tons!—capsized—right in the middle of a delivery! And with someone in your precarious condition, well, the *slightest* noise could tip the scales. Good heavens, that would be absolutely unthinkable!. . .I was there, after the last one, when the Director *warned* Dr. Silent: "If this sort of thing happens again, we will have to perform an autopsy." You know, of course, what that is—? An *autopsy?*

MR. STILL: (*Indifferently*) Post-mortem.

GRISELDA: Yes. I believe the one is Greek, the other Latin. At first, I always thought it was called autopsy with men and post-mortem with women. Really, what an incredible little dolt I used to be! Above all, I couldn't keep anything to myself. I always had to blab everything right away, like a waterfall! You see, I'm the type who must think out loud and that jars the nerves of some people. Even my own, occasionally. But sometimes, I just can't control myself. . . .However, I've gotten noticeably quieter, almost uncommunicative, at least that's the way it sometimes seems to me. And you can imagine why: one simply experiences too much—as a nurse. One fate after the other! For each man has his fate! You, too, after all; but I'm not going to become inquisitive. No, you never can reproach me for that. Nor can Dr. Klemm. He's our head doctor and he can run to the Director as often as he wishes, but he won't *ever* get rid of me! He'll go first, I'll vouch for that! There are enough doctors, but nurses—? And the Director knows that only too well, I can assure you! Just because I may talk a bit more than the others. . . Yet, there are others who talk a bit *less* than I do, so I think that balances things! Everything in life balances out. Now, how did you ever start me on this subject? Oh, yes. . .with the autopsy or, as you say, *post-mortem*. I believe the one is Greek and the other Latin. Or possibly the other way round. But it all amounts to the same thing in the end. Anyway, we're faced with a riddle: *four suicide attempts,* one after the other, and always the *same* course of events—stomach pumped, Eukraton injected—are you familiar with *Eukraton?*

MR. STILL: (*Weakly*) Yes.

GRISELDA: Very new; comes from America. They don't really have to pump out the stomach at all any more before using Eukraton. But the Director still is a bit conservative or perhaps merely conscientious. On the other hand, though, we're getting more and more modern, too. In the fall—or, it may be during the winter—we're getting a heart-lung machine. I'm awfully delighted! I hope we'll have a couple of acute cases *immediately.* I'm dying to see if the thing *really* works. Well, we'll soon find out, won't we—? If you ask me, surgery as a whole gradually is becoming one, single, giant, technical machine! I'm sure I'll live to see the day when they won't even need the patient himself any more! But what was I about to say—? (*Thinks quickly*). . . Oh, yes, with suicide attempts it's always the same with us—heart, circulation—everything in good shape—I stay with him so no one disturbs him—and after ten minutes—done for, *gone!* Except, in one case it was *twenty* minutes—and that poor man was hard-of-hearing, too: only got half of everything. Anyway, I find it very sensible of the Director to finally order that the next one be *dissected*. There must be *some* reason for all of this. . .

MR. STILL: (*Quietly*) I could tell him. . .

GRISELDA: Now, hush! You don't know any more than your three predecessors! Naturally, you'd blame everything on your wife—but we women are used to that! I always say: what use is the whole equal rights business to us. . .(*Mr. Still turns to the wall*). . .but, of course, you men don't like to hear that. You just turn away! And I'll tell you why: you all know something isn't quite right there! And that applies to you, *too,* Mr. Still! Yes, sometimes it just *has* to be said. And better today than tomorrow! Until you understand that—sincerely—there's no help for you. I can't help you, either. Until you willingly shake off this horrible distrust. Or do you think I'm going on about this purely out of curiosity? Well, I am not curious. Nor does your wife interest me in the slightest. But I can just picture everything so well—we women have a *sixth sense* for such things: how your wife sits there, opposite you—anxious to discuss everything, completely frank and unrestrained. Perhaps she has her knitting in her lap, too. . .

MR. STILL: (*Sits up, abruptly, and stares*) Absolutely right! She knits at the same time, too.

GRISELDA: Now, you see—don't I know that though! I've gone through it myself—and more than once!

MR. STILL: (*Groans weakly*) *Three times.* I know.

GRISELDA: No, no! I'm not talking about you and the others. I'm talking about *me.* After all, even as a nurse you have some sort of private life—and about that I could tell you volumes! Especially that business with the ear, nose, and throat man last summer. But after all, that belongs to my personal life, and you would be the last person to whom I'd. . .You understand, as a woman there are certain things I just *can't* bring myself to say. So please don't persist! (*Then, lapsing into it*). . .It began toward the end of June; he was always there when I was there and I thought. . .(*Mr. Still turns over on his side again*) Do you *always* sleep facing the wall? Then you ought to move the bed so that the wall is on the right. It's not healthy to sleep on your left side; it compresses your heart. But perhaps you are one of those exceptions whose heart's on the right. . .(*Mr. Still rolls over*) Is something the matter with you? Here. Let me take your pulse. (*She takes it*) It must have reached at least 150, but Dr. Silent is convinced we're going to save you! (*She puts his arm *down*) Of course, with the other three, we were *convinced,* too. . . .Do you know what I believe sometimes? No matter how tragic each individual case may be, piecing everything together, it is somehow—how shall I put it?—a comfort, especially if one is religiously inclined. And I *am*—even if I don't think about it much. I mean, superficially and all, but people like that often are more religious than all those others. Now, where was I—? Oh, yes. Sometimes I find it good, nevertheless, that there *is* something stronger than medicine. What a horrible thought—that people might live forever! Would you like that? *I* certainly wouldn't! Naturally, I'd like a little longer. After all, I'm still young—of course, not as young as I look. I'm going to let you in on a little secret: I'm twenty-six! Now—see? You're absolutely speechless! And you, how old are you really? I'd say around forty, but men don't show their age as soon, as a rule. Forty is too young, too, of course, and well, really—I can't even *bear* to think about it!—Here you are, having a perfectly harmless little conversation with a person and all the while, you know that he soon will be *dissected*. . .(*She clamps her hand to her mouth*) Good heavens, I shouldn't have said that: it probably has upset you. Let me take your pulse! (*She takes it*) Well, now, that surprises me! (*She counts very slowly*) Boom, boom, boom—I would've sworn you had a pulse of 180 before, but it's less than fifty now. How do you explain that? It's also suspicious that you still can't sleep after so much Phanodorm. They don't get everything out with that stomach pump and I don't trust this Eukraton at all! I saw *that* with the other three! And the specific conditions aren't present in your case—no, you don't fool me! To begin with, I was going to study psychology, and *I can tell:* with you, there are purely *psychic reasons*. Something or other's preventing you from sleeping and I'm determined to discover just *what* it is! However, if I'm talking too much, all you have to do is say so. . .(*Knitting away*) I know fully how it is—when you just want to lean your head back, shut your eyes and have complete silence. . .and someone sits there and talks endlessly. There *are* such people, you know, who have absolutely *no* feeling for the other person, especially one who may be more *there* than *here*.

As a matter of fact, did you know that you can literally *talk a person to death?* (*She holds up the child's jacket which she is knitting*) Do you think that's long enough? It's for my godchild, and godchildren—any children—do grow rapidly. Now you're probably wondering why I don't have any children of my own? Naturally, I would like very much to have one! Every woman wants a child, and I *am* a woman—even though I may be a nurse. But in the first place, I wouldn't want one by just any. . .(*She looks sharply at Mr. Still*) Do close your mouth! It's not healthy to sleep with your mouth open: you'll get bronchitis. And personally, it always reminds me of—but I don't want to upset you again! Yet, to me dead people just have something *gruesome* about them, the way they just lie there, don't hear anything you say any more. That happened with those others. I didn't notice right away, of course, and kept on talking cheerfully, and wondered: "Why doesn't he say anything any more? Am I talking too much for him?" Then I stopped for a minute and thought: "Now at least he'll have to ask why I've suddenly stopped." But no, absolutely nothing at all! (*Another look at Mr. Still*) Good, I think at last he's fallen asleep! Proof again that harmless conversation has something remarkably soothing and lulling about it. Something a lot of people dispute; you, too, probably! But once the sandman takes hold of you, *who* will you have to thank for it? Not that you should feel obligated to thank me. Actually, that's part of my job. But when a person is taking such pains to be considerate, it's not exactly polite to ignore her! A nurse is a human being, too, and a person expects at least something like an echo of her thoughts. You can't trick me into thinking you've fallen asleep now!. . .I can see perfectly well that your eyes are open. Instead of staring holes through the air, it would be more beneficial if you'd give some serious thought to what I've been telling you. Before it's too late! (*Holding up the little jacket*) Now, that ought to be long enough. (*Back to Mr. Still*) Please close your mouth! I don't want you to catch cold, then blame me. . .(*Pause; then, severely*) Mr. Still, I'm urging you for the last time, will you *please* close your mouth! You know perfectly well that I'm responsible for you, and if you're merely doing that to *annoy* me. . .I could very easily turn the tables and begin to annoy *you*. Oh, I have my weapon: *silence!* (*Pause*) All right! Then, you're not going to hear any more from me—not a *syllable!* (*Pause*) Unless, of course, you ask me something and even then, just "yes" or "no." Oh, I can be very abrupt! (*Pause*) Perhaps you don't believe me? Then I had better warn you. The first one. . .he didn't believe me either. . .or, rather, it was the *second*. The first one had an attack. Suddenly leaped out of bed and flew at my throat and that did him in, thank the Lord, or else I wouldn't be sitting here now taking care of you! No, it was the second. Just imagine, he claimed that I couldn't keep my mouth shut! Oh, my, what I told him! Hah!! Rather, what I would've told him—he only got the first five minutes of it. Anyway, for him death was a blessed release, for when I *really* get wound up, you've never experienced anything like it! And you may have that chance, for you're bringing me right to that point! (*Pause*) Just wait! Keep staring harder at the ceiling, with your mouth open even wider! Lying there like a dead man! You ought to be ashamed of yourself, joking about something as sacred as death! And if you don't stop being ridiculous. . .(*Rising indignantly*) Oh, no, I won't permit it! (*She takes down the mirror and holds it in front of Mr. Still*) There! Just look at yourself! (*She hangs the mirror back in place*) Attempting to intimidate me this way. Well, you can practice it in a circus or a variety show, but not here! (*Pause*) Are you all right—? Give me your pulse! (*She takes it*) Gone, too! (*She puts his arm back*) Well, if this isn't the limit! Now listen, Mr. Still, I will *not* put up with this sort of behavior. A man without a pulse—do you know what we do with him? Close his eyes and fasten his chin up! You understand what I mean—? And that's exactly what I shall do to you now and no protest in the world will help you! It's your own fault and you've asked for it! You don't think I can—? Oh, are *you* in for a little surprise! (*She gets a cloth*) Now, for the last time, will you be reasonable—? (*Pause*) As I said: you only have yourself to blame. Eyes closed! (*She presses his eyes closed*) Chin up! (*She fastens his chin*) There! (*Then, quietly*) Now don't imagine that I hadn't noticed long ago you were really dead. . .There's just one thing that mystifies me: why you just didn't admit it, frankly, right away—? Or were you concerned that I might be frightened? After all, Mr. Still, this is my business and, as you can see, it doesn't disturb me in the slightest. Oh, it doesn't have anything to do with indifference—that's just part of it, unfortunately. And when a person knows for certain beforehand—well, there's nothing much to be done about it. Of course, there is a possibility that the autopsy will show something; but that would be, so to speak, an extra dividend. For me, at least, everything became water-clear the moment we were alone together. And you never can blame me for not doing what I could! I talked my mouth half off—even after I already knew you'd surrendered, but I just didn't want to call your attention to it. You can't ask any more from a nurse—and fate is simply fate! (*She picks up the telephone and dials a number*) Mrs. K.? This is Nurse Griselda. Is Dr. Silent still with you?. . .I know, and I'm terribly sorry. But in cases of death, and especially. . .Oh, I just don't know *how* I'm going to break it to him. . .Hello? Hello—?? Oh, it's you, Doctor. Yes, as I was just saying to Mrs. K., I've been trying to summon up the courage to tell you. . .really, it's just too dreadful. . .Hello—? Oh, it's you again, Mrs. K.? He's already on his way—? I'm sure you think it's highly improper, but on the other hand, it's the *fourth* successful suicide in a row. . . .Yes, I'll be glad to tell you everything in detail tomorrow. . . .No, no, that was in February. You mean the third one—? Well, yes, I can tell you all about that one, too. I hear him at the door! Tomorrow! Goodbye. (*She hangs up, as Dr. Silent enters hurriedly, but exhausted*) It just doesn't make sense; yet, we were *certain,* weren't we—? (*Dr. Silent bends over the dead patient; then straightens up again*) Strophanthin—?

DR. SILENT: Too late. When did it happen—?

GRISELDA: Five minutes ago, perhaps. . .

DR. SILENT: Why didn't you summon me immediately?

GRISELDA: It may have been longer. I thought he was asleep. Only, when I was about to take his pulse again—well, you can imagine what a shock it gave me! For a minute or two, I wasn't able to utter a sound. I was absolutely tongue-tied!

(*Dr. Silent wearily sits down on the couch*)

DR. SILENT: Bring me a glass of water.

GRISELDA: Your heart? (*Filling the glass*) Oh, and I've been thinking of nothing else all this time: the poor doctor has to put with the babbling of that Mrs. K. for hours again, and nothing strains a person more. . .(*Handing him the water*) Let's hope *you* hold out!

DR. SILENT: (*Indicates Mr. Still*) And now this! (*He washes the pill down*)

GRISELDA: I'm still *absolutely speechless!*

DR. SILENT: (*Pensively*) We must find the cause. . .

GRISELDA: Yes, I told *him* that, too!

DR. SILENT: (*Looks up, sharply*) What—did you tell him?

GRISELDA: Exactly what you said: that we were faced with an unfathomable mystery! Three consecutive suicides—*all* ending with an exit.

DR. SILENT: Nurse Griselda! Are you crazy—?

GRISELDA: That calmed him down immediately, of course. Especially after I'd explained that all good things come in *threes*—or something similar—and we'd just wait and see, so he mustn't worry too much in advance about a post-mortem. . .

DR. SILENT: How. . .(*He sits up rigidly and stares at her*) *What?*

GRISELDA: No, I believe he already was in a coma when I came to the part about the post-mortem. So, perhaps he really didn't get that at all. Everything else I just scattered around—very carefully and casually—during our conversation, so he wouldn't become too alarmed. . .

DR. SILENT: (*Leans back*) Bring me the pillow there. I have to lie down for a minute.

GRISELDA: (*Brings the pillow*) Anyway, it's all very curious: he was certain he could explain to you. . .

DR. SILENT: What?

GRISELDA: Why the three before him—and even himself, probably—had. . .

DR. SILENT: (*Turns over and exhales*) I'm aware of it, too, now. . .

GRISELDA: Really? Then at least we *have* gone a step farther! Imagine! I didn't believe him at all: I thought he was being facetious! Oh, well, they say that shortly before their death, people have second sight. . .(*Sits down again and knits*) Personally, I've never had it, but of course that would be a bad omen. And I must say, on the contrary, I've been feeling awfully good lately. . .especially since I've started eating Knäckebrot in the evening. I'd really recommend that to you, Doctor!. . .Now that you've finally solved the riddle about the cause of death, a load really has been lifted off me. Above all, now we won't need to dissect him and, quite honestly, that's what bothered me the most. You never are assured that you yourself won't be. Naturally, you can't feel anything more then—but just the idea is simply repugnant to me—even with other people! A person you knew—even if you only had a fleeting acquaintance with him—well, it doesn't matter if it's Mr. Still or you or whoever. . .Here I'm completely different from my brother, who studies biology and is always dissecting insects—under the microscope, of course, but still—and that doesn't seem to bother him a bit. That's why I would have preferred to study psychology—and even though I didn't, I'm confident now that I can use it properly. That was obvious again today! (*She looks sharply over at Dr. Silent*) Please don't, Doctor! Stare at the ceiling as long as you wish, but at least close your mouth. That's the way it began with him, too, and one's enough for me tonight! Besides—you wouldn't have any reason at all! You're here with me and anybody who even tried to disturb you would really be in for it! Oh, yes, I can be very unpleasant!! (*The telephone rings*) Just a minute, excuse me. The telephone. (*She picks up the receiver*) Who? Oh, Mrs. Still. . .(*Subdued*) Could you lower your voice, please? There are two dead men in the room. . . .Yes, how can I tell you as gently as possible? Well, one of them is your husband. Oh, that's what you thought?. . .The doctor who attended him. (*She laughs*) No, don't worry. Something like that doesn't upset me in the least—after all, it happens to us all too frequently, unfortunately. And it's nothing like what it used to be, either—you know, cholera and things like that. No, right now, I think heart and respiratory diseases are in first place, then comes cancer, and then traffic accidents. . . .Yes, awful, they're tearing the streets up in your neighborhood? Well, the quickest way, then, would be on foot: you'd still make the funeral. Just a minute, dear, I have to get a chair. (*She gets it and sits down*) Where were we? Oh, yes, or will your husband's body be transported? Exactly, especially since the doctor—at the same time—yes! (*Laughing again*). . .Double burial, that's good—oh, heavens, if it just weren't so sad!. . .Naturally! On the other hand, there's always an ample supply of doctors—as well as salesmen—while nurses —yes, exactly, Mother Nature evens everything out! (*She presses the receiver to her ear, knitting all the while*) Those are my needles. I hear yours, too, by the way. . . .Me? I'm making a little jacket for my godchild. Yes. . .that's the way it is: some *come,* others *go!*. . .No, no, we can talk as long as we want: I'm free now for the night. . . .That's what I always say: everything has two sides! (*She speaks the following final sentences faster and faster, softer and softer, as the lights gradually fade*) Oh, that's a long story! Well, listen now. I always have the night shift on Wednesdays and the doctor was changed because the Director happens to be a hunter—yes, it depends on the weather —and then, the head doctor, Dr. Klemm, substitutes for him, and Dr. Silent takes his ward and yesterday, the weather was definitely negative—only a few drops around noon—but along toward evening. . .(*Her voice trails off and the room is in complete darkness*)

Curtain

William Inge

THE CALL

William Inge

William Inge began his reign as one of America's foremost dramatists in 1950, when the Theatre Guild introduced his compelling drama, *Come Back, Little Sheba,* to Broadway audiences. In 1953, he scored again with *Picnic,* which won him both the Pulitzer Prize and the New York Drama Critics Circle Award. At its Broadway opening, critic Richard Watts, Jr. wrote: "William Inge's new work revealed the power, insight, compassion, observation and gift for looking into the human heart that we had all expected in him. . . .Here is a dramatist who knows how to set down how people behave and think and talk, who can create the feeling of a small Kansas town, and is able to write dramatic scenes that have vitality, emotional power and heartbreak. There is a true sense of the sadness and wonder of life in this new dramatist."

In 1955, Mr. Inge added another link to his chain of successes with *Bus Stop* and, two years later, *The Dark at the Top of the Stairs*—a revision of his very first play, *Farther off From Heaven,* which Margo Jones produced in 1947 at her Dallas Theatre—was hailed by press and public as an exceptionally poignant study of family relationships. Although the latter was autobiographical, the author transferred the locale of the drama from his native Kansas, where he was born in 1913, to Oklahoma.

Rated as one of the mid-century's most perceptive and sensitive dramatists, Mr. Inge's close affiliation with the theatre originated with his tenure as stage and screen reviewer for the *St. Louis Star-Times.* In addition to the aforementioned plays, his other produced stage works include: *A Loss of Roses, Natural Affection,* and *Where's Daddy?*

He now makes his home in California and presently is at work on a cycle of seven or eight short plays bearing the overall title of *Complex,* a dramatic exploration of life in a large Eastern housing development in which crime and violence abound. A personal note from the author estimates that "the cycle should be completed within the next two years or so, for production by a leading repertory company."

Unlike Mr. Inge's earlier plays with their straightforward narratives and easily grasped characterizations, *The Call*—here published for the first time—represents the dramatist in a new and intriguing light as an interpreter of surrealistic attitudes. Similarly, his other new short play, *The Disposal,* reveals him under a bulb of considerably *different* voltage as he unequivocally strips bare the emotional and mental fibers of three condemned men awaiting execution in a state penitentiary. (*Note: The Disposal* is included in this editor's collection of *Best Short Plays of the World Theatre: 1958–67*)

A volume of William Inge's earlier short plays was published in 1962 and, in that same year, he won an Academy Award for his screenplay, *Splendor in the Grass.*

Characters

TERRY

JOE

Scene

The setting is a splendid apartment on a high floor on New York's East Side, somewhere in the fifties or sixties. Terry, a trim, well groomed man, wearing a handsome dressing gown and slippers, is talking on the house phone. He is middle-aged but youthfully fit.

TERRY: (*On the house phone*) But captain, he called almost an hour ago. Didn't you see him when he called?. . .No. He still hasn't arrived. . .Yes, I'm serious. He hasn't arrived, and it was almost an hour ago when he called me from the lobby. . . I've been waiting almost an hour. Could he have got lost? Well, maybe you'd better send one of your men around the building to. . .(*The doorbell buzzes*) Just a minute. This must be he. I'll call you back if it isn't.

(*He hangs up and goes to the door, opening it to admit Joe, a middle-aged man who has let his waistline expand, and appears all of his forty-some years. He wears a colorful Oriental uniform, something like that of the Shriners. He is physically exhausted now, lugging a suitcase that appears very heavy*)

TERRY: (*To Joe*) Well, here you are! I've been wondering what could have happened. Did the elevator get stalled?

JOE: I walked up.

TERRY: What?

JOE: I don't like those elevators.

TERRY: You walked up twenty-two flights of stairs?

JOE: Things happen in those elevators that I don't like.

TERRY: Oh. . .well, perhaps. Sometimes.

JOE: You get locked inside one of those elevators and you don't know *where* it's going to take you.

TERRY: Come now.

JOE: It's true. A friend of mine came to New York and went up in one of those elevators, and we never heard from him again.

TERRY: Well, sometimes those things *do* happen.

JOE: I walk everywhere I can. I walk.

TERRY: Anyway, welcome!

JOE: (*Looking around*) Very nice place.

TERRY: Thank you.

JOE: I can tell good furniture when I see it.

TERRY: Thelma loves antiques.

JOE: You have some of those modern paintings.

TERRY: We collect a little. It's a hobby.

JOE: They confuse me.

TERRY: Really?

JOE: They're all mixed up and wild.

TERRY: Do you think so?

JOE: What do they mean, Terry?

TERRY: Oh, I don't know that they *mean* anything, Joe. They're just. . .pictures.

JOE: I like pictures that *mean* something.

TERRY: Well, I think these pictures have *meaning,* but. . .

JOE: I like pictures of things I recognize.

TERRY: Yes. Well. . .

JOE: Those pictures just hang there and scream at you, like the world. All mixed-up and crazy.

TERRY: One gets used to them.

JOE: Where's Thelma?

TERRY: Oh, she's terribly sorry that she couldn't be here to greet you, but she's rehearsing now.

JOE: Rehearsing?

TERRY: Yes. It's a great role for her. Your sister is a great actress, Joe.

JOE: Oh yes.

TERRY: She'll be home for dinner, though. She's very eager to see you.

JOE: She isn't *here,* though.

TERRY: No. She's rehearsing. It's her work, Joe. You understand that. It's her *life.*

JOE: Oh yes. I understand. She's become very important.

TERRY: Let me take your suitcase and. . .

JOE: (*Holding onto the bag*) No.

TERRY: But let me put it in your room. Maggie will unpack it for you and hang up your clothes.

JOE: No. These are my *private* things. My keepsakes. I never let anyone open it. I just carry it with me wherever I go. It's always locked.

TERRY: But where is your luggage?

JOE: I don't think I better stay here, Terry.

TERRY: What?

JOE: I just don't think I'd better stay.

TERRY: Joe! This is a sad surprise. We're expecting you, you know. Your room's all ready. We're giving you a handsome room, right over the river. You can see all the way over to Queens.

JOE: (*Looking out window*) It's not very pretty.

TERRY: Well, it's a *view.*

JOE: I think I'd better go to a hotel. (*He sets down the suitcase*)

TERRY: Joe! Don't you think you'd be happier here with us?

JOE: Well. . .I don't know, Terry. I just don't know.

TERRY: But surely you'd be happier here than at a hotel.

JOE: (*Pondering the matter*) I just don't know.

TERRY: We've been counting on you for a visit, Joe. We've got ever so many things planned for you. Shows, and concerts and. . .

JOE: Well, I don't know. I'll be a long time resting up from the parade. (*He looks out a window*) You live pretty high up here, don't you?

TERRY: Does that bother you?

JOE: I don't know. I get dizzy sometimes, Terry.

TERRY: I'm sorry, Joe. Have you been to a doctor?

JOE: Oh, they're just spells. They don't last long, except I don't like it up high.

TERRY: Oh. Well, that does make a difference, I suppose.

JOE: Yes. I get dizzy.

TERRY: Well now, sit down. We'll just talk a while, let you relax from your long trip. Did you have a good flight?

JOE: No. You see, I. . .

TERRY: Oh, I'd forgotten. You don't like to fly, do you?

JOE: No. I don't think it's right.

TERRY: I hope the trip wasn't too uncomfortable.

JOE: There were all those teenagers!

TERRY: Teenagers?

JOE: They took over the whole tourist space. They were doing all kinds of unnatural things.

TERRY: *Unnatural* things?

JOE: Yes. . .making love.

TERRY: They do exercise a new freedom.

JOE: There's a time and a place for everything, but those teenagers don't *know* it. They don't believe in *God!*

TERRY: I don't think they believe in anything, truthfully, but maybe there's hope for them yet.

JOE: I don't like them. The plane was *full* of teenagers. They all like that LSD, and smoke that marijuana stuff. They act *wild* and *crazy*. They were having a *Love-in.*

TERRY: Well, anyway, you're *here.*

JOE: Yes.

TERRY: *Do* sit, Joe. Can I get you a drink?

JOE: (*Sitting*) It don't agree with me, Terry.

TERRY: Maybe some tea? Maggie can. . .

JOE: No stimulants, Terry. No stimulants of *any* kind.

TERRY: Maybe some soda?

JOE: Don't bother. I think I'd like a glass of water. That's all.

TERRY: Well, that's certainly no problem. (*He goes to the bar*) Ice?

JOE: No. No ice. Just plain. Cold things don't agree with me.

TERRY: Very well. Here you are. (*He hands Joe a glass of water which Joe sips at slowly as if it were wine*)

JOE: Thank you.

TERRY: I'm going to have a drink, myself. Sorry you can't join me.

JOE: Oh, it's not that I can't. I'm no alcoholic or anything. It's just that it don't agree with me.

TERRY: (*At bar*) I see.

JOE: Besides, I have to lead the parade this afternoon.

TERRY: The parade?

JOE: I lead the parade for our lodge back in Billings.

TERRY: Oh, I see.

JOE: Yes. We're having a convention here. Some very fine speakers. Yes, indeed. Men who know what's wrong with the world and intend to do something about it, because if *someone* doesn't do something about it *soon,* there's not going to be any world left.

TERRY: You may be right.

JOE: These speakers are men who really *know* what they're talking about.

TERRY: Your uniform is most colorful.

JOE: Oh! Thank you.

TERRY: Yes. Most colorful.

JOE: Some people think it's gaudy.

TERRY: Oh, I don't agree.

JOE: But I think it's good for a man's pride to wear something unusual like this. . .once in a while.

TERRY: Yes, it is.

JOE: It's made of genuine Persian silk.

TERRY: That so?

JOE: The brocade was made by hand. Some little old lady who lives in the Alps.

TERRY: Beautiful.

JOE: The boots are hand-tooled Russian calfskin.

TERRY: Russian?

JOE: But that doesn't mean I'm a Communist.

TERRY: Of course not.

JOE: No, sir. I'm no Communist. Communism is something we've all got to get out and fight.

TERRY: I agree.

JOE: Where did you say Thelma is?

TERRY: Rehearsing. She's replacing Mary Martin in *Hi, Sweetie!* It's a great show. She'll be home for dinner, though.

JOE: Thelma turned out real good, didn't she?

TERRY: Yes. I guess she's about the best actress in town now. Most of the critics think so.

JOE: That's nice. I suppose you and Thelma associate with all those people.

TERRY: *What* people, Joe?

JOE: Oh, you know.

TERRY: I'm afraid I don't.

JOE: All those *big* people you read about in those magazines.

TERRY: Oh, we have a few friends who are important people.

JOE: I suppose I should see her act sometimes.

(*Terry brings his drink from the bar and sits opposite Joe*)

TERRY: Of course you will. I've got a row of seats for her opening night, just two weeks off. And we're counting on you.

JOE: Well, I. . .

TERRY: No getting out of it, Joe. You're going. It's to be a big occasion. The play is a great hit.

JOE: Well, you see, Terry, I'm not very comfortable in theatres. Too many people.

TERRY: Oh?

JOE: People make me very nervous. Especially all those people in those magazines.

TERRY: But you're here on a convention.

JOE: I don't mix much with those other fellows. I keep pretty much to myself. I just lead the parade.

TERRY: Thelma and I will have to come see the parade.

JOE: Oh, it's a very big affair.

TERRY: I should imagine.

JOE: Every major city in all the fifty states is represented.

TERRY: That so?

JOE: My lodge in Billings brought a lion.

TERRY: That so?

JOE: We parade all through Times Square and up Fifth Avenue.

TERRY: That's quite a walk.

JOE: I get my exercise. . .I don't like crowds, but I lead the parade.

TERRY: Well, it's a shame if you don't get to see your own sister in *Hi, Sweetie*.

JOE: You say she's going to replace Mary Martin?

TERRY: Yes.

JOE: Mary Martin is very lovely.

TERRY: Well, so is Thelma.

JOE: Oh, yes. Thelma is lovely, too.

TERRY: You *must* see her. She'd feel terribly hurt if. . .

JOE: Oh, it won't make any difference to Thelma if *I* don't see her. After all, she's got *lots* of friends among all those people.

TERRY: But you're her *brother*.

JOE: Yes.

TERRY: And I'm sure she's very fond of you.

JOE: Well, maybe. But people change.

TERRY: I'm going to see to it that you *see* the show.

JOE: Maybe I can go some night and stand at the back. All alone. I like to go places alone. I *think* better.

TERRY: Well, I'm sure that can be arranged, but. . .

JOE: That's the way I'd like it, Terry.

TERRY: Very well. But Thelma's going to be disappointed.

JOE: Oh. She'll understand.

TERRY: We just thought you'd enjoy her opening night.

JOE: I don't think so.

TERRY: I see. Very well. But we do want to show you a good time while you're here.

JOE: Oh, I'll be all right. Don't worry about me. I don't think about it much anymore. I mean. . .it don't bother me like it used to.

TERRY: (*Puzzled*) What's that, Joe?

JOE: Mama.

TERRY: Oh, yes. Your mother. . .

JOE: I've got used to it by now.

TERRY: That's good.

JOE: After all. . .she was almost eighty. No one lives forever.

TERRY: That's the way to look at it.

JOE: I just go about my business now like it'd never happened.

TERRY: That's what a person must do.

JOE: And the store's doing good.

TERRY: I'm glad.

JOE: The store keeps me busy.

TERRY: I'm sure.

JOE: Keeps me from thinking too much about. . .things.

TERRY: Yes. Work is good therapy.

JOE: The world is all mixed up and *wild*.

TERRY: Yes. We live today in a state of chaos.

JOE: If it just wasn't for those damn teenagers and acid-heads and LSD.

TERRY: Do they exist out in Billings, too?

JOE: They're *every*where. They're taking over the country.

TERRY: (*Smiling*) It does seem that way at times.

JOE: (*Sad again*) I still miss her sometimes, though.

TERRY: Who's that?

JOE: Mama.

TERRY: Oh, yes.

JOE: Who did you think I meant?

TERRY: I. . .I didn't know for sure.

JOE: She was a wonderful woman.

TERRY: Yes. She was.

JOE: President of all those clubs and organizations.

TERRY: Yes. She kept busy.

JOE: Every minute, until that last *spell* came.

TERRY: Yes. It's a shame about that last *spell.*

JOE: Funny thing. . .(*He smiles*) Habit is very strong, isn't it?

TERRY: What do you mean, Joe?

JOE: I mean like. . .Well, when I got off the plane at the airport. . .I don't like to fly. . .I passed the Western Union counter and I went to it and started to send a telegram home to Mother to let her know I'd arrived OK. Isn't that funny? Just habit. You see, every time I ever went anyplace, I'd always send her a telegram the minute I got there to let her know I was OK. And now. . .I still get the feeling that I've got to send her a telegram, even though. . .she's been gone. . .ten years.

TERRY: Yes. Habit is strong.

JOE: Yes. I still get that feeling.

TERRY: Well, you were very close to her.

JOE: Yes. Very close.

TERRY: I'm sure you meant a lot to her.

JOE: I was the baby of the family.

TERRY: Yes.

JOE: The others all got away, but Mama *needed me.*

TERRY: Yes. That's what Thelma said.

JOE: Thelma, and Harry, and Alice, and Tom, they all got away. They're all doing well.

TERRY: Yes.

JOE: But I was the baby. . .and Mama *needed* me when the others went away.

TERRY: It was splendid of you, Joe, to stay and take care of her.

JOE: Oh, I just did what any man would have done.

TERRY: There are many men who'd have got a nurse for her and. . .

JOE: Oh, Mama wouldn't stand a nurse being around. (*Terry is silent*) No. I was the only one she'd let help her.

TERRY: Well, I still think it was splendid of you.

JOE: This is city water, isn't it?

TERRY: I'm afraid it isn't very good.

JOE: It's got all those chemicals in it.

TERRY: I suppose we should get bottled water like most of our friends do.

JOE: I still use the water out of the cistern at home. Nice and fresh.

TERRY: How do you feel about staying here now, Joe? Do you think you. . .

JOE: I think I'd better get me a little hotel room, Terry.

TERRY: Thelma's going to be very disappointed.

JOE: I'd just feel more myself in a little hotel room. On a low floor. I get dizzy up here.

TERRY: Well. . .you know best.

JOE: I never did get used to being in other people's houses.

TERRY: But you should regard Thelma and me as family, Joe.

JOE: Oh, I do, Terry. I think the world of you and Thelma. But just the same, I think I'd feel better in a little hotel room.

TERRY: Very well.

JOE: Sometimes I don't sleep.

TERRY: Sometimes Thelma and I don't, either.

JOE: When I don't sleep, I like to get up and walk around.

TERRY: That's all right.

JOE: Sometimes I walk around half the night, thinking.

TERRY: You wouldn't disturb us.

JOE: Oh, I might.

TERRY: Well, there's a small hotel at the corner, but. . .

JOE: You just said a song title.

TERRY: What?

JOE: "There's a Small Hotel."

TERRY: Oh.

JOE: We used to play a game. Whenever anyone said a song title, he had to make a forfeit.

TERRY: I can call and make a reservation.

JOE: What?

TERRY: A hotel. Make a reservation.

JOE: Don't bother, Terry. I don't want to be any trouble. I'll go out walking pretty soon, and I'll just stroll along until I find a place that looks right. I'll know the place when I see it. I'm funny that way. It's instinct. I just walk into a place and know if I'm going to be comfortable there. That's what I did last August when I went to the fair in Omaha. I just walked along the street until I *found* a place.

TERRY: But you'll be here for dinner, won't you?

JOE: To tell the truth, Terry, I guess you'd better not count on me. You see, I'm on a very strict diet. No salt.

TERRY: Well, I think Maggie can arrange a salt-free dinner for you.

JOE: No. It would be an imposition.

TERRY: Not at all. I'll tell Maggie not to put salt in her cooking tonight, and Thelma and I can salt our own food as we please.

JOE: That's very kind of you, but just the same, I'd feel better eating out. Then I wouldn't feel I was in the way.

TERRY: Very well, Joe.

JOE: I just never did get used to. . .other people's houses.

TERRY: But you'll want to see Thelma, won't you?

JOE: I'll drop in and see Thelma after I've had my supper. Yes, I'll come up and we'll talk about old times.

TERRY: She's been looking forward to seeing you.

JOE: Oh, I doubt very much if it'll break her heart, or anything.

TERRY: But Thelma's fond of you.

JOE: Just the same, she's got her *work*. That's her *life*.

TERRY: But she always has time for those she loves.

JOE: I *like* Thelma.

TERRY: I'm glad.

JOE: Thelma's very nice. Thelma has always been much nicer, for instance, than Alice.

TERRY: Is that so?

JOE: Alice isn't always very nice. Alice was very *grabby* about things when Mama died.

TERRY: I wouldn't know.

JOE: Alice always looks out for *Number One.*

TERRY: Some people are like that.

JOE: But maybe we should feel sorry for Alice. She didn't make a good marriage.

TERRY: Howard always seemed a good sort whenever they came here to visit.

JOE: I don't think Alice made a very good marriage.

TERRY: Well, I wouldn't know about the personal side of things.

JOE: The personal side is not good.

TERRY: That's too bad.

JOE: I don't know if Thelma told you, but he betrays her.

TERRY: Oh!

JOE: You would never *betray* Thelma, would you?

TERRY: Certainly not.

JOE: Alice has threatened to leave Howard.

TERRY: Really!

JOE: But they've been together so long.

TERRY: True.

JOE: Sometimes people just stay together that way, because they don't know what else to do.

TERRY: Yes. Some people don't know what else to do.

JOE: Alice and I don't have much in common anymore. Even though we *are* brother and sister.

TERRY: Too bad.

JOE: People grow apart.

TERRY: True.

JOE: Thelma has really made something of herself. I'm always reading about her in all those magazines.

TERRY: I'm proud of her.

JOE: She always was talented.

TERRY: I'm sure.

JOE: But then, she was one of the older ones. She got away.

TERRY: How's that?

JOE: I say, she got away.

TERRY: Oh. . .yes.

JOE: Like Harry and Alice and Tom. They *all* got away. (*A pause*) *I* had a little talent.

TERRY: That so?

JOE: Yes. I had quite a little. I used to do. . .all sorts of things.

TERRY: I didn't know.

JOE: At the university, I did some very unusual things.

TERRY: I didn't know.

JOE: People talked a great deal about some of the things I did.

TERRY: I didn't know.

JOE: I was considered *gifted*.

TERRY: Yes, gifted.

JOE: I could have developed.

TERRY: I'm sure.

JOE: I see important people today who don't have what I did. People you read about in those magazines.

TERRY: Joe, I'm most sorry that you don't feel you should stay with us.

JOE: Oh, I'll be all right, thank you.

TERRY: Well, I'll be dressing, Joe. If you'll wait, I'll have a walk with you and help you find a hotel.

JOE: Whatever you say.

TERRY: I'll be just a few minutes. There are all sorts of new magazines to keep you interested.

JOE: Oh, I never read those magazines. They're always full of stories about what those people are doing. I get tired reading about those people.

TERRY: I'm not sure I know who you. . .

JOE: Oh, you know. All those *people*.

TERRY: I'm not sure.

JOE: Oh, *you* know. Don't pretend you and Thelma don't know.

TERRY: Well, if you want anything, just go to the kitchen and ask Maggie.

JOE: I'd like to place a call.

TERRY: Go right ahead.

JOE: I don't have a credit card.

TERRY: That's all right.

JOE: But you've got to promise to bill me.

TERRY: Forget it.

JOE: No. I'm serious. I don't believe in making long distance calls at other people's homes and leaving the bill for them to pay.

TERRY: Very well. If you insist. See you presently.

(Terry exits into another room. Joe sits a few moments and then goes to the telephone at the desk. He dials. He waits. Then the sound of a voice comes from the receiver)

JOE: But there *is* such a number, Operator. I'm certain.

(The sound of a voice again. Joe hangs up. He thinks for a moment and then dials again. Again the voice comes from the receiver)

JOE: Operator, if you'd just let the number ring, I'm sure to get an answer soon. (*Pause*) But there *is* such a number. If you'd only let me through! (*Pause*) I'm certain of the number. If you'd only let me through, let me *through.* (*Pause*) Operator, you keep interfering. If you just wouldn't interfere, the call would go *through.* (*Pause. He is beginning to sound desperate*) But there *is* such a number. You can't tell me it doesn't exist. I know better. (*Pause*) That's what you always tell me, but there *is.* You just won't put me *through.* Please! Please, operator, *please* put me through. The call is very important to me. I keep trying to put it through, and you always interfere. I've got to get *through.* It's a case of absolute necessity. You might almost say, it's a matter of life and death. (*Pause*) No! Don't tell me there *is* no such number. Are you trying to tell me something I know does not exist? (*Pause. He begins to sound frantic*) But if you'd only let me *through!*

(The Operator cuts him off)

JOE: (*Frantic*) *Don't* cut me off! *Please!* You mustn't do that! (*He holds the telephone in one hand talking to it, not into it*) Don't you know what these things do to people's feelings? Are you trying to cut me off from everything I've ever known? From everything I've ever believed in? I *know* the number still exists, but you won't let me *through!* (*He is sobbing desperately*) You won't let me through! (*He looks at the receiver*) You *always* cut me off.

(*Finally, he brings himself to place the receiver carefully back into its cradle. He sits and waits. He sits for several moments, staring into blank space. Then, Terry appears, dressed now, very fashionably*)

TERRY: I hope I didn't take too long. Did you make your call?

JOE: I couldn't get through.

TERRY: That's too bad.

JOE: None of my calls get through anymore.

TERRY: What's that?

JOE: I never seem to have the right numbers.

TERRY: You can try again later.

JOE: No. It will be the same thing. They won't let me through.

TERRY: Shall we be off? (*Starts to pick up Joe's suitcase, but finds it too heavy to lift*) I say. . .that's heavy.

JOE: (*Anxiously*) Oh, don't pick it up. Those are my keepsakes. *I'll* carry it. (*He picks up the suitcase*)

TERRY: Your *keep*sakes?

JOE: Yes. In here, I've packed all my mementos, everything that's precious to me out of my memories.

TERRY: Do you have to carry it *everywhere?*

JOE: Yes. These things are very precious to me. *Very.*

TERRY: Of course. You must show them to me some time.

JOE: No. I don't show them anymore. People laugh. People nowadays travel around without their keepsakes.

TERRY: I'd consider them a burden.

JOE: Just the same, I can't let them go.

TERRY: (*Concerned*) Are you sure you can manage?

JOE: Oh sure, I can manage.

TERRY: But it's *extremely* heavy.

JOE: (*Proudly*) It's *not.*

TERRY: But I couldn't even *lift* it.

JOE: It's *not* heavy.

TERRY: But you don't want to have to carry such a heavy bag while we're strolling. Maybe you'd better call a hotel from here and make a reservation. Then we can take a cab.

JOE: No. It's not heavy, I tell you. I carry it with me all the time. It's not heavy at all.

TERRY: Very well.

JOE: Yes. I carry it with me all the time. It's no one's business, how heavy it is. It's no one's business but *mine.*

TERRY: Very well. Let's go.

(The two men go out together. Joe lugging the suitcase, its weight forcing him to drag his steps, and silently groan as he follows Terry out the door)

Curtain

Candice Bergen

THE FREEZER

Candice Bergen

On January 27, 1968, millions of televiewers were tuned in to Hollywood's annual *Stars of Tomorrow* ceremonies and toward the end of a glittering, tension-filled evening, the major award—for the most promising international female star of the year—was announced. The recipient was Candice Bergen who, at that moment, was not in the clouds, but high above them winging her way westward, via jet, to visit with her family in Bel Air, California.

Several hours earlier, this editor assisted the young star to a taxi which sped her to the airport and as she departed, she confidentially related: "The publication of my play *The Freezer* in *The Best Short Plays 1968* is my *real* hour of glory."

To the world's film-makers, Miss Bergen is regarded as a topline young actress who, within the comparatively brief period of three years, firmly has established herself in five major motion pictures: *The Group, The Sand Pebbles, The Day the Fish Came Out, Live for Life, the god game.* Yet, to the star herself, the play's the thing: "My writing and photography are the only things that give me any self-satisfaction."

Daughter of the noted Edgar Bergen, Candice was born on May 9, 1946, in Beverly Hills, a locale which she describes as "a modest suburb of Bel Air with vinyl trees and artificial grass and no garbage cans on the street." Her primary education took place in California, at the Cathedral School in Washington, D.C., and in Switzerland. Later, she majored in art history and creative writing at the University of Pennsylvania where, as a sophomore, she wrote the first draft of *The Freezer*. During the same period, she also won two major school awards for her acting and photography.

While attending Penn, Miss Bergen commuted regularly to New York for modeling assignments; these led to her first film, *The Group,* which she made during the summer of 1965, between semesters at the University.

In addition to a very busy acting career, she continues to turn out photo-stories for leading national magazines (her article, *Is Bel Air Burning?* was featured in the Christmas, 1967, issue of *Esquire*) and ultimately, she plans to develop *The Freezer* into a screenplay.

A beauteous blonde of Swedish descent, the authoress-actress also is an expert skier, tennis player, and horsewoman.

Miss Bergen was on location in Majorca, filming *the god game* (John Fowles' adaptation of his novel, *The Magus*), when she received word that *The Freezer* had been selected for inclusion in this volume. She promptly wrote of her delight: "It was the most momentous thing yet to occur in my lifetime. I've been unbearably cocky on the set since I found out. I'm threatening to retire. After all, what with the eventual Broadway production (I tried to create a new theatre form: a ten-minute play with an hour and a half intermission for people who would rather talk than listen.), the subsequent motion picture (with Julie Christie, Richard Burton, Oskar Werner), and merchandising rights: *Freezer* tee-shirts, *Freezer* ball-points and a link-up with Westinghouse on a refrigerator promotion—why work? Anyway, now that I'm a real writer, I have to stay poor. After all, it's for art. I'm going to cut off my ear."

Author's Note

The play is set in the year 2500, soon after the recent incorporation of The Freezing Method. *This is a scientific process reducing bodily temperature and suspending all metabolic functions for the period of one year, whereby* The Frozen One *undergoes organic renovation, i.e. chemistry check-up, plastic transplant tuning, bile filters, and plasma program.* The Freezing Method *is made compulsory for all members of the State at the age of 65, comparable to that of our present retirement. After the passage of a year on ice, one returns with a deficit of 40 years, a taut assemblage of new and partially plastic bodily organs, completely rejuvenated, physically perfected. Infinitely useful.*

Mankind is now under the aegis of a universal State, a worldwide urban renewal program. It is another attempt in history at a so-called Aryan *race. Men and women are genetically tested and paired for a modern age* immaculate conception; *the offsprings a product of the most calculated balance of physical and mental unity. It is the next* Age of Reason, *of linear logic uncolored by emotion, with only functional and functional state-oriented thoughts.* The Freezer, *however, is our nucleus as through our three characters the play attempts to demonstrate life's organisms without death.*

Characters

THE MAN: *He is our hero. He has no name; for that matter, neither do his wife nor* The State Physician. *The State doesn't think much of names. Anyway,* The Man *is our hero. He and his mate,* The Woman, *are a total statist incongruity. Making this a sci-fi* A Man and A Woman. The Man *epitomizes literacy and sophistication in an age devoid of reading matter and saturated with auditory permeation. He is the silver tongue in the golden silence. Characteristically British, there is a* Noël Coward *clink about him, a glibness, an effete pathos. The last vestige of sensitivity and intelligence, he is the State's glaring anachronism. He believes in death, has looked forward to its prospects, is life-saturated and curious about God. It is this that renders him an alien. He is the good guy, the consistent loser.*

THE WOMAN: *She is the State's concept of ideal beauty. Just returned from her first trip to* The Freezer, *she has shed her jowls and the wrinkled gullies of her face have undergone a* land reform, *leaving the furrows flat and sculpted. The remnant of age is her mind; now approximately sixty-seven, she admits to just sixty-six. So there is a slight senility in her actions, as if she forgets she is not sixty-seven but twenty-three. Unfettered by character or emotion, she is the acrid* Aryan, *The State Woman, definitively male. Like* The State Physician, *she is growing increasingly functional.*

THE STATE PHYSICIAN: *"The Ubiquitous Multi-functional State Physician" is the State's equal to The Woman. Probably more feminine. There is little to be said about him. He looks like the State wants him to look, thinks like the State wants him to think, and behaves according to regulations. He is akin, in creative output, to that of a guava. In a functional light, he is akin to a piece of Danish modern. He is the Khakied Caretaker.*

The Setting:

The curtain rises on the austerity of a geometrically architected set. The backdrop is a dull, splotchy antique brown and should be immediately recognized as the background of da Vinci's "Last Supper." (*Those who haven't seen it in Europe will recognize it from Forest Lawn's interpretation.*) *The wall should be cut and designed to match. The effect should be an exacting one, linear, spatial. The audience should note some sort of symbolism that at the long cubical table, Christ is absent, and that the architectural void of da Vinci's frames nothing. Instead, we find* THE MAN *seated at the right end of the table and* THE WOMAN *at the opposite end. To the extreme left is a large battleship gray door marking the entrance to* The Freezer. *For several moments after the curtain rises, the only sound is made by* THE WOMAN. *She is sitting with earphones on* (*the kind they have on TWA*) *and humming to the music she hears on the earphones. She is listening to electronic music and her humming sounds like a huge twanging rubber band. A twelve-tone hum. And very irritating.*

THE MAN: (*Growing increasingly irritated, rises; muttering intensely in a one-man discussion*) I won't. No. No, I won't do it. Never! (*The Woman continues dissonant humming, softly, face forward, engrossed. The Man crosses slowly in back of table to behind wife, then in front of her in a bid for attention, and yells*) I won't! (*The Woman glances up casually, then resumes humming; buzzing and twanging to music and moving spasmodically in rhythm to it. The Man crosses brusquely to her chair and slaps the arms of it with his fists. The Woman slowly, deliberately, removes the earphones and coldly looks up*)

THE WOMAN: Will you please stop interrupting me?

THE MAN: Funny, my dear, how they say we're all the same, isn't it? The food, the drink, no deviation. It's possible, they say, by creating one man's environment identical to the next's—they equalize our nature. Program our thought patterns. All men have the same universal wants, likes and dislikes. The State wanted nothing more from our progress than their own personal convenience. (*The Woman, assuming the attitude of having heard this often, wearily puts back her earphones. The Man turns and gestures to The Woman*) Like you, my dear, for example. No deviance. They came for you last year. I remember it. At my age it's one of the few incidents that pimple the surface of my mind; your going to *The Freezer.* Nothing ever happens to people anymore, you know. A century ago things were popping. But not us. It's that *credo of uniformity* rubbish. I can still see you last year. You looked older than I do, and not half so attractive. You *are* ten years my senior lest you tend to forget that you were no bargain when they paired us off. That day you were in the best mood in years. And it *has* been years! You rather hopped out the door, anticipation in your limpy old gimp. Twitching, you rumbled off in the arms of The State Physician. (*Crossing to The Woman in mock affection, he strokes her cheek and stares*) And here you are again, my darling. They hurled your crumpled lumps on the rack and bloated the wrinkles to the plasticine perfection that illumines the room with its prismatic glare. You've been renovated, my sweet, like an urban renewal project! But they neglected the furnishings in your barren frame; even though your heart is new, sound, a first-rate ticker; they overlooked one thing, my little Harlem, that barren cache of a mind! They slapped us together, my fellow gene, in their genetic pairing process. We have produced a gaggle of little perfects for the State. Our own private *Aryan* race. Do you recall when our first two were incubated? After inspection the State gave us a bonus. But I can't see your genes, love, so there's really nothing about you to like.

(*The Woman, with festering agitation, reaches around by her chair, sees something and yanks at it irritably*)

THE WOMAN: *Do* you mind? You're standing on my cord! I've been getting static all during the exposition and it was you! It was *you* all the time. You and your flat feet standing on my cord!

THE MAN: (*Stepping gingerly off it; cheerfully*) Well, in

a matter of minutes that cord will be cut. Figuratively, that is. He should be here soon.

THE WOMAN: (*Vaguely interested*) Who? (*She looks at him. She realizes. We see the first sign of emotion; glee, pure smug glee. Then, with a shriveled concern*) Oh? You mean today's the day? Today's the day you go on ice?

THE MAN: (*Moving downstage*) That's just it, pet! I'm not going. I am not going at all. On the contrary, you shall have to put up with me only a few years longer instead of infinitely. I'll take care to stay off your cord. I give myself five years and then I shall die. I shall die very slowly. Die a natural death and be gone from this world, this State. But most of all, my little ray of sunshine, be gone from you! Delicious for both of us. You're once again in your prime, you'll be well paired off. As for me, I'll take death, thank you very much.

THE WOMAN: You're welcome, only you haven't the choice. You're insane. You've always been an alien, your cluttered mind. What makes you think *you* can end up differently? We're State property you know and if they want to freeze us, they will. Personally, I think the idea's an excellent one. The State's been very good to us. And since The State Physician's a personal friend of mine, you can use my old private tray in *The Freezer* if you like. I don't know what more you can ask, really. It's a first-class tray. (*A high-pitched whine is heard. It is the doorbell*) Well, that's The State Physician now. Let's see if the State salutes your scheme.

(*The Woman goes to the door; it slides back and The State Physician enters, dressed, like The Freezer door, in battleship gray. He approaches The Man. They salute by jerking their heads to the right*)

THE MAN: How do you do? I've decided I'm not going. So sorry to inconvenience you like this. But I think I'll just stay and die off the way the others used to.

THE STATE PHYSICIAN: (*Patronizingly: as if talking to a Texan*) Is that correct? And what was the impetus that geared this mechanism? It is, certifiably, beyond State conception. Definitely insane.

THE MAN: And *I* challenge the supposed infallible sanity of the State! Can't they realize that mankind was founded on two basic principles? *Religion and Death?* The one motivates the other. *Both* motivate the man! A century ago religion died out. Scratch one principle. And now they've obliterated death! Even death has died out! That subconscious nagging in the back of our minds. That little voice that pushed you faster and faster. It was a safeguard. When all else failed, death was always there. It was the only dependable thing. A constant. Always there to pull you through. What is there left to rely on now?

THE STATE PHYSICIAN: The State.

THE MAN: People ordered their lives according to death. It was a time-planned guarantee! We do nothing now because we have no pressure under which to do it. There's always tomorrow. And there always is. It's not I'm one year closer to death anymore, it's I'm one year closer to life. It's preposterous! Man has always been under death's dictatorship, always questioned it, challenged it. What happens when you die? A reincarnation? An afterlife? How do we know that what we might have transcended wasn't superior? That life isn't intended misery because it's a stepping stone onto an elevated plateau? Life's gross injustice seems to indicate an after compensation. Perhaps the more unhappy the life, the more utopian the death! How do we know what our rebirth might have been? How do we know anything today, except what we're force-fed?

(*Visibly broken, he crosses to a chair and collapses into it*)

THE STATE PHYSICIAN: (*With calm assurance*) Aren't you forgetting that since the power of reason, man has also wanted to know immortality? *That* was also the divine and constant wish nagging in the back of his mind. Until now, man held it like a dream in his hand. He now clutches it as reality. You are correct, death, in its constancy, was always there. But now you have immortality. You have man's eternal dream. You can't really mean you wish to jettison that. We did away with death because death was detrimental to the State. Contrary to our philosophy. It was *unutopian, uneuphoric,* and *unfair.*

THE MAN: How considerate!

THE STATE PHYSICIAN: As for your religion—what possible use can it have for us? Religion was a chemical reaction of death; something they turned to in proximity of the moribund state. God was simply the final step in man's death—strangulation syndrome. We have rendered that obsolete. (*He moves to The Man, putting a brotherly hand on his shoulder. The Man sits, slumped, head bent*) And you *have* an afterlife. Consider yourself reborn. As the *new you,* the State you. You can be the, uh, Renaissance man. (*He pats his shoulder and lifts him up. The Man suddenly looks very old. He is crying*) You see, you've everything to gain. That's the State policy. And besides, you haven't any choice. (*He guides The Man slowly across the stage to The Freezer door and quietly swings it open. The Man stands in front of it, weary, broken, bowed to the State, sobbing pathetically, whining softly*)

THE MAN: (*Softly*) But I don't want to go. I don't want to. Please don't make me go, please. . . .(*He looks desperately, hopelessly, at his wife. Then he turns toward the door, resigned, old. He stands staring blankly at the audience*) All I wanted was to *know*. I wanted to die. To have the chance to *know!* (*He walks quietly into The Freezer. The State Physician closes the door, bolts it. The Woman crosses to him; they embrace stiffly in a kind of automated lust*)

THE WOMAN: Did you do it?

THE STATE PHYSICIAN: Of course. I should get a bonus for this from the State. He was destructive to the system. Just like his gods and his death; he was a corrosive force. Therefore, the State made him an exception. They permitted a death grant.

THE WOMAN: (*With a smile*) At least, he will get to know.

THE CURTAIN FALLS AS THE AIR CONDITIONING IN THE THEATRE IS SLOWLY RAISED TO SLIGHTLY BELOW FREEZING.

Curtain

William Saroyan

DENTIST AND PATIENT

and

HUSBAND AND WIFE

William Saroyan

An avant-courier of mid-century drama and one of America's leading (and most colorfully exuberant) men of letters, William Saroyan was born of Armenian parentage in Fresno, California, on August 31, 1908. He began working as a newsboy at eight, became a telegraph boy at thirteen; at fifteen he left public school and pruned vines alongside Japanese and Mexican laborers in his uncle's vineyards in Northern California.

Largely self-educated, he was determined to write at an early age and, as personal curriculum, digested most of the works of the great writers during his moments away from his menial chores. At the age of seventeen, he settled in San Francisco where he began to write in earnest. According to legend, the youthful author wrote a story a day in an unheated room, bundled up in woolens, the floor around him littered with discarded or torn sheets of manuscript.

When his first short story, *The Daring Young Man on the Flying Trapeze,* was published in Whit Burnett's *Story* magazine in 1934, it created something of a sensation among the literati. That same year, the story was issued in book form and from then on, his success was assured.

Two of Mr. Saroyan's prime characteristics as a writer have continued undiminishingly through the years: his intense love affair with life and his amazingly prolific output. The author of more than forty books and plays, he has declared "I wrote in a hurry for many reasons, the best of which was the simplest and I think the truest: I was impatient to reach the best in me, and I knew there was no short cut, I had to work to reach it." And reach it he did with several novels (*The Human Comedy; My Name Is Aram; Boys and Girls Together*), scores of short stories (some of which have become modern "classics") and, above all, his plays.

William Saroyan met with almost immediate success in the theater. After making a striking debut as a dramatist with *My Heart's in the Highlands* (1939), he scored doubly with *The Time of Your Life,* the first play ever to win both the New York Drama Critics Circle Award and the Pulitzer Prize (1939–40). Acording to Saroyan, the much-lauded comedy-drama was written in six days and as he later told a newspaper interviewer: "After all, the stuff in the play has been gathering ever since I was old enough to see and feel life. This isn't a 'play' in the accepted sense of the word. I think there isn't enough 'play' in plays. Something ought to be done about it, and that's what I'm trying to do. You might just as well call plays 'mechanical,' because that's what most of them have become."

The Time of Your Life was anything but "mechanical," and it fostered a new style of drama which undoubtedly has influenced many of our latter-day avant-gardists. At its New York premiere, *The New York Times'* drama critic, Brooks Atkinson, hailed the play as "something worth cherishing—a prose poem in ragtime with a humorous and lovable point of view." Critic Richard Watts, Jr., in his columnar paean, wrote: "Mr. Saroyan's new play is a delight and joy. A sort of cosmic vaudeville show, formless, plotless and shamelessly rambling, it is a helter-skelter mixture of humor, sentimentalism, philosophy and melodrama, and one of the most enchanting theatrical works imaginable."

Since that momentous year, Mr. Saroyan's dramatic works have been performed on stages in every conceivable corner of the world. To list some in non-chronological order: *The Beautiful People; Love's Old Sweet Song; Across the Board On Tomorrow Morning; Hello Out There; Sweeney in the Trees; Get Away Old Man; Jim Dandy; The Violin Messiah; Once Around the Block; Talking to You;* and *The Cave Dwellers.*

No stranger to direction, Mr. Saroyan also has staged a number of his own plays including: *The Time of Your Life* (with co-director Eddie Dowling; Booth Theatre, New York, 1939); *The Beautiful People* (Lyceum Theatre, New York, 1941); *Across the Board On Tomorrow Morning* (Belasco Theatre, New York, 1942); and *Sam, the Highest Jumper of Them All* (Theatre Royal, Stratford, England, 1960).

Versatile as well as prolific, he also wrote the scenario for a popular ballet, *The Great American Goof,* initially presented in 1940 by the Ballet Theatre and, in 1943, he won Hollywood's Academy Award for his original screenplay, *The Human Comedy.*

Four of Mr. Saroyan's earlier plays (*The Hungerers; Subway Circus; Hello Out There; The Man With the Heart in the Highlands*) have appeared in previous editions of *The Best Short Plays.*

Dentist and Patient/Husband and Wife represent two segments from his newly completed *Anybody and Anybody Else,* an evening of theater comprised of thirty-one separate episodes. The publication of these plays in this annual marks their first appearance anywhere in print.

The author has suggested that the plays be staged "as simply as possible," and in a note to this editor, he added: "As the whole work is called *Anybody and Anybody Else,* I have decided that the sensible procedure in giving titles to the separate parts be similarly straight and informative—hence, one is *Dentist and Patient;* the other, *Husband and Wife*—rather than wild, clever titles, which would be very easy, of course."

Editor's Note

Dentist and Patient and *Husband and Wife* are two segments from William Saroyan's *Anybody and Anybody Else,* an evening of theater, comprised of thirty-one separate episodes. The two segments are being published here for the first time.

DENTIST AND PATIENT

Characters

ANYBODY

ANYBODY ELSE

ANYBODY: I'm this dentist in this little cubbyhole of an office, and you're in the chair. Open wider, please.

ANYBODY ELSE: Why are you a dentist?

A: Everybody's got to be something. I always liked teeth.

AE: That's strange, why should anybody like teeth?

A: Just a little wider, please. Teeth have form, and no two teeth are alike. A new customer comes here and opens his mouth and I get a new surprise. This variety makes me stop and think.

AE: Stop and think about what?

A: This won't hurt but it may put your nerves on end. It will take only a moment or two. I have seen some amazing mouths.

AE: What can possibly be amazing about a mouth, isn't a mouth a mouth?

A: Yes, of course, but there are mouths and mouths, and each is unique. The alignment of the teeth, the size of the whole mouth, the coloration of the gums and cheek walls, the size and shape of the tongue, the tonsils—it is all fascinating.

AE: I wouldn't be a dentist for all the money in the world.

A: I am not a dentist for money. I thought I was making that clear. It is more a matter of art, or even philosophy. What are you?

AE: Well, what do you think?

A: Judging from your mouth, I'd say you are a professional man, perhaps a lawyer.

AE: Wrong. Guess again.

A: Doctor?

AE: Try again.

A: The whole mouth suggests a man of intelligence, is it possible you are in trade? A grocer, perhaps?

AE: No, try again.

A: Just a little more of this drilling, and then the annoying part will be over. Annoying to you, to me it could never be annoying, it is always fascinating. Are you a tailor?

AE: No, perhaps you had better not try any more.

A: Your mouth definitely suggests you enjoy food, the molars are quite worn from heavy chewing. Do you own a restaurant?

AE: No, you're not even warm. Give up?

A: Perhaps I'd better.

AE: I'm a millionaire, retired.

A: The mouth doesn't suggest that at all.

AE: Perhaps not, but I would never imagine the mouth could suggest anything more than itself.

A: Gold or silver?

AE: My money? It's in gold, silver, paper, stocks, bonds, and in all of the other forms it takes.

A: Shall the filling be gold or silver?

AE: Gold of course, I'm a millionaire.

A: I have heard they are thrifty. The price of gold filling has gone up, the price for this filling will be ten dollars.

AE: The best quality gold?

A: The very best. How did you ever become a millionaire? I have always wanted to ask a millionaire that question. How in the world did you ever manage such a difficult thing?

AE: Cheating.

A: That's not easy to believe. Your mouth is not the mouth of a cheater. The cheater tends to have a small tight mouth which he very much dislikes opening wide. Just a little wider, please, so I can pack the gold properly. Yours is a large open easy and comfortable mouth, not the narrow tight small mouth of a cheater.

AE: Every millionaire I know is a cheater, most of them bigger cheaters than I am, even. I try to cheat only the rich who can afford it, but some millionaires cheat widows and orphans, and fathers and mothers who have many children, and ignorant old people.

A: Why do millionaires cheat poor people?

AE: I don't believe they know why. I don't believe they even know they cheat, I believe they believe they are doing business, that's all.

A: Do they perhaps deceive themselves?

AE: They don't seem to know the difference between cheating and not cheating, so of course it isn't necessary to deceive themselves. They just go right on cheating and getting more and more money.

A: For what?

AE: To have.

A: And then what do they do, when they are old, when they are very old and know they must soon die, what do they do?

AE: They have already taught their children how to cheat, and so they leave their money to their children.

A: Clench your teeth, please.

AE: Are you finished?

A: Almost. And it's perfect.

AE: I expect the best.

A: Rinse your mouth, please.

AE: Tastes good; what is that red stuff?

A: Lavoris, dentists have been using it for fifty years.

AE: I thought I had tasted it before.

A: You may step down, now.

AE: Thank you.

A: Why—please don't misunderstand my asking—how did it happen that you came here?

AE: I was told I could get a gold filling for ten dollars here. Other dentists charge twenty, some thirty, and a few millionaire dentists charge fifty.

A: Millionaire dentists? Is such a thing possible?

AE: There are many millionaire dentists.

A: How do they do it?

AE: By overcharging, by not keeping books, and by not paying taxes.

A: Amazing.

AE: Please accept your payment, and thank you very much. Good day. (*He goes*)

A: Good day, come back again. Fifty dollars for a gold filling. Imagine the audacity of the rascals. Ten is the most I have ever charged. And he paid in crisp new one-dollar bills—one, two, three, four, five, six, seven, eight, nine. I guess two were stuck together. One, two, three, four, five, six, seven, eight, nine. Ah, well, new currency *does* stick together. It could happen to anybody.

The Lights Fade

HUSBAND AND WIFE

Characters

ANYBODY

ANYBODY ELSE

ANYBODY: You're this incredibly confusing wife and I'm her husband, six years married and six kids.

ANYBODY ELSE: The hell you say. Why should I be the incredibly confusing wife? I don't know how women think. I can't be the wife, and if you want to know the truth I don't like the idea of being the husband, either.

A: Do the wife, you don't have to know how women think. I saw your sister this afternoon.

AE: Don't speak to me of my sister. You know I can't stand the thought of her. Never could. Do you think she's more attractive than I am?

A: Well, I wouldn't say that.

AE: Then, you do. It's always been that way. Then, why didn't you marry *her?* Why deceive me all these years?

A: She came to my office to ask if we might like to leave the kids with her this summer for a month.

AE: Oh, no she doesn't. It's the old trick. Be the mother of the kids, have them all fall in love with her, and then have their father fall in love with her, too. Tell me quite plainly, I'll understand. Are you in love with her?

A: Good heavens, no.

AE: You said that very defensively, I think you are, but don't know it. Well, she *is* younger, more at ease near men, terribly clever, and she has a way of finding perfumes that make men think they want her. Well, then, go ahead have her.

A: I don't want her.

AE: Try her. Have her. If she's all that irresistible keep her for a mistress, or if that's not enough marry her! Take the kids to her for the summer and for the winter and forever. I had an idea you two were plotting behind my back.

A: Oh, now, really, stop it. I've had a bad day, and I'm tired.

AE: Well, I can imagine you might be, after a day with

my sister, the two of you drawing up your campaign to throw me out. Of course you're tired, but your campaign *is* working, I can tell you that. I'm tired, too. I'm so tired I'm almost willing to give in without a fight. If you love her and if you think the children would be happier with her than with me, their own mother, I won't stand in your way. Pack up and go to her, the whole lot of you! The children aren't so asleep they won't like being awakened and taken on a great adventure. Go ahead, wake up the children and take them to my sister!

A: Asleep already? I had counted on spending a little time with them, as I do every evening after dinner. Aren't they having dinner with us?

AE: I gave them bread and water and put them to bed at six.

A: What in the world for?

AE: They've been acting awfully unfriendly lately, and little wonder. They sense they're not going to be with me for very much longer so why bother about being friendly?

A: I don't think you should have done that. They're perfectly innocent.

AE: But *you're* not, and children sense changes in their father. They've all taken your side in this family breakup.

A: There is no family breakup, for heaven's sake. Don't you think you ought to pay Dr. Clayford a visit soon and have a talk with him?

AE: Oh, so now you want to make out that I'm crazy.

A: Not at all, you're exactly the way you've always been, but lately you've been a little unhappier than usual and I think if you have a talk with him, Dr. Clayford will reassure you and you can be your old self again.

AE: It's part of the plot. He's your friend, not mine.

A: All right, then, if you feel uncomfortable about the idea of talking to him, see another doctor.

AE: Why not a lawyer?

A: A lawyer wouldn't understand why you're unhappy and so he wouldn't be of any real help.

AE: Not to you, perhaps, but I'm sure he'd be of a lot of

help to me! I want full custody of the children, with no visitation privileges for their father because of his immoral character—the house, both cars, the bank account, and half your income for life. So you see, I have no intention of being unfair. Yes, I'll see Gordon Craterfield in the morning.

A: What's the matter, what is it, please tell me?

AE: Just *everything,* that's all! Oh, I've known for some time you've been in love with my sister, it isn't that alone, God help the poor woman, twenty-four years old and not married yet, I'd had three children when I was twenty-four, it's the simple fact that you're bored with me, with our life together, with our kids. And you'd better take out more insurance, a lot of men with personalities like yours die of heart attacks suddenly without warning. I'll expect it to be for at least $250,000. Or they suddenly write a silly note and commit suicide. Be sure it's double indemnity.

A: What's the matter, what's *really* the matter?

AE: You dare ask that question? Ask it twice? I gave the kids bread and water and put them to bed at six, and you dare ask that question?

A: Yes, because I just don't understand what's going on, what's eating you, so tell me, we've had these confusing talks before, and every time you've told me something different, so of course I haven't learned much. What is it this time?

AE: If you can't see for yourself what it is, I certainly am not going to humiliate myself by telling you.

A: What are you taking off your clothes for?

AE: It's too hot in here, and the kids are fast asleep by now.

A: I'm hungry.

AE: You take off your clothes, too. We can *always* eat.

A: And I'm tired, too.

AE: You'll feel refreshed.

A: What about your sister?

AE: Oh, I know you don't care about her. You couldn't with a woman like me in your life.

A: What about the lawyer in the morning?

AE: Can't you tell from looking at me that I wasn't serious about that?

A: Well, see the psychiatrist anyway, will you please?

AE: Oh, I'll see him, I'll see him, but what can he tell me that I don't already know?

The Lights Fade

Paul Avila Mayer

THE BRIDAL NIGHT

(Based on the short story by Frank O'Connor)

Paul Avila Mayer

Dramatic writing was a natural inheritance for Paul Avila Mayer for he is the son of the distinguished American playwright and screen writer, Edwin Justus Mayer (1896–1960).

Born in Hollywood, California, on May 28, 1928, and educated at Harvard, Paul Avila Mayer's own career as a writer began in television. As he personally notes: "At one time, about ten years ago, I wrote quite a number of television scripts for popular network shows. At that time, I had to make a choice between going on in television or writing industrial and documentary films. I chose the latter because I felt they would leave me more time for plays.

"Since giving up television, I have become prolific and very successful as a writer of industrial and documentary films and while they provide no creative satisfaction, no status, and no opportunity for real advancement, they do provide enough money for me to live very well. And, I must admit, I find them a more pleasant way of earning a living than writing for television."

Mr. Mayer's choice was profitable not only financially but also creatively, for in the past decade he has written a number of plays, original screenplays and new translations of modern classics. Foremost among the latter is his version of Luigi Pirandello's celebrated drama, *Six Characters in Search of an Author,* which ran on the New York stage (Martinique Theatre) for 529 performances in 1963–1964.

Mr. Mayer's translation now is considered the standard American version of the famous play and it has been produced throughout the country by regional theatres and universities as well as on an extensive tour by William Ball's American Conservatory Theatre.

In June, 1963, the play had the honor of opening London's new May Fair Theatre. The production, which ran for eight months, starred Sir Ralph Richardson and Barbara Jefford. In its coverage of the play, Britain's *Theatre World Annual* commented: "This new translation by American playwright, Paul Avila Mayer, is widely held to be the best. . ."

In 1966, Mr. Mayer scored another Off-Broadway success,

at the Renata Theatre, with *Three Hand Reel,* a trio of short plays based on stories by the late Frank O'Connor (1903–1966). The plays, depicting various phases of life in Ireland, are *The Frying Pan, Eternal Triangle,* and *The Bridal Night,* which appears in this volume.

In an essay dealing with the works and times of Frank O'Connor, Professor Julian Moynahan of Rutgers University wrote: "In the many stories he devoted to small town life, alienation or madness is sometimes the result of the solitary individual's struggle against the priest-money-gossip-dominated communal proprieties, but just as often the outcome involves an intricate and comic compromise."

Many years earlier, William Butler Yeats, playwright, poet and a founder of the Irish Dramatic Movement at the end of the nineteenth century, observed that "O'Connor is doing for Ireland what Chekhov did for Russia."

With *Three Hand Reel,* Mr. Mayer faithfully and winningly vivified several of O'Connor's fictional accounts of Irish realities on stage.

Presently at work on an original new play, the dramatist lives in New York City with his wife, actress Sasha von Scherler, and their three young daughters.

Characters

MRS. SULLIVAN
MISS REGAN
DENIS SULLIVAN
SEAN DONOGHUE
DANNY DONOGHUE
DOCTOR

The action takes place at the present time in a small cottage and nearby exterior areas high above a harbor on the West Coast of Ireland.

Scene:

Upstage center: the interior of a small, whitewashed cottage high above a harbor on the West Coast of Ireland. To stage right: a bedroom. To stage left: the living room-kitchen, containing a bed. A door separates the two rooms. Downstage left: a large rock.
Downstage right: a shrub tree.

At Rise:

Mrs. Sullivan, an old woman wearing very simple clothing and a shawl, is seated just outside the cottage. She speaks directly to the audience, but really to herself.

MRS. SULLIVAN: (*After looking about slowly*) Aye, it is a lonesome place. But any place is lonesome without one you'd care for. (*After looking around again*) This is the only place I've known and yet it is a bad place to bring up a boy, all alone as I was. And with the sea so violent and nothing but the bareness and the ships being lost in the storms and in the good weather the stink of the fish, it's no wonder he was taken so. (*Shaking her head*) I always knew there was violence in him but he was a gentle son to me. No one could have asked for more.

(*Crossing herself*) Blessed be His Holy Will, for there is no turning aside what is in store.

(*At this moment, Miss Regan enters and crosses slowly to the rock, downstage left. She is carrying a book and a pad of paper. Reaching the rock, she sits and reads.*

In appearance, Miss Regan is bright and cheerful, rather feminine. Yet her cheerfulness is the variety which somehow keeps strangers at a distance, which is, perhaps, where she feels they belong. Miss Regan is in her early thirties)

MRS. SULLIVAN: It was a teacher that was here at the time. Miss Regan her name was. She was a fine looking, jolly woman from the town who had never married. Her father had a shop there. They said she had three hundred pounds to her own cheek the day she set foot in the school, and I won't belie her. (*Miss Regan looks up from her book, gazes around at the sea and the sky, smiles in appreciation of all that she sees*) 'Twasn't banished she was at all, but she came here of her own choice, for the great liking she had for the sea and the mountains. (*Mrs. Sullivan gestures to indicate the path used by Miss Regan*) Now this is the story, and with my own eyes I saw her, day in day out, coming down the little pathway from the road and sitting beyond there on a rock, in a hollow out of the wind. (*Miss Regan turns back to her book*) The neighbors could make nothing of it, and she being a stranger, and with only the book Irish, they left her alone. It never seemed to take a peg out of her, only sitting in that hole in the rocks, as happy as the day is long, reading her little book or writing her letters. Of an odd time she might bring one of the little scholars with her to be picking posies. That was where my Denis saw her.

(*At this moment, Denis Sullivan enters. Denis is probably twenty, possibly twenty-five, yet he always seems younger because there is always something of the adolescent about him. As we watch him we begin to suspect that there is something wrong, but these suspicions are supported by only the most subtle deviations from normal behavior.*

Denis stands watching Miss Regan, then approaches her, rather slowly, and by an indirect route. He seems troubled. As he reaches her side, Miss Regan puts down her book and looks up at him with an expression of inquiry on her face)

DENIS: (*Not knowing what to do with his hands*) I saw you. . .from the rise. . .so I walked over.

MISS REGAN: (*Smiling*) Did you now?

DENIS: I've seen you before, all alone out here by yourself.

MISS REGAN: 'Tis very observant of you, isn't it?

DENIS: You're the new teacher. I know all about you. (*Miss Regan smiles, looks back to her book*) Four times I've seen you. Why do you sit here?

MISS REGAN: Because it is quiet and peaceful. . .and don't you think it is very beautiful?

DENIS: How would I be knowing? I've never been any place else. (*With sudden anger*) I hate it!

MISS REGAN: Do you now? And where would you rather be?

DENIS: (*Apologetic for his anger*) I'm sorry. (*Smiling boyishly; answering her question*) In the city.

MISS REGAN: And what would you do there?

DENIS: I'd have a little shop—two shops, maybe—with the electricity, but where's the good without money?

MISS REGAN: True for you.

DENIS: Why do you read so? Will you be taking an examination?

MISS REGAN: (*Indicating her book and pad of paper*) These are my companions. They keep me from being alone.

DENIS: (*Frowning*) Will I be going away, then?

MISS REGAN: (*Slowly*) Well, I would imagine so. Haven't you some place to be?

DENIS: No. I could sit by you, so quiet you wouldn't know I was here, and you could do your reading and writing. I wouldn't be a bother to you. I'd be like a dead bird, I'd be so quiet.

MISS REGAN: Don't you go out on the boats?

DENIS: Ah, no, I do no work. I have to look to the mother.

MISS REGAN: Oh.

DENIS: We have the pension, and the hens. And herself needs me. I must stay with her. She has explained it to me.

MISS REGAN: (*Understanding*) Ah, well then, you must do that, mustn't you?

DENIS: Yes.

MISS REGAN: (*After a moment; nodding "yes"*) Tell me your name.

DENIS: (*Smiling now*) Denis. Denis Sullivan. (*Rather shyly*) Will I be sitting down?

MISS REGAN: I see no harm in it. (*Mrs. Sullivan flinches. But the scene continues without pause*)

DENIS: (*Sitting*) And will I come and sit with you tomorrow?

MISS REGAN: If you like.

DENIS: I will, then.

MISS REGAN: My name is Miss Regan.

DENIS: I know.

(*He looks at her for a moment, then smiles.*
Now, as Mrs. Sullivan speaks, Miss Regan gathers herself together and walks with Denis on a promenade across the stage, moving very gradually until they reach Mrs. Sullivan. During this movement, we see Denis behaving almost like a puppy while Miss Regan is warm and kind and gently affectionate)

MRS. SULLIVAN: And that's how it was. Whenever he saw her he'd be off and spend part of the day or evening with her, and now and then he would take her out with him in the boat. And she'd say, with that big laugh of hers. . .

MISS REGAN: Sure it looks as if I've got me a fellow! (*Turning to Mrs. Sullivan*) And a good evening to you, Mrs. Sullivan.

MRS. SULLIVAN: Good evening to you, Miss Regan. Will you be having a bit of tea and toast with us tonight?

MISS REGAN: 'Tis kind of you, Mrs. Sullivan, but I've my school papers still.

MRS. SULLIVAN: Perhaps tomorrow, then. (*As Miss Regan looks out at the countryside with pleasure, takes a deep breath, smiling*) It is a lonesome place that draws you so, is it not, Miss Regan?

MISS REGAN: I am used to being alone.

MRS. SULLIVAN: You do not miss the town?

MISS REGAN: (*Answering the unasked question*) Mrs. Sullivan, I grew up in a large house with only my father. Just us two. I did not go much among people when I was a child so perhaps I never formed the habit. I enjoy being alone and have few needs for people.

MRS. SULLIVAN: Do you not miss your father?

MISS REGAN: My father. . .is growing old. I never thought it would happen to him. I could not stay and watch.

MRS. SULLIVAN: (*Solicitously*) Well, now, I hope my boy has been treating you kindly, then.

DENIS: (*Embarrassed*) Ah, mother. . .

MISS REGAN: Why, he's treating me like the princess. Why a big, strong, handsome lad should want to spend his time with me, I don't know. He should be courting a girl of his own.

DENIS: I don't want a girl of me own. That is, I'd rather pass the time with you.

MISS REGAN: (*With a laugh; teasing again*) Why then you really are my beau, aren't you, Denis?

DENIS: (*Embarrassed*) Ah. . .

MRS. SULLIVAN: Sure Miss Regan's only being foolish with you, Denis. Why should you be carrying on so? (*As Denis continues to look embarrassed; to Miss Regan, gesturing toward the rock*) 'Tis a quiet corner you've found, isn't it, Miss Regan, almost as if it had been waiting for you?

MISS REGAN: Mrs. Sullivan, leave no one near it. It is my nest and my cell and my little prayer-house, and maybe I would be like the birds and catch the smell of the stranger and then fly away from ye all. (*She laughs*)

DENIS: (*Alarmed*) But where would ye go?

MISS REGAN: Where do the birds go?

DENIS: (*Controlling himself; but still alarmed*) Now you wouldn't really. . .

MRS. SULLIVAN: (*Interrupting*) Miss Regan was only making a little joke, Denis.

DENIS: (*Continuing*). . .you wouldn't really go away?

MISS REGAN: (*Sensing Denis' panic; in a soothing tone*) Ah, where would I be going, Denis? And why should I be leaving when I've such very fine friends right here?

DENIS: Perhaps. . .in the town where you came from. . . you've a fellow?

MISS REGAN: (*Soberly*) No, I've no fellow, Denis. (*Picking up her earlier tone; gesturing toward the rock and the sea beyond*) And where else would I find the mountains and the sea swept together in such a wild way? God had a fine palette when he painted this scene, don't you think?

DENIS: (*Relieved*) Just so long as you would never want to leave it. For if you were to go, what would happen to me?

(*Miss Regan starts at this remark, and turns away from Denis, obviously concerned. Mrs. Sullivan does not seem to put any special stress on it*)

MRS. SULLIVAN: Isn't he the foolish lad, now, worrying about what hasn't happened at all?

MISS REGAN: (*Turning back to Denis*) Now, Denis, can you think about it this way: yesterday you didn't see me at all. . .

DENIS: (*Nodding; interrupting*) You were late to the school.

MISS REGAN: (*Going right on*). . .but I was just as much your friend as if we'd been together, wasn't I?

DENIS: (*Very simply*) You mustn't ever go away.

MRS. SULLIVAN: (*With a laugh*) Listen to him. All right, then, we're all agreed: Miss Regan is never to go away.

MISS REGAN: (*With a laugh, but worried*) Never, never, never. Except this instant for I've still my papers to do. (*As she rises and exits*) The blessing of God on you.

(*Denis crosses and sits in the kitchen area of the cottage. His shoulders slump*)

MRS. SULLIVAN: But soon after that it all turned hem side out. It was not to this cove Miss Regan came at all, but to the little cove beyond the headland, and all at once Denis was stopping at home, idle and moping, always underfoot. (*Mrs. Sullivan turns into the kitchen, moves to Denis*) Here now, Denis, get out of me way. Have you nothing better to do than going around the house with a face as long as a wet week?

DENIS: Leave me be.

MRS. SULLIVAN: How can I, boy, the way you're looking. . .

DENIS: (*In a rage; shouting suddenly*) What difference is it how I would be looking? What difference so long as I tend to the hens and do the few jobs?

MRS. SULLIVAN: (*Worried*) Denis, boy. . .

DENIS: (*Interrupting; still shouting; pounding one fist over and over again on a table top as he speaks*) Is it only a lackey I'm ever to be, doing a woman's work the whole of my life?

(*He suddenly sweeps the table clear of cups and saucers; then looks up at his mother, breathing in deep, heavy gasps. Mrs. Sullivan stares at him without speaking, then his breathing slows and when he speaks he is in control again, plaintive and close to tears*)

DENIS: (*Despairingly*) Mom, Mom, shouldn't I be doing something else? Shouldn't I be trying to make something of myself?

MRS. SULLIVAN: But you're only a boy.

DENIS: There's far younger than me on the boats.

MRS. SULLIVAN: But you tried the boats—have you forgotten? And the stink of the fish was more than you could bear. (*Denis hangs his head*) And who would be looking after me?

DENIS: (*Rising; starting to pick up the cups and saucers he swept to the floor*) Ah, that's it, isn't it?

MRS. SULLIVAN: I couldn't be getting on without you and that's a fact, but perhaps it must be. If I'm only a selfish old woman keeping you from whatever it is you should be doing, then I must stand aside and open the door to you. But what is it you want, Denis? And where will you have to go to find it?

DENIS: I wish I knew.

MRS. SULLIVAN: I could always go into the county home, like Mrs. O'Ryan. They say there's always a bit of toast with your tea and that's all I ever needed. Is that what you want me to do, Denis?

DENIS: Now, Mother, you know there wasn't anything like that in my mind.

MRS. SULLIVAN: It isn't as if I ever asked much from life.

DENIS: (*They have had this conversation before*) No, Mother.

MRS. SULLIVAN: And you know I've always had your good in view.

DENIS: Yes, Mother.

MRS. SULLIVAN: There's nothing I wouldn't do for you, Denis. I hope you're never doubting that?

DENIS: Sure don't I know it, the way you've been telling it to me all these years?

MRS. SULLIVAN: But we've been happy together here, haven't we, Denis? (*Denis nods*) Only the two of us. What could be kinder than a boy and his mother.

DENIS: It is true, only. . .

MRS. SULLIVAN: Yes?

DENIS: (*Hesitating*) Shouldn't I. . .have a wife?

MRS. SULLIVAN: (*Saddened for him*) Oh, that's it, isn't it? (*Denis nods "yes"*) And what would you be knowing about girls and have a wife?

DENIS: What could I be knowing in this lonesome place?

MRS. SULLIVAN: It isn't only the place. (*Gently*) Don't you know, son, there's some are never meant to marry?

DENIS: And is it I'm never to have any life but this?

MRS. SULLIVAN: (*Slightly chiding*) Ah, there's many a lad sweating out the years in a shop or a mine who'd gladly change. . .

DENIS: (*Interrupting; tense but still in control*) Is this all there is to be in the world for me?

MRS. SULLIVAN: Denis, Denis, you shouldn't be bothering your head with such thoughts. (*Lightly*) Where's your Miss Regan? Isn't it the great stranger she's becoming?

DENIS: (*Menace in his voice*) How would I know where she is?

MRS. SULLIVAN: Why wouldn't you go out and find her

and pay your attentions to her and all saying you are her intended?

DENIS: (*In a sudden rage again; taking one menacing step toward his mother, then stopping*) Must you be going on and on about Miss Regan? What is it to do with you? Am I never to have a moment's peace in this house?

MRS. SULLIVAN: (*Shocked by his anger*) It was only a little joke.

DENIS: (*Picking up his coat and crossing to the door*) Well, I've no taste for your little jokes and that's a fact!

(*Denis storms out of the kitchen. He pauses, just outside the cottage, looks around him, debating which way to go. As he does so, Miss Regan enters downstage and sits, reading*)

MRS. SULLIVAN: And it was only then that I knew why Miss Regan had become the great stranger. She'd seen before I did that Denis had more in mind than company. And instead of coming to our little cove, she was going to another place even farther out from the town. (*Denis now begins to search for Miss Regan, finally finding her as his mother finishes her speech*) But in the daytime or the dusk, whenever he could find some reason for being out of the cottage, he would take his coat and. . .looking here and there, seek out the spot she was at. (*Denis throws himself on the ground in front of Miss Regan*) Little ease that was to him, poor boy, for he'd throw himself on the ground before her and there he'd stay, chewing on a piece of dirty grass, hardly able to say a word, for the madness was on him, even then.

MISS REGAN: (*Looking up; sadly*) Ah, is it you again, Denis? You've come a far way to find me this time. (*Continuing as Denis does not respond; gesturing toward the sky*) Do you see those lovely birds? Can you imagine what it feels to be up there, riding the winds, never having to come down. Don't you know I'm a lone bird that wants only to stay far up in the skies, and will never come to the nest? (*Pausing; then continuing again as Denis still does not respond*) You're a kind boy, a good boy, Denis, but it makes me so unhappy to see you looking at me like that. . .

DENIS: (*Angry for a moment*) Why should I be making you unhappy?

MISS REGAN: Denis, please. . .

DENIS: (*Softly; awkwardly*) All I've wanted. . .is to be near to you. . .

MISS REGAN: But don't you see it's all in vain? Not even the sight of your terrible sadness will melt my resolution. Don't you know the harm you're doing to yourself, eating your heart away for something you could never have.

DENIS: I'd rather suffer for the sight of you than die for the lack of it.

MISS REGAN: Ah, you won't die. (*Quoting*) "Men have died and worms have eaten them, but not for love." (*Trying to be light about the situation*) You'll pass me by on the street soon enough, without a pang.

DENIS: Is it to be forgetting my life you think I'll be?

MISS REGAN: Denis, be reasonable! Don't you know you're hurting me as well? (*Denis hangs his head*) You're such a boy still, Denis. Life is a big, grand thing and not so easily forgotten as you might think.

DENIS: Sometimes I'm afraid that it's life that is forgetting me. Sometimes there's such a blackness in my head that I don't know where I am at all. . .like a man who's been swept overboard in the night. . .and you're my only lifeline.

MISS REGAN: Denis, what are you saying—a blackness?

DENIS: It's. . .a blackness. That's the only word for it. . . when I cannot find the edges of things. . .like times my mother talks to me and I see her mouth moving and the feelings in her face, but there are no words. . .it's as if I'd slid back a little, inside my body, into a terrible, churning kind of blackness. . . (*With greater intensity*). . .and from the first day you went away from me I've had to fight it more and more. . .

MISS REGAN: Ah, poor boy, poor boy. I would never have let you sit down beside me that first day if I had dreamt it could come to this. But now that it has I couldn't let it get any worse for fear my heart would break. You've got to go away from me, Denis, and never come to me again. You've to find a fine young girl from the town and have your love with her. There's nothing I could do for you but hurt you more than I have already.

DENIS: (*Rising onto his knees in front of her*) But there is no fine young girl for me. Haven't you seen that? Don't you know there are some never meant to have a fine young girl? You must ask my mother and she will explain it to you. (*Moving awkwardly toward her on his knees; seeing her pull back from him*) Why do you move away when I come near you? What is it about me that is so wrong? I wouldn't bother a hair on your head. All I want is. . .(*He stops, unable to express what it is he wants*)

MISS REGAN: Denis! Sit down!

DENIS: (*Sitting*) What is it that's so dreadful wrong with me?

MISS REGAN: (*Almost in tears*) I won't be coming out to the sea again. When I'm not in the schoolhouse, I'll be keeping to my room. I can't go on letting you make yourself so. . .uneasy over things that never was and never will be.

DENIS: You couldn't be doing that to me!

MISS REGAN: It is the only thing I can do!

DENIS: I'll come out anyway. I'll find you.

MISS REGAN: I won't be here.

DENIS: But you must! 'Tis everything to me!

MISS REGAN: Don't you know it would be no good. I can't stand the hurt inside me when I look at you. (*More gently*) There's nothing I can do for you, Denis. I'm a lone bird. I cannot help myself so how should I help you? Now, please, for the love of Almighty God, won't you go to your home?

DENIS: I cannot.

MISS REGAN: (*Rising*) Then I'll be on my way. (*Gesturing for him not to rise*) Stay where you are, dear Denis. (*Very gently*) I'll hope to be hearing happy things about you soon. (*Deeply disturbed, Miss Regan exits*)

(*Tears well up in the eyes of Denis as he looks after her. He is still kneeling on the ground*)

DENIS: (*After a pause*) Whatever is it I've done so wrong? Whatever did I do? Whatever did I do?

(*Mrs. Sullivan rises and moves about the kitchen now, folding a quilt and making other preparations for bed. The lights gradually lower until it is night. As she moves about and speaks, Denis rises and enters the kitchen, seating himself in a dejected manner, but holding his head as if he is listening for something*)

MRS. SULLIVAN: And from that day she never went to the coves again. The madness was on him, even then, and when I saw the plunder done I knew there was no cure for him except to put her out of his mind entirely. Another might have taken pity on him, knowing he would make her a fine, steady husband but she was not that sort and I knew it from the first time I laid eyes on her, that her hands would never rock the cradle. (*As evening falls*) And then those terrible nights began.

(*Denis stirs suddenly, raises his head toward the window*)

DENIS: Do you hear it?

MRS. SULLIVAN: Sure there's nothing to hear.

DENIS: There! There 'tis again!

MRS. SULLIVAN: (*Crossing to him*) 'Tis only the boats knocking against the wharf. (*Putting her hand on his forehead*) Ah, your head's on fire, lad!

DENIS: (*Shaking her hand off*) I was sure I heard it. (*Starting to the door*) I'll only just climb a minute to the top of the cnuceen.

MRS. SULLIVAN: (*Gently; blocking his way*) Son, get to your bed. (*As he tries to go past her; hesitates*) There's no looking for Miss Regan's coming or going for she's not out to the coves these many days, and you know it very well.

DENIS: (*Hazily*) 'Tis more than a fortnight. But I must do something. . .only I'm not sure just what it is. (*Now Denis permits Mrs. Sullivan to lead him into the bedroom*) Mother, what will I do?

MRS. SULLIVAN: If only you could be putting her out of your thoughts. She is not for you and you must learn to bear it. Denis, Denis, no man will bring her to the bridal bed—don't you see that? (*As he looks despondent*) Go to your bed, boy. Try to sleep. Sometimes things look better in the morning. Certainly things never look so dark as they do in the night.

(*During the speech that follows, Mrs. Sullivan moves into the living room–kitchen, locks the door, turns down the lamps, and lies down on her bed.*

Denis sighs as she leaves his room. As she is preparing for the night, he tosses on his bed, moans aloud ever so softly, then again, louder)

MRS. SULLIVAN: Jesus, Mary, and Joseph, you could almost see it getting worse. The heavy sigh he gave when I was bolting the house for the night and he with the long hours of darkness forninst him—my heart was broken thinking of it. All the night I would hear him, turning and groaning as loud as the sea on the rocks. (*During the speech that follows, Denis rises from his bed, crosses through the cottage in the dark, unlatches the door, and goes out*) It was then, when the sleep was a fever to him, that he went walking in the night. (*She sits up in her bed*) Denis, boy, is that you? (*During the speech that follows, Mrs. Sullivan gets out of bed, throws a shawl around her shoulders and barefooted goes out of the cottage after Denis. She follows him through a long movement around the stage until he reaches the rock*) I put on my few things and went out after him. What else could I do, and this place terrible after the fall of night with rocks and hills and water and streams, and he, poor soul, blinded with the dint of sleep. He traveled the road a piece and then took to the hills and I followed him with my legs all torn with briars and furze. It wasn't till he came to the little cove where he'd first seen her that he gave up. I saw him begin to weep. (*Coming up to Denis; softly*) Denis! Denis, my own darling boy! My a lannav, my storeen bawn, it's your own mother calling to you. What is it, son? What is it?

(*Denis turns to face his mother. He approaches her, then drops to his knees in front of her and puts his arms around her legs*)

DENIS: (*Clinging to her*) Mother, we'll go home now. (*Rising, moving with her back to the cottage*) There's nothing out here but sand and rock and it's cold. I will never have what I want, never in my whole life. I never have and I never will. (*Almost in tears*) What is the purpose of my being alive if I can never have what I want? (*Turning into his bedroom, leaving her in the kitchen*) It was the bad day you ever brought me into the world.

(*Denis lies down on his bed with a great sigh. As he does so, Mrs. Sullivan turns to a table where she sinks to her knees in front of a small, inexpensive, plaster image of the Blessed Virgin.*

As she begins her prayer, Denis lies quietly on his bed. But as she continues, he begins to see something, something threatening at the base of the bed. At first, he only mumbles softly and gestures for the spectre to go away. Then he draws his knees up in a protective gesture.

By the time Mrs. Sullivan reaches the end of her prayer, Denis' emotions have built to a paroxysm of fear. He is crouched against the headboard, like an animal at bay)

MRS. SULLIVAN: Blessed Virgin, Mother of Grace, spare my poor boy! Sure he's always been a good boy, a quiet, kind, gentle boy. Don't let them take him from me now! Blessed Mary, save him for me, for he is all I have. Don't let him go on suffering for the faults of others. His father before him had a touch of the queerness and I'm to blame as well. I should have taken him to the city 'stead of rearing him here in this desolate place, all alone as I was. But I did the best I knew. When they were jeering and throwing rocks at him in the schoolyard, didn't I take him home to me, to care for him. And if I was wrong, it was me, not him. Blessed Mary, why should he be taken? What did he ever do? When did he ever hurt a single living creature? Why should it be him? Why, why, why? (*She weeps for a moment, then speaks with greater strength*) But if it is God's will that it must happen, if the veil of madness is to come down on him day by day and night by night, then let it happen while the light of life is still in me, that I would not be leaving him lonesome and half mad in a place like this. Ah. . .

(*At this moment, in the bedroom, Denis gives a cry, half human, half snarl, and begins to lash out at some unseen enemy. Mrs. Sullivan breaks off her prayer, rushes in to the bedroom, stares at Denis.*

During all that follows, except for whimpering and snarl-

ing, Denis does not speak again until he says: "Mother. . . will you leave me. . .," etc.

(*Approaching Denis*) Denis! Denis, boy, what is it? There's nothing there, Denis, there's nothing there! (*He lashes out at her and she retreats*) Don't you know me, Denis? Denis, Denis, it's me. . .(*Approaching him again*). . .your own mother, your own mother, boy!

(*Denis lashes out again, half man, half animal, slapping her outstretched hand roughly; Mrs. Sullivan retreats*)

Stop it, Denis! Stop what you're doing! Behave yourself, son! Oh, darling, darling son, won't you stop it, please?

(*Unable to reach Denis, Mrs. Sullivan turns and hurries out of the cottage and exits.*

Denis remains on the bed, cornered, cowering, mad. Once he covers himself with the bedclothes and weeps in panic and rage. Then, after a few moments, when he hears returning footsteps, he throws off the covers, snarls and prepares himself to fight to the end.

Mrs. Sullivan enters followed by Sean Donoghue and his son, Danny. They are large, muscular men and carry heavy ropes)

MRS. SULLIVAN: You're a good neighbor, Sean Donoghue, and I'll not belie you. And I'll be obliged to you if you'll be gentle with him, for he is all I have.

SEAN DONOGHUE: We'll look to it, Mrs. Sullivan. Perhaps it isn't as bad as. . .(*He stops, looking at Denis cowering on the bed. Sean Donoghue crosses himself, as does his son, Danny*) God Almighty, look at him! (*Very gently*) Denis, lad, it's me, Sean Donoghue. We're going to make you lie down, lad. It's for your own good, lad.

(*Sean Donoghue and his son, Danny, approach slowly, then throw themselves on Denis and attempt to subdue him and tie him with the ropes. Denis seems to have an unnatural strength as he throws off the two husky men, again and again. Finally, however, they succeed in fastening first his feet and then his hands with their ropes.*

During the action, the two men continue to speak sooth-

ingly (if breathlessly) to him and his mother watches in agony. Then she leaves the room, goes to the fireplace in the kitchen.

At last, when the final knot is in place, Denis suddenly lies still, relaxing, looking up at the ceiling. As he does so, Mrs. Sullivan enters with a hot stone, slips it into the bed near Denis' feet)

MRS. SULLIVAN: Here, Denis, son, this will help take the chill of the cold floor off you. (*Looking at him carefully*) You're back to yourself now, boy, aren't you? You know me and what I'm saying? (*He does not reply*) Tell me what you want me to do?

SEAN DONOGHUE: (*As Denis does not reply*) You'll have to have the doctor, Peg.

MRS. SULLIVAN: I know. (*Turning to Denis*) Go to sleep darling son, my darling, my darling son. (*Knowing what she is saying is untrue*) Perhaps it will all be different in the day.

(Denis smiles sweetly, then closes his eyes and drops off instantly into a calm, childlike sleep)

SEAN DONOGHUE: He's off, just like that. (*Leading Mrs. Sullivan back into the other room. She sits on her bed; he sits on a chair*) We've a long night ahead. You get some rest, Peg. Danny will run along and I'll just sit here until morning in case there be anything you might be needing. (*He gestures at Danny who turns and exits*)

MRS. SULLIVAN: You're a fine man, Sean Donoghue. And I wouldn't know how I would ever repay you.

SEAN DONOGHUE: God protect us all and let's not talk of repayments. Close your eyes now. In the morning I'll go along on the train and get the doctor.

(Mrs. Sullivan nods, closes her eyes. The lights go down to darkness. Then we hear her speak)

MRS. SULLIVAN: When I think of that sweet darling little boy that I loved as if he was the dozen children I should have had, when I think of that trusting little face that I took into my heart as if he was the only child ever born, when I think of all his little hopes and plans and dreams come to this. . .ah!. . .

(*Mrs. Sullivan weeps. The lights come up full. Sean Donoghue prepares tea, placing a cup in front of Mrs. Sullivan who looks at it and then up at Sean Donoghue*) They'll bless you in heaven. (*They both sip their tea silently for a moment. As they do so, Denis stirs*)

DENIS: (*After a moment; sharply*) Mother!! (*Pausing; then plaintively; holding up his wrists as if she were in the room to see the ropes*) Mother. . .would you leave me this way against the time they come for me?

MRS. SULLIVAN: (*Hurrying into the bedroom*) You'll be quiet now?

DENIS: I should hope to be.

SEAN DONOGHUE: Don't do it, Peg.

MRS. SULLIVAN: Ah, I haven't the heart to leave him like this all the day.

SEAN DONOGHUE: If 'twas a hard job trussing him before, it will be harder the next time and I won't answer for it.

MRS. SULLIVAN: You're a kind neighbor, Sean, and I would never make little of you, but he is the only son I ever reared and I'd sooner he'd kill me now than shame me at the last.

(*Slowly, Mrs. Sullivan releases the ropes from Denis' wrists. The boy is very tense. With a shrug of resignation, Sean Donoghue releases the ropes from Denis' feet. Once he is freed, Denis seems to relax. He lies back in bed, quite calm, and smiles.*

Mrs. Sullivan stands looking down at Denis. Sean Donoghue tips his hat to her)

SEAN DONOGHUE: It will take a good while but I will be back before dark with the doctor, Peg. (*Mrs. Sullivan nods and Sean Donoghue exits*)

MRS. SULLIVAN: After I loosened the ropes on him he lay there very quiet all the day without breaking his fast. But I wasn't a bit afraid. I knew Denis was a good boy and would do me no harm. Come to evening he asked me for the sup of tea and he drank it. (*Sean Donoghue enters followed by the Doctor. Mrs. Sullivan moves into the kitchen where she sits with Sean*

Donoghue. The Doctor moves past her into the bedroom where he sits beside Denis and looks at him) It was soon after that Sean Donoghue brought in the doctor to see him. For a long while the doctor was talking with Denis and looking him all over. And all the while Denis never said a word. (*The Doctor rises, comes out into the kitchen*)

DOCTOR: Mrs. Sullivan? (*Mrs. Sullivan rises to face him. The doctor writes a few words on a piece of paper, gives the paper to Mrs. Sullivan*)

DOCTOR: This is the place where he'll be going. It will be tomorrow before they come for him.

MRS. SULLIVAN: (*Knowing the answer*) He. . .couldn't stay here with me?

DOCTOR: (*After shaking his head "no"*) Now you want him well looked after, don't you? To receive professional care? Of course, there isn't any charge. (*Mrs. Sullivan nods. His tone becomes guardedly optimistic*) There's no telling for certain. Perhaps, in a few months, a year or two, there's just no telling. . . (*More businesslike*). . .but 'tisn't right for you to be alone in the house with him.

MRS. SULLIVAN: I'll stay here all the same.

SEAN DONOGHUE: There's no need for her to be alone. I'll be with her.

DOCTOR: Very well. Good night to you both. (*The Doctor exits.*

Outside we hear the wind rising and the tide running high. Mrs. Sullivan and Sean Donoghue sit in the living room-kitchen)

MRS. SULLIVAN: (*To Sean Donoghue*) There's a wind blowing up from the sea.

SEAN DONOGHUE: (*Nodding*) It comes along with the darkness. (*Uncomfortable; as Denis begins to roll his head from side to side in the bedroom*) It'll be the bad night, Peg. See how dark it is already. (*Mrs. Sullivan nods.*

In the bedroom, Denis is lapsing into an increasingly wild delirium which continues through the remainder of the scene. At first, he mumbles incoherently)

MRS. SULLIVAN: (*Listening to Denis*) What is that he's saying? I can't make it out.

DENIS: Ah. . .ah. . .ah. . .'tis so dark. . .the blackness. . . where's Winnie? Ah. . .Winnie. . .Winnie!!. . .

SEAN DONOGHUE: Who is that he's calling?

MRS. SULLIVAN: It is the schoolmistress.

SEAN DONOGHUE: 'Tis a bad sign. He'll get worse as the night goes on and the wind rises. 'Twould be better for me to get the boy to put the ropes on him again while he's quiet.

MRS. SULLIVAN: Sean, Sean, he's only a boy. . .(*Suddenly struck by an idea*) Perhaps if she came to him herself for a minute he would be quiet after.

SEAN DONOGHUE: Perhaps. If the girl has a kind heart, she'll come soon enough.

MRS. SULLIVAN: Go quickly now and ask her before he's getting any worse.

SEAN DONOGHUE: (*Rising*) As quick as I can! (*Sean Donoghue hurries out of the cottage and exits. Mrs. Sullivan stands waiting tensely. In the bedroom, Denis is more and more agitated*)

MRS. SULLIVAN: I would not have had the courage to go to her myself. Her little house is there on the edge of the hill; you can see it as you go back the road with the bit of garden before it the new teacher left grow wild. And it was a true word Sean said for 'twas worse Denis was getting, shouting out against the wind for us to get Winnie for him. Sean was a long time away or maybe I felt it long, and I thought it might be the way she was afeared to come. (*Mrs. Sullivan turns toward the door as she hears Sean Donoghue and Miss Regan approaching*) Then I heard the step that I knew so well on the boreen beside the house. . .(*Mrs. Sullivan runs to the door as Sean Donoghue and Miss Regan approach the cottage*). . .and I ran to the door, meaning to say that I was sorry for the trouble we were giving her, but when I got there. . .

(*As she opens the cottage door, Denis cries out from the bedroom, "Winnie!!" Mrs. Sullivan breaks into tears. Miss Regan hurries past her into the bedroom.*

Dennis is rolling about on his bed and ranting but the moment Miss Regan enters his vision clears and he is suddenly calm)

DENIS: (*Seeing her enter; shouting*) Winnie!! (*Suddenly calm; holding up his two wrists so that she can see the marks of the ropes*) See the marks of the ropes, Winnie! Look what they did to me!

MISS REGAN: Shussh. Quiet yourself, Denis. Quiet.

DENIS: (*In a whisper*) Winnie, asthore, isn't it the long time you were away from me?

MISS REGAN: It is, Denis, it is indeed. But you know I couldn't help it.

DENIS: Don't leave me any more now, Winnie.

(*Mrs. Sullivan has approached the bedroom and is standing in the doorway. As Miss Regan puts her hand on Denis' forehead, the boy relaxes even more*)

MISS REGAN: I'll be right here beside you.

(*Denis smiles, lies down in the bed looking all the while at Miss Regan*)

MRS. SULLIVAN: Ah, it's a miracle, a miracle! You're going to be all right now, aren't you, Denis, son?

SEAN DONOGHUE: (*To Miss Regan*) God will bless you for coming.

MISS REGAN: I'm a friend to Denis. Why in God's name wouldn't I come?

DENIS: Winnie, lie down here beside me.

SEAN DONOGHUE: Oye, don't you know the poor girl is played out after her day's work. She'll visit with you but then she must go home to bed.

DENIS: (*The terrible mad light appearing in his eyes again*) No! No! There's a high wind blowing and 'tis no night for one like her to be out. Leave her sleep here beside me. Leave her climb in under the clothes to me the way I'll keep her warm.

MRS. SULLIVAN: Oh, oh, oh, oh, indeed and indeed, Miss Regan, 'tis I'm sorry for bringing you here. 'Tisn't my son is talking at all but the madness in him. I'll go now and bring Sean's boy to help put the ropes on him again.

MISS REGAN: (*Quietly*) No, Mrs. Sullivan. Don't do that at all. I'll stop here with him and he'll go fast asleep. Won't you, Denis?

DENIS: I will, I will, but come under the clothes to me. There's a terrible draught blows under that door.

MISS REGAN: I will indeed, Denis, if you'll promise me to go to sleep.

MRS. SULLIVAN: Oye, whisht, girl, 'tis you that's mad. While you're here, you're in my charge and how would I answer to your father if you stopped in here by yourself?

MISS REGAN: (*Worried but determined*) Never mind about me, Mrs. Sullivan. I'm not a bit in dread of Denis. I promise you there will no harm come to me. You and Mr. Donoghue can sit outside in the kitchen and I'll be all right in here.

(*Mrs. Sullivan and Sean Donoghue move slowly out of the bedroom into the living room–kitchen of the cottage. Denis watches Miss Regan as she removes her shoes and her shawl, then slowly gets into bed beside him*)

DENIS: Won't you be putting out the candles?

MISS REGAN: (*Getting out of bed*) Yes, Denis.

(*She blows out candles leaving only one burning beside the bed; then she gets into the bed a second time.*

Denis and Miss Regan play the remainder of this scene in lowered voices while Mrs. Sullivan and Sean sit, with lowered heads, in the kitchen. The kitchen is fully lit)

DENIS: Ah, Winnie, you've come to me at last. I waited such a terrible long time.

MISS REGAN: Never you mind, Denis, dear. I'm here with you now.

DENIS: Such a long time. You can't imagine what it's been like. I've had no appetite for food or sleep or even to go out on the sea for the thought of you. You wouldn't ever go away again, would you, Winnie?

MISS REGAN: Never, Denis. Never again.

DENIS: Ah, my love, my love. I knew it from the first day I looked at you, that you would be the only girl in the world for me, that very first day down by the hollow when you spoke to me, I knew it then.

MISS REGAN: I knew it then, too, Denis, love.

DENIS: I love you, Winnie. My love for you is like the very sea, so grand you cannot see its length or depth but you know it will be there for all times, the first in the creation and the last on Judgement Day. Tell me that you love me; say it that I may hear you say it.

MISS REGAN: I love you, Denis. I love you.

DENIS: Ah, the pain of it. I feel that I would burst from the ache of happiness inside me. Say it again you won't ever go away. Say it again you'll never leave me, Winnie.

MISS REGAN: I'll never leave you, darling Denis. I'll be with you forever and beyond. Wherever you are, you'll never be without me.

DENIS: Never again?

MISS REGAN: Never again.

DENIS: I will be all right again, if you're with me, Winnie. You're all I need, all I've ever needed.

MISS REGAN: I'll be with you, Denis.

DENIS: Ah, it's so sweet and I was so afraid it would never be like this. The blackness was getting worse, Winnie, so that sometimes I was afraid I would not be able to come back out for all the terrible churning inside me. But all the while I was thinking of you and knowing that if you would only come to me I would be whole again. (*Becoming agitated again*) Tonight was the worse ever. They were all around me. They were making the bed move, Winnie.

MISS REGAN: Hush, hush, my darling man.

DENIS: (*Forgetting his fears*) Am I a man, this minute? Is it so, that I'm not a boy any longer?

MISS REGAN: You're a man; the grandest man in the world, Denis.

DENIS: (*Relaxing*) I never thought it would happen. I never thought that in this lonesome place and us with only this poor kind of a house that there would be a girl for me. For you are the girl for me, aren't you, Winnie?

MISS REGAN: (*Tears flowing down her face*) I'm the girl for you and you're the man for me. I'll never have another love but you.

DENIS: And you'll never leave me, for some fellow in the city. . .

MISS REGAN: There is no fellow in the city, for me, Denis. You are the only fellow I will ever have. You are all the loves I will ever know.

DENIS: And you will never have another love but me?

MISS REGAN: I will never have another love but you. (*Weeping*) So come, put your head against me and go to sleep. My love. For there is no sleep like that with the one you love. And 'tis a joy not often known in this cruel world.

DENIS: (*His arm around her; putting his head on her bosom; closing his eyes*) Then aren't we the happiest couple under the sun?

MISS REGAN: Aren't we, though. Sleep, sleep now, Denis. Sleep.

DENIS: (*Sleepily*) Blow out the candle, Winnie.

(*Miss Regan blows out the candle by the side of the bed. A single shaft of moonlight throws a soft beam of light across their faces. Denis' eyes are closed, his breathing is slow and easy. Miss Regan is a study in torment, staring wide-eyed at the ceiling.*

There is a pause. Then the moonlight softly fades out and, simultaneously, the light of dawn appears.

A cock crows somewhere. Mrs. Sullivan raises her head at this sound, rises, moves to the doorway of Denis' room, hesitates, then enters and moves to the foot of the bed. Sean Donoghue stirs, begins to pour tea.

When Mrs. Sullivan enters, Miss Regan moves slowly away from Denis, then pauses to adjust the bedclothes so that he is fully covered)

MRS. SULLIVAN: In the morning when I went to the room door to see him, she did not speak to me and I did not speak to her. My heart was too full. (*Looking at Denis; softly*) Look at him, sleeping like a child, sleeping like he slept in his good days with no worry at all on his poor face. God help us, it was a song of my father's that was going through my head: "Lonely Rock Is the One Wife My Children Shall Know."

SEAN DONOGHUE: (*Calling from the other room*) I have the tea ready for you now.

(*Mrs. Sullivan puts her head to one side in a questioning manner, and Miss Regan responds by nodding "yes" ever so slightly.*

Then, loosening Denis' arm from around her, she gets out of the bed, picks up her shoes and shawl. As she does so, Denis awakens)

DENIS: Winnie, where are you going?

MISS REGAN: I'm going to work, Denis. Don't you know I must be at school early?

DENIS: But you'll come back to me tonight, Winnie?

MISS REGAN: I will, Denis. I'll come back, never fear.

DENIS: I'll be waiting.

MISS REGAN: (*After a moment*) Yes, Denis. . .love.

(*Miss Regan goes out into the other room followed by Mrs. Sullivan.*

Sean Donoghue sets out cups of tea on the small table. Silently, Miss Regan draws a chair up beside the table. Mrs. Sullivan drops to her knees in front of Miss Regan and kisses her hands.

After a moment, Miss Regan pulls Mrs. Sullivan to her feet and Mrs. Sullivan takes her place at the table.

There is a long silent moment as the three sip tea.

Then, Mrs. Sullivan turns and speaks in the direction of the person to whom she was speaking at the beginning of the play. As she does so, she moves away from the table and into her original position. The lights go down leaving her in a single spotlight and the rest of the stage in black)

MRS. SULLIVAN: There would no words come to me, and we sat there, the three of us, over our tea, and I declare for the time being I felt 'twas worth it all, all the troubles of his birth and rearing and all the lonesome years ahead. It was a great ease to us. Poor Denis never stirred, and when the police came he went along with them without commotion or handcuffs or anything that would shame him, and all the words he said to me was, "Mother, tell Winnie I'll be expecting her." (*Slight pause*) It is in the asylum in Cork he is on me these twelve years. (*Crossing herself*) God save us all, far enough. Too far for an old woman. There was a nice priest here one time drove me into the city to see him. It is a place I was never used to, but it eased my mind to see poor Denis well-cared-for and well-liked. It was a trouble to me before that, not knowing would they see what a good boy he was before his madness came on him. He knew me; he saluted me, but he said nothing to me until the Superintendent came to tell me the tea was ready for me. Then poor Denis raised his head and says, "Leave ye not forget the toast. She was ever a great one for her bit of toast." It seemed to give him ease and he cried after. A good boy he was and is. It was like him after all that time to think of his old mother and her little bit of toast. (*Shaking her head*) And it made me feel that good, as if I'd found my mislaid love. (*After a slight pause*) Mislaid love. Isn't that what it's all about? I wondered, that moment when he asked about my toast, if all of them that are fortunate enough to have their loves cross themselves every morning for the gladness of it. (*After pausing again*) Denis said nothing about Miss Regan. And do you know, from that day, to the day she left us, there did no one speak a bad word about what she did, and the people wouldn't do enough for her. Isn't it a strange thing and the world as wicked as it is, that no one would say the bad word about her?

(*There is a pause. Mrs. Sullivan sits motionless. Then, the lights black out*)

Curtain

Norman Ginsbury

THE SHOEMAKER AND THE DEVIL

(Based on the short story by Anton Chekhov)

Norman Ginsbury

A British dramatist of international stature, Norman Ginsbury was born in London in 1903. His initial success in the theatre came with the West End production of *Viceroy Sarah* in 1934. The play, renamed *Anne of England,* was brought to the Broadway stage in 1941 with Flora Robson and Barbara Everest who, according to theatrical chroniclers, "gave two of the season's most striking performances as, respectively, the Duchess of Marlborough and Queen Anne."

An exceptionally perceptive and accomplished dramatic interpreter of historical characters and events, Mr. Ginsbury achieved his finest hour with the London presentation of *The First Gentleman,* in which Robert Morley scored a tremendous personal success. The drama opened at the New Theatre in 1945, and it ran there and at the Savoy for over a year. The play was honored on V-E night by no less a personage than Winston Churchill. As Mr. Morley recalls the notable occasion: "In a speech at the end I told the audience that the 'First Gentleman of Europe' was in the stalls. Churchill asked the manager to tell me that he had appreciated my words. 'But what,' I asked, 'did he say about my performance?' 'Nothing whatever,' came the reply. We have to remember that Churchill, first and foremost, was a politician, not a diplomat."

Regardless, Mr. Morley's performance as the Prince Regent in Mr. Ginsbury's drama still is regarded as one of his finest portrayals. (*The First Gentleman* opened at the Belasco Theatre, New York, in 1957, with Walter Slezak in the title role. The production was directed by Sir Tyrone Guthrie.)

Mr. Ginsbury's own plays (as well as his translations and adaptations from other sources: Ibsen, Chekhov, Strindberg) consistently have been magnetic lures for players of the front rank. Perhaps the most luminous company of all appeared in his version of Ibsen's *Peer Gynt* as presented in 1944 by the Old Vic Theatre Company. The roster of performers who participated in the Tyrone Guthrie production indeed reads like a Who's Who of the British Theatre: Sir Laurence Olivier, Sir Ralph Richardson, Dame Sybil Thorndike, Margaret Leighton, Joyce Redman, Nicholas Hannen, Harcourt Williams, George Relph and George Rose, among others. The Old Vic's sensational London season (which also included Shakespeare's *Richard III* and Shaw's *Arms and the Man*) was followed by a continental tour which ended at the Comédie Française at the invitation of the French Government.

In 1960, Mr. Ginsbury's version of *Peer Gynt* was presented in New York by the Phoenix Theatre with a cast headed by Fritz Weaver and Inga Swenson.

The author's many produced and published stage works also include: *Walk in the Sun, The Firstcomers, School for Rivals, The Happy Man, Portrait by Lawrence* (in collaboration with Maurice Moisewitsch), *Ladies for You,* and new translations of Ibsen's *Ghosts, An Enemy of the People, A Doll's House, Rosmersholm, The Pillars of Society,* and *John Gabriel Borkman.*

In 1966, his new version of Strindberg's *The Dance of Death* was produced at the Tyrone Guthrie Theatre, Minneapolis.

Norman Ginsbury (who resides in Eastbourne, a seaside resort in Sussex, England) has made the initial dramatizations of a number of popular Chekhov short stories including *The Shoemaker and the Devil* which appears in print for the first time in this volume.

Characters

FYODOR PANTELEITCH NILOV

MARYA, HIS WIFE

THE CUSTOMER

THE FOOTMAN

THE MAID

KUZMA LEBYODKIN

A WOMAN

POLICEMAN

Scene:

A cobbler's shop in a small town in Russia, in 1900.

Fyodor Panteleitch Nilov, the cobbler, is making a new boot. He is about 40, dirty and unkempt. His wife Marya, about the same age and just about as dirty, is opposite him. A lamp is flickering on a small table. It is Christmas Eve but the Christmas spirit is not in evidence. Fyodor is grumbling.

FYODOR: It's Christmas Eve and look at me. I'll never finish this boot in time. Look at me!

MARYA: You look just the same as always. Unwashed, unkempt, stinking of vodka.

FYODOR: Well, I shouldn't look the same as always. Not on Christmas Eve. I shouldn't be working my guts out here the same as always. Not on Christmas Eve. I ought to be out in the street singing or playing the concertina like everyone else. Open the window.

MARYA: It'll blow the lamp out.

FYODOR: Open the window, I tell you. (*She opens the window. Outside, people are singing and a concertina is going full blast*) Listen to them! Everyone's enjoying themselves. Except me. Every time I hear a laugh I get more miserable. (*He takes a swig from a bottle of vodka*)

MARYA: If you stopped drinking that vodka. . . .

FYODOR: Everyone's out there. Except me! All day long I sit here and sew and stitch and sew and hammer. (*He hammers a nail into the sole of the boot*) Even on Christmas Eve! Work, work, work!

MARYA: Drink, drink, drink! (*He takes another swig from the bottle*)

FYODOR: Close the window. (*She closes it and shuts out the voices and concertina*) If that swine from Kolokolny Lane hadn't come in and told me he'd wring my neck if his boots weren't finished before the morning service, I'd have been out there with the rest of them. Everyone's having a good time. Except me! (*He takes another swig*)

MARYA: None of them's as drunk as you are.

FYODOR: All of them are having a good time, drunk or sober. And here am I working till I drop for the Devil-knows-who! Money! It's at the bottom of everything. If you've got no money you can't enjoy yourself. So I have to sew and stitch and sew and hammer so that I can get a bit of cash to enjoy myself. But I never get enough. (*Another swig*) No matter what I do there's never enough cash. Everyone else has got money to burn. Except me. I'm the only poor swine with nothing. (*Another swig*) Nothing! (*He wipes his mouth on his sleeve*) How long is it since I've had some real, solid food inside me?

MARYA: There's no *room* for solids in your inside; it's so full of liquids.

FYODOR: I could go to sleep now, but I mustn't. I could go to sleep, I tell you. Forty winks to make me forget how hungry I am! But I mustn't. If I go to sleep, my customer goes without boots and I go without cash. (*He hammers in more nails in a fit of fury*) I hate 'em, I hate 'em all, especially the one from Kolokolny Lane.

MARYA: Is he the one with the black hair?

FYODOR: Yes, and a yellow face.

MARYA: And dark glasses?

FYODOR: Yes, and a horrible German name no one can

pronounce. That's him all right. No one knows what he does for a living even. Mysterious. . .

MARYA: He hasn't been here long. No one knows anything about him.

FYODOR: *Very* mysterious, if you ask me. A fortnight ago, I went to measure his boots and there he was sitting on the floor pounding something in a mortar. Before I had time even to say good morning. . .

MARYA: It all flared up. You told me.

FYODOR: There was a bright red light everywhere and pink smoke and a stink of sulphur and burnt feathers. I sneezed five times. Very mysterious, in my opinion.

MARYA: (*Cackling*) He sounds like the Devil to me.

FYODOR: Well, his boots are nearly finished, thank God! (*He drains the vodka bottle*)

MARYA: So is that bottle of vodka, thank God! I wish he'd come and collect his boots.

FYODOR: I wish he'd come and pay for them. Money! That's what I want. *Money!* Everyone's rich. Except me! Everyone's got big houses and carriages and fur coats. Except me! And hundred-ruble notes. *Except me!* (*Viciously*) I wouldn't care if their houses fell in and their carriages fell in the river and their hundred-ruble notes caught fire!

MARYA: And their fur coats went mangy.

FYODOR: I wouldn't care. If there was any justice in the world the rich would turn into beggars and the beggars like me would get rich, and I'd be the richest of the lot. I'd lord it over them, that's what I'd do! I'd show 'em. Open the door so we can see what's going on out there.

MARYA: It'll blow the lamp out.

FYODOR: Open the door, will you! (*She opens the door. He joins her in the doorway*) Look at them! Driving around in their carriages! They've all got a great big ham inside and vodka. Lots and lots of bottles of vodka!

VOICES: (*In street*) Get inside, you dirty old drunk! Go and have a good wash, you smelly old tramp! What a sight for

Christmas Eve! Go and hide your filthy face! etc. etc. etc. (*He bangs the door shut and goes back to his last*)

FYODOR: Did you hear them? That's their Christian charity. On Christmas Eve, too! Oh, I'd like to. . .(*He shakes his fist*) I hope they all choke. . .

MARYA: . . .eating their Christmas dinners.

FYODOR: D'you know who I met yesterday?

MARYA: Who?

FYODOR: Kuzma Lebyodkin. The idiot!

MARYA: Idiot? He's a master-bootmaker now. He's nearly as rich as the czar.

FYODOR: Only because he married a woman who's nearly as rich as the czar. D'you know what he said to me?

MARYA: What?

FYODOR: He said, I've got men working under me now. And look at you, he said, you're *still* a nobody, a *beggar*.

MARYA: What did you say?

FYODOR: Nothing.

MARYA: *Nothing?* You let him talk to you like that and you said nothing?

FYODOR: I ignored the remark.

MARYA: (*Gasping*) You let him insult you and you said nothing?

FYODOR: I said nothing, but I spat in his eye!

MARYA: And what did he do?

FYODOR: He knocked me down. By the time I'd got up he'd disappeared. I'll get him yet. You see. (*He yawns*) But not now. What I need *now* is a good sleep. (*He yawns again, then he nods and begins to snore. The door opens and the Customer from Kolokolny Lane enters. Marya's description of him was correct. He has black hair and a yellow face and he wears dark glasses. Fyodor starts up*) Who's there? Who's there? Who is it? Ah! My customer from Kolokolny Lane!

CUSTOMER: Here I am!

FYODOR: Good! Good! And very pleased I am to see you. A merry Christmas to you! (*He waits a moment for the usual response but it does not come*) Here are your boots, Sir, all ready and waiting.

CUSTOMER: So they ought to be! Let's try them on.

FYODOR: Certainly. Take a seat.

CUSTOMER: (*Sitting*) Help me get these off.

FYODOR: Certainly, Sir. (*He takes hold of the Customer's boot and starts to pull*)

CUSTOMER: Pull, man, pull!

FYODOR: I'm pulling.

CUSTOMER: Not like that! Ease it off!

FYODOR: That's what I'm doing. Here we are, it's off! (*For a moment he stares, petrified, then he springs up and staggers back in horror*) Your—your foot. . .

CUSTOMER: What about it?

FYODOR: It's—it's a *hoof!* (*Marya takes one look at the hoof and rushes into the street in terror*)

MARYA: (*As she goes*) Oh, God in Heaven!

(*Fyodor pulls himself together. He makes the sign of the Cross and starts to mumble a prayer. He changes his mind. He puts his hands determinedly behind him. Then he coughs*)

CUSTOMER: Who was that who rushed out just now?

FYODOR: My wife, Marya.

CUSTOMER: Well, she's skedaddled.

FYODOR: Who can blame her? I mean—well, you know. . . (*He coughs*)

CUSTOMER: Well?

FYODOR: Well, you must admit it's a bit of a shock. So unexpected! And people do say that the wickedest and most horrible person on earth *is* the *Devil.* (*Hurriedly*) But I'm not so sure, myself.

CUSTOMER: Oh?

FYODOR: I don't think the Devil's nearly as black as he's painted. No, Sir, I don't. Oh, I know he has hoofs instead of feet and I know he wears a tail under his clothes—excuse me, I'm not being personal—but he's got more brains and education than any of those University students who go swaggering around here with their books under their arms.

CUSTOMER: Oh, them! They might have books under their arms, but they've got bottles in their pockets and sawdust in their heads. All the same, thank you for the compliment, my friend. I'm sure it was well-meant.

FYODOR: The Devil knows how to use his brains, what's more. He never lets them get rusty.

CUSTOMER: Do you know, I like you, Mr. Shoemaker. You're a very *perceptive* person. What can I do for you?

FYODOR: Oh, well, I. . .

CUSTOMER: Come, come, don't be shy.

FYODOR: I don't like to ask.

CUSTOMER: People who don't *ask* don't *get*. An opportunity like this may never occur again.

FYODOR: That's true! All right then. Ever since I was so high. . .(*He measures from the floor with his hand*). . .I've envied the rich. In my opinion, everyone should be equal, as equal as possible. We should *all* live in big houses with servants and drive around in our own carriages. Everyone! Why should I go on being a pauper for the rest of my life? Answer me that.

CUSTOMER: The answer's simple. You *shouldn't*.

FYODOR: Am I any worse than Kuzma Lebyodkin?

CUSTOMER: Of course you're not.

FYODOR: There you are then! And, believe it or not, he's got his own house now and his wife wears a hat.

CUSTOMER: Does she really?

FYODOR: Yes. Take a look at me. I'm as good as he is any day in the week.

CUSTOMER: Better.

FYODOR: I've got eyes just like rich people. I've got ears, a nose, a head, a back, a front. I'm just the same as they are so why should I have to work my inside out while they live in the lap of luxury? Why am I married to Marya instead of a lady who smells of scent? Marya's all right, mind you, I'm not saying she's not, and she works hard, but she's not educated and she's heavy-handed and if I ever discuss politics or anything intelligent and she happens to be near by she always butts in and talks a lot of nonsense in front of other people and makes me feel ashamed.

CUSTOMER: It's very hard on you, very, very hard.

FYODOR: Now you see how I'm placed?

CUSTOMER: Yes, I do, and you have all my sympathy. What would you like me to do for you?

FYODOR: I beg you, Sir, to be so good as to make me a *rich* man. Let me know what it's like to have all the rich food and all the money I want. Let me know what it's like to have all the drink I want without being scowled at. And let me know what it's like to have a woman who smells of scent.

CUSTOMER: (*Pause*) You know my terms of course?

FYODOR: Well, I. . .

CUSTOMER: You must give me your *soul* in payment. That's all I ask.

FYODOR: Well, I. . .

CUSTOMER: I've got an Agreement in my pocket. (*He whips it out*) Here. Read it. It's perfectly straightforward. I guarantee to give you all that you ask for. All I ask in return is your soul.

FYODOR: (*Cagily*) They say the Devil dances on an empty pocket. When you ordered a pair of boots from me I didn't ask for payment in advance. A businessman carries out the order to his client's satisfaction *before* he asks for payment.

CUSTOMER: All right, we won't quibble. Now, prepare yourself. . .

FYODOR: There'll be the Devil to pay later, I'm quite sure. (*There is a sudden clap of thunder and a blackout, then rolls of thunder and a smell of fireworks and burnt feathers. The lights gradually come up again. The room has been transformed. It is most elegantly furnished. Rather incongruously, a concertina stands on a small table. One part of the stage serves as a dining room. Fyodor, looking somewhat startled, is sitting by another table, eating a sumptuous meal. He is well-dressed and wears a fancy waistcoat. A Footman and a pretty Maid are serving him*)

FYODOR: (*To himself*) I say, look at me! I'm wearing a fancy waistcoat. *Me!* A fancy waistcoat! (*He laughs. Suddenly he becomes aware of the Footman and Maid and stops laughing*) Who are you?

FOOTMAN: Your footman, Sir.

FYODOR: Footman my foot! (*To Maid*) And you?

MAID: I'm your maid, Sir.

FYODOR: My maid! Well I never!

FOOTMAN: *Bon appetit,* Sir.

FYODOR: What?

FOOTMAN: A healthy appetite, Sir.

FYODOR: What am I eating?

FOOTMAN: Roast mutton, Sir, and you're drinking vodka.

FYODOR: Am I? Well, fill up. (*The Footman fills Fyodor's glass. Fyodor takes a long drink. The Maid places a dish of cucumbers on the table*) What did you say I'm eating?

FOOTMAN: Roast mutton, Sir, with onion sauce. I'll bring the next dish. (*He goes out*)

MAID: (*Piling up his plate*) These are cucumbers, Sir, washed in Angora goats' milk.

FYODOR: (*Eating heartily*) Very good, very good! Pretty ankles you've got.

MAID: Thank you, Sir. (*She leaves as the Footman returns with a large roast goose. He removes the mutton and helps Fyodor to a huge portion of goose. Fyodor tucks in*)

FYODOR: Where's the maid gone?

FOOTMAN: Only to the kitchen, Sir.

FYODOR: You're not taking that mutton away, are you?

FOOTMAN: You must leave room for the goose, Sir.

FYODOR: Goose?

FOOTMAN: Roast goose, Sir. You're eating it now.

FYODOR: (*Faintly*) Roast goose? *Me!*

FOOTMAN: Roast goose with stuffing of chestnuts, sliced bacon, and duck's liver.

FYODOR: (*Murmuring*) Chestnuts! Sliced bacon! Duck's liver! (*He takes a pull at the vodka*) Very tasty! (*The Footman goes while Fyodor eats voraciously. The Maid returns with another dish*) What have you got there, my girl?

MAID: Côtelette de porc panées au raifort.

FYODOR: And what might that be?

MAID: Pork chops. And horseradish with cream.

FYODOR: But I'm still on the goose.

MAID: You must leave room for the pork chops, Sir.

FYODOR: All right, I will. (*She removes the goose while he tosses down more vodka*) Excellent vodka, this!

MAID: Yes, Sir, so are the chops.

FYODOR: You've got a luscious little bottom. (*He smacks it*) There! It asked for that.

MAID: Don't let the chops get cold. (*He tucks in. She goes with the goose as the Footman returns*)

FYODOR: You're back now, are you?

FOOTMAN: Yes, Sir.

FYODOR: What have you brought me now?

FOOTMAN: Boiled grain, Sir, fried in goose fat.

FYODOR: But I haven't finished the chops.

FOOTMAN: You must leave room for the grain, Sir.

(*The Footman whisks away the chops and puts down the grain. He goes off with the chops while Fyodor makes succulent noises with the grain*)

FYODOR: Delicious! (*The Maid returns with another dish*) What is it now?

MAID: Omelette, Sir, with pimento, mushroom and chopped garlic.

FYODOR: I'm only halfway through the grain.

MAID: But you can't say "no" to the omelette.

FYODOR: You're right, I can't. (*She takes the grain away. He shovels in the omelette with gulps of vodka*) It's marvelous. (*He belches*) Tell me, my girl, are we in heaven?

MAID: Good God, no, Sir!

FYODOR: You don't get food like this anywhere else.

MAID: Oh, yes, you do! This dinner was cooked in his Satanic Majesty's own ovens. (*She goes with the grain as the Footman approaches with yet another dish*)

FYODOR: What's that, may I ask?

FOOTMAN: Fried calves' liver in cream, Sir.

FYODOR: Fried in his Majesty's own ovens?

FOOTMAN: Of course, Sir. His Satanic Majesty supervises *everything.*

FYODOR: Well, well, well!

FOOTMAN: In your case, he even stoked the fires. (*He goes with remains of the omelette*)

FYODOR: (*Eating*) Stoked the fires, did he? (*The Maid returns*)

FYODOR: What, *more?* (*She removes the liver and places the new dish in front of him*)

MAID: Onion pie, Sir, with steamed turnips and kvass. (*Fyodor belches*)

FYODOR: That made room, anyway. I'll have it. (*He munches very audibly. She goes with the liver. The Fooman returns with a large jar of honey*)

FOOTMAN: Honey, Sir.

FYODOR: Leave it there. (*The Footman puts it down on the table*) A tasty dinner, very tasty indeed! Not too filling! It would have been nice if Marya could have shared it with me, but she skedaddled off. She'd have been out of place, anyway. She doesn't know how to behave in society, poor woman! (*He belches*) To tell you the truth, Marya's got no table manners. Absolutely none! It's not her fault. She's never had a chance. No education, either! The pity of it is—she doesn't realize it. She'll never learn to keep her place. The way that woman sticks her blabber in every time I talk politics is quite wicked. She just shows herself up in front of other people. It makes me look ridiculous. (*The Customer, still wearing his dark glasses, appears*) Hallo, hallo, hallo, where did you spring from?

CUSTOMER: Well, Fyodor Panteleitch, how did you like your dinner?

FYODOR: Good enough, good enough! The mutton was a bit stringy and the goose was a bit greasy and the liver was burnt down one side but I'm not complaining. All in all, it was quite enjoyable. It's a pity that Marya wasn't here to share it with me.

CUSTOMER: Marya?

FYODOR: My wife.

CUSTOMER: The woman who ran away when she saw my foot?

FYODOR: Yes, but you mustn't blame her for that. She's got her good points even though she *will* hold forth on subjects she knows nothing about.

CUSTOMER: You can do better than Marya, don't you think?

FYODOR: Well, yes, I suppose I can in some ways.

CUSTOMER: You will, too, if I know anything about it.

FYODOR: I say, I've only just noticed. I've got new boots on. Brand new boots! I wonder who made them. I certainly didn't.

FOOTMAN: Kuzma Lebyodkin made them, Sir.

FYODOR: Oh, he did, did he? Send for him. (*The Customer clicks his fingers. Kuzma Lebyodkin appears, very respectful*)

FOOTMAN: He's here, Sir.

KUZMA: You have some orders for me, Sir?

FYODOR: Hold your tongue! Remember your place! Show some respect! *Idiot!*

KUZMA: But, Sir. . .

FYODOR: Stand to attention! Speak when you're spoken to! Stick to your last! *Donkey!*

KUZMA: But, Sir. . .

FYODOR: And don't dare to argue with me or I'll knock your teeth into the back of your neck. (*Kuzma cringes*) Now! What do you want?

KUZMA: You sent for me, Sir, and as you haven't paid for the boots. . .

FYODOR: Haven't paid for the boots? I like that for impertinence! Get out of here! You? Footman?

FOOTMAN: Sir?

FYODOR: Biff him one!

KUZMA: No, no, no, please don't hit me!

FYODOR: Throw him out! (*The Footman makes for Kuzma who flees, the Footman in pursuit. They disappear. Fyodor turns to the Customer*) Now, my friend, I need money.

CUSTOMER: Look inside your pocketbook.

FYODOR: (*Taking it out and looking inside*) How much is here?

CUSTOMER: Five thousand rubles.

FYODOR: I deserve more than this. (*The Customer gives him another, larger, pocketbook*)

FYODOR: (*Looking inside it*) How much is here?

CUSTOMER: Ten thousand rubles.

FYODOR: Not enough! (*The Customer gives him yet another pocketbook, still larger and fatter*)

CUSTOMER: Twenty thousand rubles.

FYODOR: That's more like it! (*Fyodor tries to stuff it in his pocket but it won't fit*) I can't get them in my pocket.

CUSTOMER: We'll soon put that right. (*He snaps his fingers. A large moneychest appears*) Pile it in there.

FYODOR: In you go, my lovely rubles. (*He piles them in*) A key? I must lock it. (*The Customer gives him a key. Fyodor bangs the lid down and locks the chest*)

CUSTOMER: You'll find more money in every room in the house. Keep the doors locked.

FYODOR: So I'm rich, really rich at last!

CUSTOMER: Yes. And now I'm going to give you something even more *valuable* than money.

FYODOR: What's that? (*The Customer clicks his fingers*) A new wife! (*A Woman with full bosoms and bright red dress appears. Fyodor rubs his eyes*) Well, I never! She's beautiful! She looks like a lady, too. (*To Woman*) Do you ever talk politics?

WOMAN: Not to my husband.

FYODOR: That's sensible. Do you smell of scent?

WOMAN: I drip with it.

FYODOR: (*Sniffing*) So you do! Come here and sit on my lap. (*She sits on his lap*) That's right. Nice and comfy!

WOMAN: Lovely!

FYODOR: Good! Now you can give me a nice, big kiss. (*She gives him a big, loud kiss*) Another one! Another! (*Another big, loud kiss*) More! *Lots of them!* (*She gives him more*) Mr. Customer?

CUSTOMER: Yes?

FYODOR: Don't you think it's time you went?

CUSTOMER: I've gone! (*A loud click and he is gone*)

WOMAN: The dear man has left me a lovely box of sweets. Have one.

FYODOR: I don't think I will, thank you very much. I've got indigestion.

WOMAN: This one's a peppermint. It'll do you good. (*She pops one in his mouth*)

FYODOR: It's getting late. Time for bed, don't you think?

WOMAN: Oh, dear me, no, not yet! It's much too early.

FYODOR: Is it?

WOMAN: Of course it is! (*Very refined*) No one in our station in life goes to bed before *midnight.*

FYODOR: That reminds me. We're rich. There's lots of loose money lying about the house. Thieves might try to break in. You'd better go and look in all the rooms with a candle. Lock up everything.

WOMAN: Oh, all right then, if you want me to! (*She takes a candle and goes*)

FYODOR: (*Calling after her*) *Every room,* mind you! And come straight back here when you've finished. Don't be long. (*To himself*) I've got indigestion. That's what comes of eating the Devil's dishes. I should have gone to Church. But I've bartered my soul and I'm not so happy about it. If I went to church I'd say "God forgive me, a sinner." But that's what I used to say when I was a *poor* man. And now I'm a *rich* man and I still say it. What's the difference? When I die, they won't bury me in glittering gold or sparkling diamonds. They'll bury me in the black earth, the same as the poorest beggar. So what do I get for being rich except worries about money? When I'm poor I worry because I haven't got any and when I'm rich I worry because I don't know where to hide it. Rich or poor, it's worry all the time! Sometimes, when you sing, you can drive your worries away. Sing, sing, sing, sing out to the whole world. (*He goes to the window, throws it open and sings at the top of his voice*)

FYODOR: (*Singing*) Tatiana,

Haughty, haughty,
Lifts her head and cuts me dead,
But Dunyasha,
Naughty, naughty
Little tart, she wins my heart.
Then Irina,
Fat and forty. . .
(*Outside, in the street, a voice shouts up at him*)

POLICEMAN: You up there, you're creating a disturbance!

FYODOR: Who's that?

POLICEMAN: *A policeman.* You're creating a disturbance.

FYODOR: What, me? I've never done such a thing in all my life.

POLICEMAN: Nobody sings in this part of the town, Sir. Not out of the window!

FYODOR: Where do they sing then?

POLICEMAN: In their bath, perhaps.

FYODOR: I never take a bath and if I did it would be the last place in the world I'd want to sing in. What a funny idea!

POLICEMAN: If you go to the slummy part of the town, you'll hear people singing in the streets or in the taverns. But not here! Never here, Sir! It's not done. *You're upper class here.* You're gentlemen. You can sing in church, of course.

FYODOR: So, gentlemen never sing in their own homes! Only in their baths! They must have a screw loose. All right then, I'll stop singing.

POLICEMAN: Thank you, Sir. Goodnight, Sir.

FYODOR: Goodnight! (*He closes the window with a bang*) All the same, I must have music. It'll drown my sorrows. I *need* music. Where's that concertina? Where is it? (*He grabs it and plays a few notes*) They can't object to this. Not even in this high-class neighborhood. Let them *all* hear it! Let them *all* enjoy themselves! (*He opens the window and starts playing. After a while, the Policeman shouts up at him again*)

POLICEMAN: You up there! You're creating *another* disturbance!

FYODOR: Why? I'm not singing.

POLICEMAN: You mustn't play the concertina here. Not in this district! It's not done, not the thing. . .

FYODOR: Don't gentlemen play the concertina?

POLICEMAN: Not like that, Sir. Not out of the window. Not in this part of the town. *It's very select here.*

FYODOR: Do they play it in their bath?

POLICEMAN: (*At a loss*) You've got me there, Sir!

FYODOR: They play it in the slummy parts, you must admit?

POLICEMAN: Oh, yes, and in the taverns. But not in church, not the concertina.

FYODOR: In our church, the organ sounds exactly like a concertina.

POLICEMAN: (*With finality*) That may be the case, Sir, but gentlemen never play the concertina in their own homes, not out of the window.

FYODOR: Thank you, my man. I've learned a lesson that wasn't worth learning.

POLICEMAN: Goodnight, Sir.

FYODOR: Goodnight! (*He closes the window with a bang*) Oh dear, dear, dear, dear, dear, dear! (*The Woman returns. She has changed into a very alluring negligee*)

WOMAN: Here I am, darling!

FYODOR: Oh, so you're back at last!

WOMAN: Yes, darling, and everything's all right. I've searched all the rooms and locked them up.

FYODOR: What's that you're wearing?

WOMAN: It's a negligee.

FYODOR: What's a negligee?

WOMAN: It's a gown that ladies wear in their homes. On informal occasions. (*She is standing close to him, playing with his hair*)

FYODOR: Informal occasions, eh? Well then, let me give you a friendly informal slap on the bottom.

WOMAN: Don't be silly, darling. (*He gives her the slap, a very hearty one. She jumps*) Oh! Don't be so common! You don't know how to treat a lady.

FYODOR: Different gentlemen have different ways of treating different ladies.

WOMAN: If you were a gentleman you would have kissed my hand when I came into the room.

FYODOR: Kiss your hand? What next? What a life! Kissing hands! It's not natural! It seems to me that nothing that's natural is good manners. I mustn't sing, I mustn't play the concertina, I mustn't even give my own wife a playful slap on the bottom. (*Roaring at her*) I don't want to kiss your hand! It looks as though it hasn't done a day's honest work all its life. You've got nothing my Marya hasn't got except a strong stink of scent. Artificial, that's what you are!

WOMAN: And you're common! Just common! A *moujik!* I was brought here by false pretenses. I won't stay, I won't, I won't! You're deplorable! (*She rushes out*)

FYODOR: If she comes back here I'll throw her out of the window. The policeman can have her! (*There is a loud click and the customer reappears*)

FYODOR: (*Sourly*) Well, what are you after?

CUSTOMER: Fyodor Panteleitch, I've carried out *my* part of the bargain.

FYODOR: That's what you think.

CUSTOMER: You asked me to make you a rich man. I did. You asked for all the rich food you could eat. I provided it. You asked for all the vodka you could drink. I supplied it. You wanted a woman who reeked of perfume. You had her.

FYODOR: Bargain, did you say? Bargain? Your goose gave me indigestion and your woman gave me goose pimples. She made me understand what a treasure I have in my *Marya.* As for your money, looking after it would be enough to give me a nervous breakdown. *Bargain? It's a swindle!*

CUSTOMER: Here, don't try that game on me! You just come with me now. . .

(*He grabs Fyodor. There is a clap of thunder and a blackout, then rolls of thunder. The lights gradually come up again. We are back in the cobbler's shop. Fyodor is dozing with the Customer's boot in his hand. The lamp is smoking and there is a smell of kerosine. The Customer in dark glasses is standing in front of Fyodor, shouting at him*)

CUSTOMER: You fool! You idiot! Blockhead! Imbecile!

FYODOR: What's happened? Where am I? I—I must have dozed off. Who are you?

CUSTOMER: I'm your customer from Kolokolny Lane, you damned fool, and if I hadn't come in when I did, it would have been the end of you.

FYODOR: There's a stink of kerosine.

CUSTOMER: If I hadn't moved your lamp the whole place would have been on fire.

FYODOR: And I'd have gone up in smoke.

CUSTOMER: So would my boots. That's more important. Where are they? You've had them a fortnight. . .

FYODOR: One of them's ready.

CUSTOMER: What about the other one?

FYODOR: Give me five minutes.

CUSTOMER: They were promised for last week.

FYODOR: I'll finish it now. A few more stitches and you can take them both away with you.

CUSTOMER: If you didn't drink so much and drop off so often you might be a richer man.

FYODOR: What makes you think I *want* to be a richer man?

CUSTOMER: Everybody wants to be richer than they are.

FYODOR: Are you a rich man?

CUSTOMER: Not yet, but I'm going to be.

FYODOR: What do you do for a living?

CUSTOMER: I make chemicals and drugs. I'm not rich yet, but just you wait.

FYODOR: Take my advice. I've had a *taste* of it, a taste of it, no more, but it was *enough*. I was no happier and no better off when I was rich than I am now.

CUSTOMER: When I want advice from a shoemaker, I'll. . .

FYODOR: You're going to get it all the same. Do you know what I'm going to do the moment I've finished this boot of yours?

CUSTOMER: No, and I can't say I care particularly.

FYODOR: You'll care a little more when you've heard me out. When I've finished your boot I'm going to get up, wash myself and go to church. On my way, I'll see carriages and sledges with bear-skin rugs. I'll see rich merchants and gentlemen and lovely ladies walking along the pavement, and I'll see people as poor as I am trudging along in the snow. Some people can drive in their carriages and eat eight-course dinners without getting indigestion, some can sing at the top of their voices without getting interrupted, some can play the concertina and some can't, some can have beautiful wives smelling of perfume and some can't, but they're all as badly off as I am because one and the same fate is waiting for the lot of us—the grave. In the end, my friend, we're all equal, rich and poor, prince and pauper. So while you're alive, make do with what you've got and be satisfied because the only thing that matters is your *soul*. Life must come to an end but your soul goes on for ever and there's nothing in life, nothing, which is worth even a tiny scrap of your immortal soul.

(*He starts putting stitches in the boot. The Customer is staring at him, round-eyed*)

Curtain

Peter Weiss

NIGHT WITH GUESTS

(*English translation by Laurence Dobie*)

Peter Weiss

In 1964, a comparative newcomer to the theater garnered international headlines and acclaim with a startling play. The man and the event: Peter Weiss and *Marat/Sade*—or, to give the play its complete title, *The Persecution and Assassination of Marat as Performed by the Inmates of the Asylum of Charenton Under the Direction of the Marquis de Sade*. Hailed as "an electrifying experience," the drama instantaneously established Peter Weiss as a major new force in the modern theatre.

Born in Germany in 1916, Mr. Weiss left his homeland shortly after the Nazis instituted their verminous era of infamy. In 1939, he settled in Stockholm and has since made that his home. Now a Swedish citizen, he continues to write in the German language.

Although he is an accomplished painter and has made many successful documentary films (as well as a full-length movie, *The Mirage*), his world renown has come as a dramatist. *Marat/Sade* had its premiere in April, 1964, at the Schiller Theatre in West Berlin. The English-language version opened in London in August, 1964, under the auspices of the Royal Shakespeare Company. Subsequently, this same production, directed by Peter Brook, was taken to New York in 1965. One of the outstanding theatrical events of the decade, it swept the seasonal awards including the New York Drama Critics Circle citation as the year's best play; two major Tony Awards, for best play and direction; and seven categories in Variety's annual poll of the New York theatre critics. A filmed duplication of the Royal Shakespeare Company's memorable production was released in 1967.

In 1965, Peter Weiss' succeeding play, *Die Ermittlung* (*The Investigation*), had its simultaneous premiere in thirteen West German theaters, at the East German Berliner Ensemble, and a midnight play-reading by the Royal Shakespeare Company in London. Taken directly from German court records of the 1964–65 trial of twenty-one persons who participated in the destruction of four million people at the infamous concentration camp at Auschwitz, this dramatic confrontation of man's inhumanity to man was presented on the New York stage in 1966. Well received by the press, its stark and brutal truths of a disreputable era in history were too close for audience comfort and the presentation expired after 103 performances. A network television production of the play, however, later was viewed by millions.

Early in 1968, Mr. Weiss' *Song of the Lusitanian Bogey* marked the enormously successful Off-Broadway debut of the newly organized Negro Ensemble Company. In reviewing the production, the drama critic for *The New York Times,* Clive Barnes, observed: "Mr. Weiss does not write plays as other people do. He creates a highly dramatic framework, or perhaps better a magnetic field of dramatic force, offers this to a director and the actors, and invites them to pin the audience's ears back, stab it with facts, karate-chop it with the passionate blows of insensate statistics."

Night with Guests, published for the first time in the English language in this anthology, is a striking case in point. Its framework is deceptively simple; its doggerel verse unashamedly theatrical. Yet, between and behind the lines, this "canvas woven out of children's nightmares" has frightening implications. The author's suggested staging (see *Production Notes*) as a blend of the stylized Japanese *Kabuki* and the exaggerated tones and contrasts of a *Punch and Judy* show vividly offers the director and his company a "magnetic field" for dramatic invention and interpretation.

The play originally was presented at the Schiller Theatre, Berlin, in 1963 and, later, at the Traverse Theatre Club, Edinburgh, in 1965.

The Tower, another recent short play by Peter Weiss, was published earlier this year in this editor's volume of *Best Short Plays of the World Theatre: 1958–1967.*

PRODUCTION NOTES

Style of Production:

Both the Kabuki Theatre (*of Japan*) *as well as the traditional* Punch and Judy *puppet shows could serve as a source of inspiration.*

From the Punch and Judy *shows you have the grossness, coarseness, strong effects of boisterousness and, often, false emphasis due to the aggressive and cruel undertones of gaiety.*

From the Kabuki Theatre *you have the control of movement, the unnatural and strange voice controls which often produce hisses and groans, as for instance in the final scene of our play—the duel—which should almost resemble a ballet.*

Design and Costuming:

The strong, glaring colors, with mask-like characters (example: the exaggeratedly bushy beard and red nose of the guest) as well as the highly stylized movements and gestures of the actors and the stark simplicity of the decor, with only the most essential objects, resemble each other in both theatre forms.

Dialogue and Text:

The nursery rhymes are a pervading theme, to be recited throughout in singsong fashion, just like a mechanically solemn hurdy-gurdy voice.

The text should be presented in a mean, vicious, fearful and cunning manner rather than as a lyrical interpretation. (Example: in mentioning the "treasure chest," the audience should be made to realize that this is intended as a deceptive trick or by referring to the "pink ribbon," it becomes obvious that the uninvited guest will be strangled.) Also, the deceitful insinuations of the children should be strongly emphasized when speaking to the guests.

Music:

The musical accompaniment is very important. It must not consist of vignettes. The most effective accompaniment would be a complete composition for instruments similar to those used at country fairs such as a barrel organ, shawm, shepherd's flute or a drum.

Characters

MAN

WIFE

TWO CHILDREN

GUEST

WARNER

MAN AND WIFE (*Softly*)
Who's this creeping to our door?
He hides his face from sight
He tiptoes up—we can't be sure—
And steals in from the night!

CHILDREN
Eeny meeny mink mank
Pink pank pink pank
Roly poly peely pi
Hicky dicky dock

MAN AND WIFE (*Softly*)
Is this stranger Peter Wright—?
Standing quiet, big eyes bright?
But why so late and why so grim
Bearded, silent—is it him?

CHILDREN
It's Peter Wright in his red shirt
He will see we don't get hurt!

GUEST (*Enters*)
Jasper Ruddigore is here
Bringing blood and death and fear!
My knife will flash, in and out
Before you know, I'll snuff you out!

CHILDREN
Oh, spare us, Jasper Ruddigore
What would you want to kill us for—?

MAN AND WIFE (*Softly*)
Now in our house he firmly stands
He turns and shuts the door
Our blood will soon drip from his hands

We know the fate in store!
(*Loudly*)
Come in, dear Jasper Ruddigore
And share a meal with us four. . .

GUEST
I do not like your tasteless dish
My table's amply laid
Sit in the light and eat your fish
I'll sharpen up my blade!

MAN AND WIFE
Your coming pleases us a lot
We fear you'll go away
We'll give you everything we've got
Please say that you will stay.

GUEST
Anything you could display
I have—and more indeed
Tomorrow, I'll be far away
Carrying all I need!

MAN AND WIFE (*Softly*)
How can we sit and eat a bit
Although we're nearly starving—?
We do not feel much like a meal
When we are in for carving!

CHILDREN
Eeny meeny mink mank
Pink pank pink pank
Roly poly peely pi
Hicky dicky dock

GUEST (*Sharpening his knife*)
Strop strop oft!
The steel is hard, the flesh is soft. . .

MAN AND WIFE
Dear Jasper, if you'd come and live
We'd give you all we've got to give
But kill us and you'll never know
All that we would love to show

GUEST
What, my dears, do you have then
Some scraggy goats, a scrawny hen?
MAN AND WIFE
We haven't got a comb
Or soap to clean our home
And wash ourselves, although
We do have a nice pink bow!
A bowl, a cup, a key
As you can easily see
And then we have a bed
With blankets we can spread
A table and four chairs
And beer and fish and prayers
Oh, we're so poor it's clear
There's not much for you here
GUEST
You think I'll listen to these lies?
My knife will stop your sniveling cries!
MAN
Dear, good Mr. Ruddigore
It's really true that we are poor
We'd long have given up our hold
But for a casket full of gold!
GUEST
Where is this casket full of gold
Of which I've only just been told?
MAN
A reedy pond that's overgrown
You'd never find it on your own.
GUEST
Strop strop oft!
The steel is hard, the flesh is soft. . .
First your children, then your wife
You may be sure, I'll use the knife!
MAN
Dear Jasper, all I've said is true!

How could I think of fooling you?
I'd just be tossing away my life
When you're so handy with your knife!

GUEST
The casket's near; we'll have it here
The kids can go. .

MAN
Oh Jasper, no!
I mean, the casket's such a weight
Two men might well find it too great

GUEST
If the casket's such a size
How did you come by such a prize?

MAN
Soldiers left it when they fled

GUEST
You must be rich, from what you said
And yet, you hide this gold instead
Of using it to be well fed—?

MAN
Ah, times are bad for us, dear guest
With all the plunder and unrest
Robbers pass by, day by day
Take every egg our hen may lay
And strip the ripening apple tree
Of all the fruits we'd hoped to see
And pluck the berries while still green
Until the raspberry bush is clean
And dig potatoes from the ground
Then mount their horses with a bound
To gallop quickly on their way
Why, if they knew of this array
Of gold and silver, rings, a crown
Surely, then, they'd chop us down!

GUEST
I see you are a clever man
For your affairs, a proper plan

Therefore I'm sure you're strong enough
To bring alone the gold and stuff
And I will stay with your good wife
My twitching hand upon my knife

CHILDREN
Where is Peter Wright—?
His red shirt blazing bright
He's kind in word and deed
He helps all those in need

GUEST
Huff puff fleshyflim
Look and look, you won't find him!
It needed just a whiff of me
For him to turn his tail and flee. . .
If he sees my glittering knife
You'll be forgotten in his life
So don't have any hopes he's near
He runs faster than the deer

MAN
Dear guest, I'm weak but you are strong
Come with me, and with you along. . .

GUEST
Shut up! And tie your wife's hands tight!
I've mighty far to go tonight
So make it quick; I've little time
Or patience left. And I'm. . .
Not in favor of this delay
Now see her hands cannot get free
Or with her life she'll swiftly pay. . .
Then you be on your merry way!

MAN
But if it's true as I tell you
To fetch the casket will take two. . .

GUEST
I'll count up to ten
If she's not tied by then. . .
One!

CHILDREN (*Softly*)
Inky pinky cockaloo
GUEST
Two!
CHILDREN
Higgely piggely bugaboo
GUEST
Three!
CHILDREN
Hanky wanky tackatee
GUEST
Four!
CHILDREN
Wiggely waggely huggaree
GUEST
Five!
CHILDREN
Hunky spunky peekaboo
GUEST
Six!
CHILDREN
Hobbely gobbely wibbaloo
GUEST
Seven!
CHILDREN
Hurly whirly bellabye
GUEST
Eight!
CHILDREN
Bobbely bubbely winkatye
GUEST
Nine!
CHILDREN
Licky spicky hickaray
GUEST
Ten!
CHILDREN
Wonky tonky lackaday

GUEST

Show me your hands; has he obeyed my commands?
Are the knots firmly tied—?
I'll be satisfied
Once they're tested and tried
Now, do as you're told and bring me the gold!

WIFE

And if the weight's too great
What, pray, will be our fate?

GUEST

Strop strop oft!
The steel is hard, the flesh is soft. . .
I shall count quickly to fifty, by when
If he hasn't arrived with the casket, why then
Your throats will be cut; you'll be one bloody gout
And you, do you hear, take good care while you're out
You can't escape from me and if you tried
I'd soon overtake you; and don't attempt to hide
For, I'll look in each nook and I'll see at a glance
Just where you are; so face it, you haven't a chance!
You've only one choice and you can discount
Any hopes you may have—I'm starting to count. . .

CHILDREN

Oh, father, father, don't leave us!

MAN

Be quiet, children, and don't fuss
It's not my fault; now do your best
To please and entertain our guest
(*He goes, hurriedly*)

WIFE

Be quiet, children, things aren't black

You've heard, your father's coming back
I know he'll find the strength of two
To do the job that he must do
He'll bring the casket full of gold
The one we pushed and dragged and rolled

CHILDREN

Yes, we were forbidden
To say where it was hidden
If someone knew—pink pank
Of all the gold—clink clank
And the crown—pick pock
Hicky dicky dock
He'd fish the casket out
With sticks and scout about
For a lonely rock
Where he could break the lock
And then he'd hold—mink mank
Our lovely gold—pink pank

GUEST

Did you see the treasure chest?

CHILDREN

We peeped in on tiptoe, dear guest
And saw the dancing diamonds flitter
Amid the precious golden glitter

GUEST

Is this true?

CHILDREN

As true as true!

WIFE

Children, don't disturb our guest
While he counts to fifty, lest
He gets confused and loses track
Oh, my hands, the skin will crack. . .

CHILDREN

Dear mister guest, sir, wouldn't you
Feel better and more comfy, too
If you put your knife down while

You rested in this chair awhile—?
With all this traveling here and there
You must be tired, in need of care

WIFE

Children, will you leave him be!
His counting will go wrong, you see. . .
Oh, my veins are bursting, mercy me!

CHILDREN

Mother, mother, why does he
Stand so still, so quietly
And watch the door so carefully?
Does he think he hears the sound
Of clattering scythes as they surround
Our little house—and he'll be found?

WIFE

Children, leave our guest in peace
No one will come to effect our release
Oh, how I wish the fire would cease!

CHILDREN

Mother, why's his nose so red
Why do his eyes roll in his head
Why is his face so horrid and bloated
Why are his boots so filthily coated?

WIFE

Children, dear, I do not know. . .
No doubt he grieves and tries to show
He's lonely and would rather be
With his wife and family

CHILDREN

Perhaps poor Jasper has to roam
Because he hasn't got a home—?
Or, maybe all his family's died
And he can't bear to be alone outside—?

WIFE

Children, you have heard us say
If he wishes, he can stay
He owns whatever we have here

The chairs, the table, fish and beer
He owns the bed, he owns the key
He owns the bowl, and even we
Whose bar of soap is fantasy, are his; and lo,
He even owns our nice pink bow!

CHILDREN

Oh, mother, dear, he looks so grim
Are we good enough for him—?

WIFE

Perhaps he will make do with us
Now that your father's lost to us!
I fear he found the weight too great
It dragged him to a watery fate
Oh, Frederick, my Frederick. . .
The pond is dark, the reeds are thick
I'll never see your face again
Your tracks will vanish in the rain
And now I cannot bring to mind
The place we once took pains to find
And tipped the casket from the barrow
To see it sink swift as an arrow. . .
Oh, Frederick, my husband, dear
Now you've left me with this stranger here!

CHILDREN

Please, dear Father Ruddigore
Forgive our faults and like us more
Drink our beer and eat our fish
Though it may not be what you wish
Be our guest, or if you'd rather
Stay for good and be our father!

WIFE

Oh, dear Jasper, look at me
Share my bed, my husband be!

CHILDREN

Eeny meeny mink mank
Pink pank pink pank
Roly poly peely pi

Hicky dicky dock
GUEST (*Shouting*)
You've betrayed me!
You have made me
Listen to a pack of lies!
Your husband dead—?
Hah! He has fled
To rouse your neighbors with his cries!
He's fetching aid
To blunt my blade
So to your throats the steel now flies!
WIFE AND CHILDREN
Please, dear Jasper Ruddigore
Let us warm your heart. . .
Our corpses strewn on the floor
Could not push a cart!
But we could pull, we could drag you. . .
Serve you, night and day
We'd be happy wearing harness
And never run away!
We'll beg for you and keep you dry;
Save you from the cold. . .
You'll have a crowd forever by
To do as they are told!
It's lonely walking all alone
Through this mud and rain. . .
Oh, Jasper, if we're mercy shown
We can ease your pain!
GUEST
I'm aware of your cunning thought. . .
Praying that I'd soon be caught!
But I shall never, never fall!
(*As he intensifies the sharpening of his knife*)
The moment's come to kill you all!
WIFE
Oh, Jasper, dear, you must believe
What Frederick said; he'd not deceive. . .

But, alas, he was not strong enough
Now you're our master, firm and tough
GUEST
Be quiet! I hear steps outside. . .
(*To Children*)
Be quick and stand by her
Quicker, closer, woe betide
If you dare to even stir—!
(*Pause*)
Where is the key?
WIFE
It lies in the bowl. .
GUEST
Where is the bowl?
WIFE
I cannot see. . .
1ST CHILD
It stood in the mink mank
2ND CHILD
Now it is pink pank
GUEST
Give me the bowl!
(*A knock*)
Now don't move a hair
Or utter a sound
For if you dare
It will need just a bound
And not one will I spare!
(*Another knock*)
It is late, who is there—?
WARNER (*From outside*)
I only want to know how you are—?
GUEST
We only want to know who you are—?
WARNER
There are robbers round about
Better keep a close lookout!

GUEST
Do not worry, we're all right
Robbers will be killed on sight!
WARNER
Are you sure your door's secure—?
GUEST
We're not that stupid, yes, I'm sure!
WARNER
Then if all is well in there
I'll go away, but do take care. . .
GUEST
Yes, you idiot, you can go!
And take all that you think you know
Of villains—hah, it can't be much
If you're concerned with doors and such!
CHILDREN
Perhaps it was dear Peter Wright
His red shirt flowing in the night. . .
GUEST
I must think quickly about your offer
The hospitality you did proffer!
. . .Perhaps I *do* have time to spare
I might as well be here as. . .there!
CHILDREN
Oh, Jasper, dear, you know we'll do
Anything you want us to!
Put father's slippers on your feet
And we will shine your boots a treat
And here's the shirt he wears in bed
The softest pillow for your head. . .
Now just lie down—oh, here below
In case of need we'll put the po
Oh, dearest Jasper Ruddigore
You'll want for nothing evermore!
WIFE
I'd make the fire glow warm and red
If I could move my hands—instead

They feel as though they're nearly dead. . .
GUEST
Hold them out and I will show
How I can free you with one blow
There! The rope just flew in two
Remember what this knife can do!
WIFE and CHILDREN (*Softly*)
Oh, no, oh, no, we won't forget
How he can wield the knife
He is our Lord and Master set
To order Death or Life
His shining blade will be obeyed
Because we are indeed afraid
CHILDREN
Inky pinky cockaloo
Higgely piggely bugaboo
Hanky wanky tackatee
Wiggely waggely huggaree
The ragbone man has got a sack
He carries it upon his back
He takes the old and gives the new
Bubbely bobbely out goes you
How he stretches out his legs
How he throws his cap
How his hair stands up and begs
How his beard can flap
It grows and grows so when it snows
It can keep him warm
And when he blows his big red nose
It's like a thunderstorm
Now his boots are taken off
His black socks do look neat
Oh, no, ahem, excuse our cough
They're just his dirty feet!
Now his trousers are removed
(*They giggle*)
He's broad as he is long

In fact, he couldn't be improved
He is so big and strong
And now we take him to the bed
As quickly as we can
A yawn, a scratch, he rests his head
Our fat, good, lovely man!

WIFE
Has he put his knife down yet?

CHILDREN
He's holding tight its shiny threat

WIFE
Has the dear man gone to sleep?
Feel his hands—but gently—creep. . .

CHILDREN
The steel is in an iron grip
His fists are clenched so it won't slip

1ST CHILD
Should we pinch his nose?

2ND CHILD
And tickle his big toes?

1ST CHILD
And give his beard a tweak?

2ND CHILD
And blow upon his cheek?

1ST CHILD
And make his tummy itch?

2ND CHILD
And make his red nose twitch?

CHILDREN
He's sunk into the bed
Just like a lump of lead
And isn't moving, so
We'll go and bring the bow
His neck we can entwine
Three times three is nine
Round and round we'll go
And quickly tie the bow!

(*Pause*)
You know what we mean—?
To look pretty and clean
We'll fetch that pink bow
And tie it just so. . .!

GUEST

Ha!!
(*Angrily*)
I know what you are playing at!
Get over there and lie down flat!
And not another sound from you
Or else I'll beat you black and blue!
Woman, you come over here
And lie where I can feel you near!

CHILDREN

Oh, Jasper, see how quick we run
To show how your commands are done!

GUEST

Now pull the blanket up, you pair!
Until I cannot see one hair
Woman, blow the candle out
So it is dark both in and out!
Come closer, so I won't feel cold. . .

WIFE

How can I, when you will keep hold. . .
Of your knife—if you dropped it though. . .

GUEST

No, I will not let it go!

WIFE

But it makes me shake like jelly
When I feel it prick my belly!

GUEST

Do as I say or else I'll freeze. . .
I'll hold the knife just as I please!

CHILDREN (*Whispering*)

Eeny meeny mink mank
Pink pank pink pank

Roly poly peely pi
Hicky dicky dock
(*A knock*)

GUEST
He's back again, the stupid pest!
He's woke me up and spoiled my rest

WARNER (*From outside*)
Forgive me for disturbing you
But if what I am told is true
There is a robber very near
He has a casket, so I hear. . .
He's really huge, I understand
He lifts a horse with just one hand!
I haven't seen him, but they say
He was seen to head this way!
The sky is dark, the stars can't play. . .
If you need help, I'll gladly stay

WIFE
Who can this be? Oh, do come in. . .

GUEST
Be quiet, woman, stop your din
Or else I'll make your belly grin!
(*The door opens*)

WARNER
I don't expect you are to blame
For unlocked doors, but all the same
There's lots of thugs who walk about
With guns and knuckledusters out. . .

GUEST
How dare you come in here; get out!
I can deal with thugs without. . .
The help of an ill-mannered lout!

WARNER
Forgive me, but your wife did shout. . .

GUEST
No one called, I know you're wrong!
It was the wind, it's very strong

WARNER

There isn't any wind out there. . .
Not a puff disturbs the air. . .

GUEST

I will not stand for any more
You busybody—there's the door!

WARNER

But it isn't safe outside
Someone lurks, he groaned and sighed
And now he's creeping through the murk
I see him twist and lurch and jerk. . .
It's someone large, so turn the key
Oh, how brave we'll have to be!

CHILDREN

You cannot turn the key
Eeny meeny mink
For here, as you see
Pink pank pink
Is an empty bowl
Roly poly roll
There isn't any key
Where there used to be
The key was for our door
It's not there any more!
Roly poly peely pi
Hicky dicky dock

WARNER

I've got my knife and I am ready!
See my hand, it's very steady
If I stand here, why then, I trust
I can kill him with one thrust!

WIFE

Oh, no! Oh, no!

GUEST

Shut up! You know. . .
What I can do to silence you!

CHILDREN
We wonder who this man can be
Who's come into our place—?
It makes it worse we cannot see
The look upon his face
But if the shirt he wears is red
We'll know it's Peter Wright
Please turn around or nod your head
And tell us we are right!

GUEST
Go back to where you were, you two!
And pull the blanket over you

WARNER
Be quiet, or we'll all be dead!
He's just outside, I hear his tread
He puts the casket down, the knave!
And now he walks into his grave!
(The door squeaks open. Then, the sound of a violent blow)

WIFE *(Dying)*
Oh, Frederick!
(Another blow)
Oh, Frederick, ohhh. . .!

MAN *(Dying)*
Oh, not like this! Oh, no. . .oh, no. . .!

CHILDREN
Stop it, stop it; please, no more!
You've got the gold, it's by the door

WARNER
If there's gold, then it is mine. . .
Because *I* killed the thieving swine!

GUEST
I live here, so the property. . .
The gold and all belongs to me!

WARNER
You remain in your bed of sin. . .
I'll take the gold—now, I win!

GUEST
Oh, yes, I know that's what you'd like
To take what's mine, you dirty tyke!
WARNER
Don't make me laugh; you look a farce. . .
Your nightshirt flapping round your arse!
GUEST
You watch your mouth or I'll kick yours. . .
You'll hit the dung heap on all fours!
WARNER
You piddling dwarf; you think you're big. . .
I'll slit you open like a pig!
GUEST
Hear him yap, the puny pup. . .
Come over here, I'll shut you up!
WARNER
No, you come here, that's if you dare. . .
You'll taste my knife, by God, I swear!
GUEST
Your little knife is blunt as wood. . .
The one I've got is twice as good!
WARNER
Ha, ha, you come and I will bash you!
GUEST (*With short, sharp, hissing sounds*)
Ha, ha, I'm coming and I'll smash you!
WARNER
Ha ha ha ha ha ha—just come!
GUEST
Ha ha ha ha ha ha—I come!
(*Sound of blows and clatter of knives*)
GUEST
Ha ha ha ha ha ha hum. . .!
WARNER
Ha ha o o ha ha o. . .!
GUEST
Ha ha so so ha ha so. . .
WARNER
Ha au au ha au au. . .

GUEST

Au ha ha au ha ha au. . .

WARNER

Au au o au au o. .

GUEST

O au o au o o. .

WARNER

O o au o au o. .

GUEST

O au oo—!

WARNER

Au o o—!

(*The fighting sounds continue more subdued during the following:*)

1ST CHILD

Come quick!
We'll leave them while they kill
Each other, as we know they will!
They'll fall upon the corpses there
So we can creep along—take care
You do not slip upon the blood. . .
We'll tiptoe round the crimson flood. . .
Softly now, hold my hand
Here's the wall to follow and. . .
We'll find the door, yes, this is it. . .
Ah, look—the dawn is nearly lit!
Mind the body, stiff and grim
Carefully step over him!
Here's the casket which was hid. . .
It isn't locked, so lift the lid. . .
We'll need a lot where we are going. . .
And we'll use it while we're growing. . .
Plunge your fingers deeply in
And fill your pockets to the brim!

2ND CHILD

It doesn't clink, and I feel soil. . .
Can this be the golden spoil?

It isn't gold, it's much too light. . .
Dried turnips—how can that be right?
1ST CHILD
The box of fodder from the stable. . .
Alas, the gold was just a fable!
Take a few which we can chew. . .
The road is long for me and you!

Curtain

Albert Bermel

THE MOUNTAIN CHORUS

Albert Bermel

Albert Bermel is a man of multiple talents who successfully has juxtaposed four separate though interrelated careers as playwright, theatre critic, translator, and teacher.

Born in London on December 20, 1927, and now an American citizen, Mr. Bermel prepared for his multi-faceted professional life at London University.

A recipient of a Guggenheim Fellowship in playwriting (1965–66), his plays have been performed in many of the world's leading theatre centers including New York, London, Edinburgh, Berlin, and Spoleto, Italy.

Four of Albert Bermel's plays have had their premieres in London: *One Leg Over the Wrong Wall* (Royal Court, 1960); *Herod First* (Saville, 1965); *The Workout* (Questors); and *The Mountain Chorus* (New Arts, 1967). The latter play appears in print for the first time in this anthology.

In addition to his own plays, Mr. Bermel has translated many classic and modern foreign stage works including Jean Cocteau's *The Infernal Machine* (produced at the Phoenix Theatre, New York, 1958, under the direction of Herbert Berghof and with a cast headed by June Havoc, John Kerr, Philip Bourneuf and Jacob Ben-Ami); *Horatius* by Pierre Corneille, France's first great tragic dramatist; Georges Courteline's popular farces (*Boubouroche; The Commissioner Has a Big Heart; Badin the Bold*); and new versions of seven of Molière's principal short comedies which frequently are staged and televised in the United States and Canada.

Among his books are: *The Genius of the French Theatre,* an anthology of plays and criticism; *The Plays of Courteline* (co-translated with Jacques Barzun); and *One-act Comedies of Molière.*

His essays and critiques on the theatre, films, and literary topics have appeared in *Harper's Magazine; Tulane Drama Review; Arts in Society; Kenyon Review;* and *Midstream.* From 1961 through 1963, he was performing arts editor for *Horizon* and for the past four years, theatre critic for *The New Leader.*

Mr. Bermel also is a prominent member of the faculty of

Columbia University's School of the Arts where he teaches playwriting and theatre history.

A resident of Manhattan, he is married and the father of two young sons.

Characters

NIGEL
DOROTHY
HACKER
SIMP
TAPPY
FONEY
LASSIE
SHEILA

Scene:

A mountaintop; the present.

Nigel enters leaning into the wind, heavily laden, wearing a climbing outfit. He unstraps a pack from his back.

NIGEL: Dorothy, can you make it?

DOROTHY'S VOICE: I'm trying.

NIGEL: Brave girl. This looks like *it*. I'll check. (*He takes triangulation equipment from his pack and surveys the site*) Pretty near perfect. Look at that tree. Who could ask for more? On top of a mountain. . .(*He unfastens his pack. Dorothy staggers in*)

DOROTHY: Finally.

NIGEL: Exactly what we hoped for. You're not too pooped?

DOROTHY: Only slightly.

NIGEL: Shall I disengage you from your pack?

DOROTHY: Bless you, Nigel.

NIGEL: Worth the climb, eh?

DOROTHY: Mm.

NIGEL: There you are. Away with the ballast. No, don't sit on your pack.

DOROTHY: I sort of folded.

NIGEL: You'll squash something. (*Lays a handkerchief on the ground for her*) How's that?

DOROTHY: Homey.

NIGEL: Happy birthday.

DOROTHY: Thank you. Coming here was sheer inspiration.

NIGEL: I can't take all the credit.

DOROTHY: Thank you.

NIGEL: Fine place to revive the old bliss.

DOROTHY: Oh, Nigel.

NIGEL: And a tree to ourselves. A darn good tree. Pine, maybe.

DOROTHY: Gorgeous.

NIGEL: Sort of a windbreak, too. Bring the binocs?

DOROTHY: In your pack.

NIGEL: No, yours.

DOROTHY: Excuse me, Nigel.

NIGEL: You didn't forget them?

DOROTHY: Wasn't my responsibility.

NIGEL: Let's not bicker about responsibilities.

DOROTHY: Please, Nigel. On my birthday.

NIGEL: Well, dammit, we need the binocs. How will we know we're alone?

DOROTHY: Here they are. In my pack.

NIGEL: Ha. (*He takes them from her*)

DOROTHY: Nigel.

NIGEL: What are you worried about now?

DOROTHY: Love me?

NIGEL: Love you. And me?

DOROTHY: You too. Yes, much.

NIGEL: (*Using the binoculars*) Well and truly alone. All those other mountains. But miles away. Swarming with tourists. Wanted to make sure. Now I'll see to the tent.

DOROTHY: Will it be out of sight of the other mountains?

NIGEL: In the hollow here. (*He begins to erect the tent*)

DOROTHY: But from the air? Planes and so forth?

NIGEL: Sturdy fabric. Very opaque. I asked the salesman.

DOROTHY: Don't you want a drink first?

NIGEL: Later.

DOROTHY: Even a little one?

NIGEL: I said later.

DOROTHY: Nigel.

NIGEL: What now?

DOROTHY: Love me?

NIGEL: Love you.

DOROTHY: And. . .?

NIGEL: And me?

DOROTHY: You, too.

NIGEL: Damn awkward with this wind.

DOROTHY: Can I help?

NIGEL: No. It's your birthday.

DOROTHY: It's a pretty tent.

NIGEL: If you say so.

DOROTHY: Expensive?

NIGEL: Nothing's too expensive for your birthday.

DOROTHY: Thank you.

NIGEL: Blast this wind. And the ground is solid rock. How do they expect you to put up a tent in a place like this?

DOROTHY: Leave it till later.

NIGEL: I will not. Tent's the first thing we need. If a tree can stand here, so can a tent.

DOROTHY: Unroll the mattresses?

NIGEL: If you like.

DOROTHY: I brought the blue sheets with the pattern. Not the white ones. And the blue pillowcases.

NIGEL: Why the blue?

DOROTHY: Matches the top of the mountain.

NIGEL: There it is. Our tent.

DOROTHY: Stunning.

NIGEL: Oh. . .

DOROTHY: Nigel, what is it?

NIGEL: Should've made up the beds first. How are we going to fix them inside that dinky little tent?

DOROTHY: I'll do it.

NIGEL: You'll knock the tent over.

DOROTHY: No, I'm careful with tents.

NIGEL: Forget it. (*He takes the mattresses and slides them into the tent*)

DOROTHY: I'll be fixing the drinks.

NIGEL: My job.

DOROTHY: I want to be useful.

NIGEL: Chill the glasses.

DOROTHY: Where's the insulated bag?

NIGEL: Your pack. Top left compartment.

DOROTHY: Do we have enough ice?

NIGEL: We're strong on cubes. Not sure about the crushed. (*Pause*) The beds just about fit.

DOROTHY: Goody.

NIGEL: Which way up do our heads go? If we put them next to the entrance flap we'll catch a draught. If we have them at the other end, how will we ever get in?

DOROTHY: I'm for lots of breeze. These winds stimulate me. Glass chilled enough?

NIGEL: Next to my cheek, please.

DOROTHY: Yes?

NIGEL: Could be a mite cooler. There are the beds. Not the most thrilling bedmaking job I've ever seen, but sleepable.

DOROTHY: Nigel, they're darling.

NIGEL: Now for the rug. (*He spreads it out in front of the tent*)

DOROTHY: Nigel, a white fur rug.

NIGEL: For the you know, preliminaries.

DOROTHY: How considerate. Where did you get it?

NIGEL: Sporting goods store.

DOROTHY: Real fur?

NIGEL: Imitation polar bear. Washable. Static-free.

DOROTHY: It's all gruff and grumpy. I love it.

NIGEL: What next? The banner.

DOROTHY: Yes, please. Nigel, why don't we. . .?

NIGEL: What?

DOROTHY: Put it on the tree?

NIGEL: Let me think. Yes, the tree would work. (*He takes out a college banner and nails it to the tree*)

DOROTHY: The tree suits it.

NIGEL: What about the suntan oil?

DOROTHY: I brought lotion. Didn't want to grease up the sheets. But Nigel, you're not sunbathing in this wind?

NIGEL: Might get a windburn.

DOROTHY: A good point.

NIGEL: On the other hand, the sun may come out later. Time for refreshments. What're you having?

DOROTHY: What are you?

NIGEL: Vodka martini.

DOROTHY: Japalac, please.

NIGEL: One dash of raspberry syrup? Have two. It's your birthday.

DOROTHY: One and a half. Light on the rye.

NIGEL: (*Mixing*) How are the glasses coming along?

DOROTHY: Try.

NIGEL: Good. Keep them at that temperature.

DOROTHY: (*Looking through the binoculars*) Astounding view. In every direction.

NIGEL: Very varied.

DOROTHY: Hors d'oeuvres. Caviar or whitefish dip?

NIGEL: A nibble of both.

DOROTHY: On an onion biscuit?

NIGEL: Why not?

DOROTHY: I'll risk the health pumpernickel.

NIGEL: Where's the tray? (*She gives him a silver tray. He arranges the drinks and the hors d'oeuvres. He sets up stack tables and unfolds a pair of chairs. They put their drinks on coasters*)

DOROTHY: Whose toast?

NIGEL: It's your birthday.

DOROTHY: That's hard. I'm thinking. Got it. To *everything.*

NIGEL: I'll drink to that. (*He does*)

DOROTHY: The Japalac is overpoweringly good.

NIGEL: The raspberry syrup. I put in one and three quarters.

DOROTHY: Nigel, you shouldn't've.

NIGEL: The caviar isn't bad.

DOROTHY: Nor is the whitefish.

NIGEL: Another toast?

DOROTHY: Interesting idea. Your turn.

NIGEL: To a successful conclusion.

DOROTHY: Nigel, you're so risqué.

NIGEL: Oh.

DOROTHY: What?

NIGEL: A mark on the silverware.

DOROTHY: Tarnish?

NIGEL: Looks like it.

DOROTHY: Borrow mine.

NIGEL: It doesn't matter.

DOROTHY: Not quite hygienic. But my lipstick has practically worn off.

NIGEL: I said it doesn't matter.

DOROTHY: Nigel.

NIGEL: Yes?

DOROTHY: Love me?

NIGEL: Love you.

DOROTHY: You forgot again.

NIGEL: And me?

DOROTHY: You too. Nigel, this is heaven.

NIGEL: Thank you. Must keep up with the sexual revolution.

DOROTHY: The what?

NIGEL: You know, the younger generation.

DOROTHY: It's better than our honeymoon.

NIGEL: Higher up, anyway.

DOROTHY: Remember that Bermuda beach hut where you. . .?

NIGEL: I could really wear swim shorts.

DOROTHY: Nigel, you're awfully well preserved.

NIGEL: Thank you. I'll get out the transformer.

DOROTHY: Nigel, shouldn't we. . .?

NIGEL: What?

DOROTHY: Be at it.

NIGEL: Must get in the mood first. Radio or TV?

DOROTHY: TV, please. More to look at. (*He takes out a portable set and twiddles*) Oh, dear. Nothing but soap opera.

NIGEL: We'll try the stereo.

DOROTHY: No, leave this on. Something to look at.

NIGEL: Contrast is only so-so. Brightness not much better.

DOROTHY: One of those other mountains getting in the way?

NIGEL: Impossible. This is a mountaintop model.

DOROTHY: They think of everything.

NIGEL: For a price.

DOROTHY: Can you up the sound?

NIGEL: On full already. Better hook up the stereo. We ought to get plenty of dimensional resonance with the valley down there, the sky up there.

DOROTHY: There's a beautiful cloud.

NIGEL: Don't see it.

DOROTHY: Behind the TV antenna.

NIGEL: Nasty-looking fellow.

DOROTHY: Has a head like a unicorn. Would you refresh my Japalac?

NIGEL: Must clear up this wiring first. You got the leads from the preamp tangled in your pack with the audio cable. (*Dorothy helps herself to another drink*)

DOROTHY: That unicorn. It has two horns.

NIGEL: If the transformer's not in shape, we're sunk. I wouldn't be surprised if the connections took a hell of a jolting up that hill.

DOROTHY: Not two horns. Three. And three heads. Four, five, six, seven. . .Believe it or not.

NIGEL: For God's sake, Dorothy. Don't keep on with your horns while I'm concentrating.

DOROTHY: The next mountain on the right has a peach of a waterfall. Most exhilarating to watch. All that foam. Bunching up at the edge. Then—whoosh. Nigel, what would happen if this mountain turned into a volcano? Right underneath us? Would we be swallowed up? In boiling lava?

NIGEL: No.

DOROTHY: Why not?

NIGEL: This isn't volcano country.

DOROTHY: How can you be sure?

NIGEL: I found the red terminal.

DOROTHY: I'm having another Japalac. Nigel!

NIGEL: Go ahead. It's your birthday.

DOROTHY: I'm putting in three raspberry syrups and two ryes.

NIGEL: Where's the outlet for the black terminal? That's all I ask.

DOROTHY: Come and sit down. You're all tense on my birthday.

NIGEL: So. Now we'll see if the whole thing goes up in smoke.

DOROTHY: That would be a shame. Personally I couldn't care less.

NIGEL: Hear that? (*Violinny dance music begins*) Reception's terrific. I'll move the other speaker three or four inches.

DOROTHY: Have another vodka martini.

NIGEL: Are you hearing balanced sound?

DOROTHY: I'll say. Sit on the polar bear rug.

NIGEL: Give me a couple of minutes. To unlax.

DOROTHY: Put your head in my lap.

NIGEL: I won't be able to see the screen.

DOROTHY: Turn it. (*He does, then sits in the folding chair. She tries to take his head in her lap*)

NIGEL: Don't think much of the color. The folding chair is folding under me.

DOROTHY: How about this? (*She lies on the white rug*)

NIGEL: Be over before long. Pity. For soap opera this is quite respectable.

DOROTHY: The unicorn cloud's gone. Surged away. Here comes its baby.

NIGEL: Unicorns are out in force today. What's happening to the stereo? The automatic frequency control must have slipped to manual. Dorothy, we're skidding between stations.

DOROTHY: It does sound weird. To hell with it.

NIGEL: And the tuner's new. Paid on the spot for it. The check's gone through by now. Should have taken out a charge account there.

DOROTHY: I think it's another radio. Somebody else coming.

NIGEL: Christ! I made sure we'd have this peak to ourselves.

DOROTHY: Snub them bitterly. Keep watching the TV. (*She gets up and joins him*)

NIGEL: Why should they enjoy the privileges of our TV and stereo? Who lugged them all the way up—? (*Nigel switches off the radio, turns down the television sound*) Here's a book. Read.

DOROTHY: I'm off books lately. No ads or anything.

NIGEL: *The New Yorker?*

DOROTHY: That's more like it. Lots of color. Nigel, they couldn't have chosen a worse time to invade us. I was getting receptive. Tell them it's my birthday. If they take the hint.

NIGEL: Won't be for long. We'll freeze them out. (*The other radio approaches. Six young people appear. Four are boys: Hacker, Tappy, Simp, Foney. Two are girls: Sheila, Lassie*)

HACKER: By the tree. (*To Nigel*) Hi, Pops. (*To the others*) In a clean, gentleman-type circle.

TAPPY: Is this for a war council?

HACKER: Don't get brighty with me. (*Hits Tappy in the face*)

TAPPY: What did I say?

HACKER: (*To Simp, who has the radio*) And cut that radio.

SIMP: I could make it like low.

HACKER: I said cut it. (*Throws the radio over the edge*) A nice drop. Must be six, seven hundred feet down. Made sweet music all the way.

SIMP: But Hacker. . .

HACKER: I told you you wasn't to bring it. Take the roll call.

SIMP: My brother bought that radio.

HACKER: Take the roll call or your brother will have to buy a new brother. (*Lassie leans against the tree and decorates her eyes with a green pencil. Foney necks with Sheila*) Foney, get off that chick's chest while we're taking our roll call.

DOROTHY: Are they planning to stay here?

NIGEL: If they are I'll have a stern word with them.

HACKER: Say, Pops, you don't have to breeze or nothing. Stick around with the broad.

NIGEL: This lady is my wife.

HACKER: Nice going, Pops. Simp, did I hear you not reading the roll call?

SIMP: Hacker, honorary president.

HACKER: Here.

SIMP: Simp, honorary secretary. Here. Foney, honorary treasurer.

FONEY: What? Here.

HACKER: I told you: stop chewing at that chick.

SIMP: Tappy, honorary advisory observer.

TAPPY: Here. What's all this about?

HACKER: Ask me one more question. Just one more. Okay, Mr. Secretary. Take the minutes of the last meeting.

(*Nigel stands up*)

NIGEL: Pardon me. My wife and I purposely chose this isolated peak.

SIMP: This what?

HACKER: You stiff. Keep your ears ungummed. The man said, "Peak." That's right, Pops: Peak?

NIGEL: And if you intend to remain here. . .

HACKER: We intend, Pops. But that don't give you no reason to blow. Is somebody hustling you? Simp, why did you quit reading?

SIMP: "The exec committee met. . ."

SHEILA: Haw.

SIMP: Shut your goddam lip.

SHEILA: Go stuff.

SIMP: Hacker, shall I give it to her?

HACKER: Mr. Secretary, I didn't like that word "goddam." That is not a gentleman-type word. Get going with the minutes.

SIMP: I keep thinking about that sonofabitching radio.

HACKER: Any more slang like that out of you while we got company and I'll take your face apart.

SIMP: "The exec committee met in conclave at the corner table in Kuppenheimer's Drugstore & Paperback Jamboree. Present were the following Toreadors. . ."

SHEILA: Haw.

HACKER: Give it to her.

SIMP: Me?

HACKER: You. Anybody. Everybody. (*The boys all strike Sheila*)

LASSIE: You scum. Hitting a girl. What you want to do that for?

HACKER: That's not my idea of a quality-type word. Scum. Give it to her.

(*They strike Lassie. She sits and weeps, the green running down her face*)

SHEILA: Foney, after that, don't you never come near me again.

FONEY: It was a little hit, baby. Here, I'll make it better.

NIGEL: I don't wish to intrude on your deliberations. I must remind you, though, that first claims come first. I expect you to honor ours.

HACKER: Sure, Pops. You sit back and make like you're in your own mansion. Simp?

SIMP: "Present were the following Toreadors from the exec committee: Hacker, Simp, Foney. Also, Lassie, Sheila and Tappy, observers. . ." Ahh. . .

NIGEL: And I don't approve of your striking girls.

HACKER: Anything you say, Pops. Simp, if you quit reading them minutes one more time you'll get my toe where you can't wear it.

SIMP: "The exec committee agreed with the honorary president that the proposed rumble between the Toreadors and their deadly foes, the Muckrakers, will, shall, and should take place as heretofore decided by the honorary president. The meeting thereupon ended."

HACKER: Who put in that word "deadly"?

SIMP: Me, I guess.

HACKER: Is that a gentleman-type word?

SIMP: I'll take it out.

HACKER: Gink. You delete it.

NIGEL: Are you ignoring my request? Perhaps I should warn you that I can enforce it. As a former fullback who has maintained his condition by climbing and other activities—

HACKER: Does everybody accept the minutes? Minutes accepted.

NIGEL: And further, as an amateur boxer of no mean prowess—

HACKER: Pops, you're the champ. So we Toreadors have to make up our executive mind why said rumble didn't take place.

FONEY: Somebody ratted.

NIGEL: Threats don't seem to deter them. Should I take action?

DOROTHY: Nigel, they're young.

TAPPY: Look, is this a war council?

HACKER: Give it to him. (*The boys descend on Tappy and strike him*) One warning ought to be enough, Tappy. Now, like Foney explained, *somebody* ratted. Except ratted is not a quality-type word. Somebody *betrayed*. Some canary flew to the boys in blue and said, "The Toreadors figure to rumble." And the blue boys greased him up good. He took away all the green he could handle.

TAPPY: Don't we have no idea who done it?

HACKER: We have a very fine idea.

TAPPY: Then what?

HACKER: Then we're holding an official-type inquiry.

FONEY: Great!

HACKER: Shut your ugly-type yap.

FONEY: Maybe I want to confess.

HACKER: Yes—?

FONEY: . . .I was kidding.

HACKER: At an inquiry? (*Striking him*) Do I have to keep all the order around here with my two single hands?

SHEILA: What you want to hit him for?

FONEY: Now you give me a black eye or something.

HACKER: We better level that off. (*Striking him in the other eye*) We don't want our treasurer losing his honorary balance.

LASSIE: He lost it when he come out of his mother's whatever he come out of.

HACKER: Lassie, one more squawk and I'll hand you the straight treatment. I'm still waiting for this confession. It better fly out quick. And it better be a clean in language Toreador-type confession all the way.

NIGEL: This is intolerable.

DOROTHY: Nigel, let's move on.

NIGEL: Uproot the tent? Set up the stereo again after it's going so beautifully? I give them five minutes. After that, I boot them off this peak.

DOROTHY: They've taken over.

HACKER: (*His eyes fixed upon Simp*) Who's about to confess?

SIMP: (*Squirming*) I don't have nothing to confess. Except if I confess on somebody else.

HACKER: You want to sing a song—? Point a finger?. . . That's a bad sign.

SIMP: If the guilty one don't confess I mean I'll confess on him.

HACKER: What you say to that, Foney?

FONEY: Me? It's not true.

HACKER: You never spoke to no blue boys?

FONEY: I was a gentleman-type Toreador all the way through.

HACKER: Get your hand outa her skirt when you tell me that.

FONEY: I swear on my mother's coffin.

HACKER: Your mother is alive and living.

FONEY: She's got to go into a coffin some day, don't she?

HACKER: How about Tappy there?

TAPPY: You picking on me again?

HACKER: Don't throw me a question when I throw you a question.

TAPPY: How *about* me? And how about *you,* Hacker?

HACKER: After I warned you. You threw me two questions. I'm going to push your mouth where it ought to go, down your ignorant-type throat.

NIGEL: Four minutes up.

DOROTHY: Nigel, before you explode give them fair warning. Listen to me, you boys. How long are you staying here with these games?

HACKER: Games, lady? If this is games I like to know what's for real. Right, Pops?

NIGEL: Do you mind not calling me "Pops." I'm old enough to be your father.

FONEY: How old would that be, Pops? You must be damn near thirty.

HACKER: Foney, apologize to the old folks for that word you said there. Or I'll rub your nose on that tree till one of them wears out.

FONEY: I apologize.

HACKER: (*Turns back to Nigel*) Like I said, Pops, you can sit around.

NIGEL: I mean to, I assure you.

DOROTHY: How did you get up here?

SIMP: We come in the *convertible.*

NIGEL: I suggest you scramble back into your *convertible* and take off instantly.

DOROTHY: A road. Nigel, we may get crowded off this mountain by more hooligans. Let's pack.

HACKER: Stick around, Pops. You might see something you can tell the world.

NIGEL: Be sensible, Dorothy. We can't unmake the beds in front of these snickering infants.

HACKER: It's a straight invitation. You wouldn't want to reject me, would you, Pops?

DOROTHY: How long will you be here?

HACKER: You know how it is, lady. When you have something on your executive mind. What you do, Pops? You a lawyer? Our defendant could sure use a hot lawyer. It might shorten this inquiry up.

TAPPY: What you mean, defendant, Hacker?

HACKER: You been in plenty big law cases, Pops? The newspaper-type kind of cases?

NIGEL: I am not a lawyer.

HACKER: Okay, Pops, you're the like citizen-type.

NIGEL: Will you please refrain from calling me "Pops"?

HACKER: Refrain?

NIGEL: Yes. Desist.

HACKER: Desist, refrain, desist. Did you clunks hear them dignity-type words? Simp, you better took them down in your minutes.

SIMP: Just wrote them, Hacker.

HACKER: Pops, you certainly are the class we need around here.

DOROTHY: Nigel, don't let them provoke you. . .

HACKER: Look at it this way, Pops. Nobody's hanging on to you by the short hairs or nothing. You want to breeze—

NIGEL: By God, Dorothy, just step out of sight and I'll. . .

HACKER: Nothing is going to like happen, Pops. Be our guest.

NIGEL: We were here first.

HACKER: Sure you was. (*Turns, ominously*) So, we come back to Tappy. . .

(*Tappy starts to dash away. Hacker dives at his legs and brings him down, then sits on his head*)

HACKER: You slobs see how slowball you are around here? If I wasn't on the team everybody would like cut out. Now. What's with Tappy? He afraid of this legal-type inquiry? Maybe he's sorry he ratted on his colleague-type buddies.

TAPPY: I didn't do nothing. You're breaking my neck.

HACKER: Tap, take it easy. All that bouncing makes me not comfortable.

NIGEL: You have no right to squash that boy's head.

HACKER: Cool it, Pops. Let's not get all busy before we investigate what this inquiry is going to prove.

TAPPY: You're killing my neck.

NIGEL: Let the boy rise and speak for himself.

HACKER: You hear that, Tappy? You got yourself a lawyer. One of the biggest. Pops here is the king of the brighty lawyers.

SIMP: Let's swing. I'm getting the chills.

(He idly punches Foney's arm. Foney comes out of his necking trance with Sheila, and punches back. They beat away at each other's biceps.

Hacker gets off Tappy's head and pulls him to his feet by the collar)

HACKER: Okay, let the inquiry roll.

NIGEL: Release that boy.

TAPPY: I didn't squeal. Not one word.

HACKER: You'll squeal plenty before this deal is through. Okay, you gentlemen of the jury. Unsuck your face from that cheap-type broad. This is big business for we Toreadors. Let's have respect for the law. Go ahead, Tappy. Spill.

NIGEL: Release him. I shan't say it again.

TAPPY: What you going to do to me?

HACKER: Now, Tappy, could I tell you that before I knew if you was like one thousand per cent guilty or less?

TAPPY: I mean, if I was to confess on myself, would I get a reprieve-type sentence?

HACKER: What you think this jury is for? Making bargains with a prisoner? Either you confess or. . .

TAPPY: Mister, will you protect me?

NIGEL: Before I say another thing, my boy, I want you to understand that whatever you've done or have not done is hardly my concern.

DOROTHY: (*Apprehensively*) Nigel! Beds, banner, tent, everything. . .

NIGEL: (*To Tappy*) I don't envy you your fate but perhaps this incident will teach you to select thoughtful companions, not roughnecks.

HACKER: Hey, Pops, watch out for the foul-type language. Like we can lose our cool, too.

TAPPY: Crud on the lotta you. So I betrayed! You was always coming down on me. I was the youngest nobody around. Now I count. I went to the cops. I cut that rumble dead. I was on the both sides at the same time. All the world trusted me. That was pretty good, hey?

HACKER: Everybody's friend. A very sweet-type arrangement.

TAPPY: You bet your butt it was. (*Nigel steps forward. Dorothy clutches at him*)

HACKER: And no fuzz didn't hand you no bread—? No crumbs. . .?

TAPPY: No.

FONEY: Clobber the truth out of his guts.

SIMP: I knewed it was him all along.

HACKER: You see what these Toreadors are asking for, Tappy? They want a bit of your like blood. Keep them unhappy. Spit up the truth.

TAPPY: I am.

HACKER: Fix him against the tree. For a total confession. (*Foney and Simp pin Tappy against the tree*) And here we have a rock with kind of edges. (*He presses the edge into the small of Tappy's back. Tappy cries out, painfully*) Tappy, what's all the yelling? We didn't even start yet. . .A bit of friendly pressure. Until we come to the full truth.

TAPPY: (*Relenting*) Okay. Okay. All the getting cut up and beat up all the time. . .

HACKER: (*Ignoring Tappy's attempted explanation*). . . Not only did you rat. You lost your respect for the decent things in life. It don't twist your insides when the Muckrakers cross up our honor?

TAPPY: Get that rock thing outta my back.

HACKER: You was afraid you might be the somebody got hurt in the rumble.

TAPPY: Not only me. (*More pained*) That rock. . .

NIGEL: Dorothy, I don't want to push you aside, but. . .

HACKER: We Toreadors wouldn't destroy a colleague's backbone. Get that rope and tie him a very fine noose.

NIGEL: That's my mountain rope.

HACKER: We pay you for it, Pops.

NIGEL: To lynch him with?

HACKER: No question of a lynch. We just tie him to this strong-type tree and let him dangle his yelling tail. We wouldn't damage him. He's an associate. Except he ratted. He'll be safe as home hanging over this nature-type cliff.

TAPPY: How come it's always my buddies get cut up? Beaten? Never one of you exec committee guys for a change? The whistle blows, you're out there in back of us.

HACKER: Hear that, Pops? That's the type criminal mind you're facing here. I mean, *mean.*

NIGEL: Let that boy go! (*He pushes Dorothy aside, strides over to Foney and Simp, and pulls their arms away. Tappy darts behind the tree and escapes*)

HACKER: (*Stalkingly*) Why'd you want to do a thing like that, Pops—? (*He leaps at Nigel and knocks him to the ground. Foney and Simp join in. Dorothy screams. After a struggle, the boys tie Nigel with the rope*) Pops, you're mean, like Tappy. Letting him cut out. It could waste a whole 'nother day before we capture him. We thought you was more polite. . . .

DOROTHY: Take your hands off him!

HACKER: We don't use our hands, lady. This like rope does it all.

DOROTHY: It's my birthday.

HACKER: All the very best, lady, from all of us on the exec committee.

DOROTHY: You degraded young ruffians, you animals, you shit!

HACKER: I could of swore you was a gentleman-type lady. And here you bust out with them kind of personal statements.

NIGEL: You're not to lay a hand on her, you hear?

HACKER: What's all this about hands? (*Holds out his hands*) Here's my hands, Pops. Not fooling with a thing. You're just too heated, Pops. (*He ties the other end of the rope to the tree*) We'll just hang you out in that fresh air.

DOROTHY: He's done nothing to you!

HACKER: . . .Only let our "defendant" cut out. Only broke

up our proceedings. But we don't got a thing against old Pops. . . .You interested in space, Pops?

NIGEL: Whatever you do, let my wife go! She's a woman. . .

HACKER: Oh, I seen that, Pops, all the way up and down. You know? Like my personal mother is a woman. A very refined-type woman. You refrain and desist, Pops. And just don't rock the rope.

NIGEL: If you touch her—!

HACKER: Shame on your snazzy head, Pops, for thinking such-type things. This isn't my age of pickle. Okay, let him sink.

(Foney and Simp lower Nigel over the edge. Dorothy rushes toward them. Hacker places himself in her way. He steps forward. Dorothy sinks down onto the ground silently, just staring blankly ahead. Nigel's voice is heard, but not his words)

SHEILA: Anybody would think they was feebs the way it takes the both of them to lower one poor schnook who isn't no bigger than either one of them put together.

LASSIE: Some musclemen.

SIMP: *(Straining)* I'll talk to you later, you hairy hooker.

(He and Foney finish letting the rope out. They stand back)

FONEY: It's a powerful-type rope.

SIMP: A cinch.

FONEY: Hold forever.

(The tree suddenly comes out of the ground and topples over the edge after Nigel)

LASSIE: You Toreadors forget about the thin soil around here?

(Dorothy looks up, sees that the tree is missing, screams, and goes back into her stupor)

FONEY: It was this wind must have done it.

LASSIE: You geek-type murderers! Poor old guy. . .

SHEILA: He wasn't so old. . .

FONEY: *(Approaching Dorothy)* Lady, it was a accident. Right, Hacker?

HACKER: That's right, lady. The boys didn't mean a thing.

FONEY: What you mean. . .*the boys?*

HACKER: (*Ignoring him*) Listen, lady, a deal. We wouldn't let you carry him home alone in that wet state. We was like attached to old Pops. We'll bring him up here. And, if they ask you, we was the witness. We saw, see? The whole mess. . .

FONEY: Boy!

SIMP: Boy, ahoy! Wow!

FONEY: This looks like *it!*

HACKER: Quit the brighty talk! You two slobs was the ones tied the knots. First, we got to bring back old smashed-up Pops. Don't move a toe, lady. We'll be up here again in one second flat, so you don't have to be without old Pops on your birthday.

(*They look back at Dorothy. Then they run. There is the sound of their car racing away. After a moment, Dorothy rises and slowly crosses back to the encampment*)

DOROTHY: All this sun. So cold. Must be. . .late. . .(*Then, suddenly*) Nigel! *Nigel!* (*Weeping*) And the banner. Your forlorn banner. . .(*After taking a long drink and finishing Nigel's, she notices the television set which is still on. She crosses to her chair and sits down, staring blankly and sobbing. Gradually, the television begins to interest her*) Can't hear a thing. . .(*She turns up the volume. She continues to sob now and again. The television program takes hold of her. She stares at it, intently. Her sobs diminish. She smiles. She laughs. . .*)

Curtain

Michael Almaz

EVERY NUMBER WINS

(an entertainment)

Michael Almaz

Born in Tel Aviv, Michael Almaz prepared for a theatrical career by studying drama in New York City. After matriculating, he returned to Israel where he founded and managed his own theatre. The success of the venture was immediate and from 1953 through 1958, he directed more than thirty productions of plays by leading international dramatists. Indeed, he is credited with "first introducing the Israeli public to the modern theatre."

In 1958, Mr. Almaz went to England and for seven years was employed by the British Broadcasting Corporation's European Service as script writer and producer. Since 1966, he has devoted most of his time to playwriting and production work in the theatre.

A satiric entertainment with its rapier-like thrusts at human vanities, *Every Number Wins* has been successfully produced in a number of European countries. Its publication in *The Best Short Plays 1968* marks its first appearance in the United States.

Another of Michael Almaz's short plays, *In the King's Bosom,* which the author describes as "a serious comedy with farcical elements," has been widely performed on the British stage.

Characters

ADOLPHUS
GUARDIAN ANGEL
GRANNY
DAD
MUM
TWO WOMEN
TWO MEN
ANGELA
FRIEDA
MISTRESS
MODEL
CRITIC
TWO BEATNIKS
GIRL
GOSSIP WRITER
PHOTOGRAPHER
MILLIONAIRE
CALYPSO SINGERS
LORNA
JAMES
SMITH
REGGIE
CAMERMAN
CLAPPER BOY
"YES" MEN
PRIEST
RIX
DAUGHTER
BOY SCOUT
FITZIE
VOICES

Note:

Most of the characters can, and should, be doubled or trebled.

Scene One

Celestial music.

The curtain rises, revealing a very grave-looking, schoolmasterly, gorgeously plumed Angel, seated at a table with Adolphus, at present a pre-brat. On the table are plates, glasses, cutlery etc., but no food.

ADOLPHUS: (*For some reason or other*) Oh boy oh boy oh boy.

ANGEL: Now now, Adolphus, behave. Let's resume our lesson in table manners.

ADOLPHUS: I'd rather play table tennis.

ANGEL: The gong has gone. We're at table now.

ADOLPHUS: I don't care about the gong. I want to play Ping-Pong.

ANGEL: Later, perhaps, when we have balls.

ADOLPHUS: What kind of balls?

ANGEL: Proper balls.

ADOLPHUS: (*Sings*) *I want to play with a Ping-Pong ball*
I want to win twenty all.

ANGEL: Twenty all is a draw, my boy.

ADOLPHUS: There ain't no draw in Ping-Pong.

ANGEL: Back to our table manners! Let's have a good look at them.

ADOLPHUS: No.

ANGEL: Why not?

ADOLPHUS: There ain't no food on the plate.

ANGEL: Pretend there is and that you're hungry. Come on, my boy, eat. . .no, not with your fingers. . .no, don't bend over the food like a dog.

ADOLPHUS: I wish I was a dog.

ANGEL: Were. You wish you were.

ADOLPHUS: Were?

ANGEL: That's the subjunctive mood. "I wish I were a dog."

ADOLPHUS: You, too?

ANGEL: Not I. You.

ADOLPHUS: Yes, I wish I. . .

ANGEL: . . .were. . .

ADOLPHUS: . . .were a dog. (*Barks*)

ANGEL: Stop this nonsense. Stop it right this minute.

ADOLPHUS: Can I please be a dog?

ANGEL: No, you can't.

ADOLPHUS: Why not?

ANGEL: God knows why not. . .but He never tells us anything. I couldn't care less, to be sure, if you turned out to be a rat—which, in a way, you probably will—but *He* seems to mind. You are going to be a little b-boy whether you like it or not. Now, back to our pre-natal education, though I'll be blasted if I know what I've done to deserve *you.*

ADOLPHUS: It's going to be great fun.

ANGEL: What is?

ADOLPHUS: *Life.*

ANGEL: Sez he.

ADOLPHUS: When I'm born I am. . .Could I have some sweet music, please? I feel like being sentimental.

ANGEL: Schubert's "Serenade in D Minor". . .(*Music. Adolphus speaks over music*)

ADOLPHUS: I'll be a boy. . .a good boy. . .'cause I was raised in heaven by a real angel of an angel—

ANGEL: Please, Adolphus, desist.

ADOLPHUS: And this angel taught me how to love me mum and me dad and all the neighbors and play nice games and help old ladies cross the road and give milk and crumbs of bread to sick cats and delouse stray dogs and swat flies and screw all the girls—(*The music stops abruptly*) What's the matter?

ANGEL: Never mind. Back to our lesson. Repeat after me: when I eat—

ADOLPHUS: When you eat.

ANGEL: All right. When one eats.

ADOLPHUS: When one eats. . .Do angels eat?

ANGEL: They sometimes have to attend dinners, to keep up their position.

ADOLPHUS: What do you eat at those dinners?

ANGEL: Oh, stuff.

ADOLPHUS: What stuff?

ANGEL: Ambrosia. They treat us to the food of the Gods.

ADOLPHUS: It sounds like heaven.

ANGEL: It tastes like hell. When one eats. . .

ADOLPHUS: When one eats. . .

ANGEL: (*Demonstrating*) One uses a (*articulates slowly*) spoon. . .a toothpick, a mustard spoon. . .a fork. . .a knife. . .

ADOLPHUS: A spoon. . .a poothtick. . .

ANGEL: Toothpick.

ADOLPHUS: Toothpick. . .a mustard spoon. . .a fork. . .a knife. . .a knife. . .(*With a sudden rage*) I hate you. I hate you! (*Stabs the Angel in the back several times*)

ANGEL: Careful, you fool, the knife's sharp! You'll hurt yourself.

ADOLPHUS: Ouch, I cut my tootsie wootsie thumbie.

ANGEL: (*Kisses Adolphus' finger*) I told you to be careful. There, there, you'll be all right in a minute, and now you'll have a nice little birthmark when you arrive. Ah, I wish they would bring back the birch. In the old days we had some capital punishments in the schools.

ADOLPHUS: Oh, angel darling, did I hurt you? What have I done? Such a terrible thing! What have I done?!

ANGEL: You stuck a knife in my back.

ADOLPHUS: It's treachery.

ANGEL: Not at all. It's *instinct.* But next time don't try your instincts on an angel. Knives, pea-shooters, the Mills or stink bombs, guns, rockets, all the infernal human rigamarole of arms can't do a thing to an angel. Where's the knife?

ADOLPHUS: In your left wing.

ANGEL: Pull it out. Careful. . .Don't uproot any feathers; new ones don't grow as fast as they used to. In a million years' time I'll be as bald as the old Bloke himself. Our next lesson—economics.

ADOLPHUS: I don't wan' no lessons, I wanna have fun. I wanna help old ladies cross the road.

ANGEL: Sit down and shut your bloody stupid mouth, you foolish son of a bitch.

ADOLPHUS: I—

ANGEL: Another word out of you and I bugger you up.

ADOLPHUS: (*Hurt*) What kind of language is that?

ANGEL: English. Sit down.

ADOLPHUS: (*Sits*) I don't love you any more. I wanna be born. I wanna go to me dad and mum.

ANGEL: Well, you can't just yet.

ADOLPHUS: Why not?

ANGEL: Because your mother and your father have first to. . .

ADOLPHUS: (*Salaciously*) Yeah. . . ?

ANGEL: It's not what you think. Come this way, this way. (*They go out and we are now in a squalid room. On one side, in an invalid's chair, sits Granny, her head and body covered by a blanket. On the other side stand Mother and Father*)

GRANNY: Da da da da—(*Stops suddenly*)

FATHER: (*Not looking*) 'Ave you done it?

MOTHER: No. I thought you was goin' to do it.

FATHER: Me? Ye're daft, woman. (*To audience*) Y'see, I'm Adolphus' expectant dad.

MOTHER: I'm his expectant mum.

FATHER: Now for to 'ave 'im come at all—

MOTHER: We 'ave to commit—

FATHER: Death

MOTHER: —control—

FATHER: Which means—

MOTHER: Do—

FATHER: —in'

MOTHER: a—

FATHER: —way

MOTHER: wiv—

GRANNY: Da da da da da.

FATHER: The ol' 'ag!

MOTHER: (*To Father*) She wants 'er cigar.

FATHER: Aw, blast 'er.

MOTHER: Nice way you 'ave of talkin' av yer own mum.

FATHER: Me own mum? Ye're 'round the bend, woman.

MOTHER: What d'ye mean?

FATHER: She's *your* mum.

MOTHER: What?

FATHER: Don't ye remember as 'ow she came along wiv ye'er dead dad's dinin' room set?

MOTHER: Wasn't 'ow she come 'ere?

FATHER: Sure. Down't ye remember?

MOTHER: No.

FATHER: Well, she did.

MOTHER: Well, I'll be blowed. Anyway, you said you'd do it.

FATHER: Do what?

MOTHER: Ye know.

FATHER: Death control?

MOTHER: Yeah.

GRANNY: Da da da da.

FATHER: What's ailin' 'er now?

MOTHER: What is it ye want, Mumsie?

GRANNY: Da da da da da.

MOTHER: I reckon it's one of yer cigars she's after.

FATHER: The greedy ol' cow.

GRANNY: Da da da da.

MOTHER: Got a cigar?

FATHER: Yeah. (*Takes one out of his pocket*) But I reckoned on smokin' it meself after. . .after death control.

MOTHER: Aw, give it to 'er.

GRANNY: Da da da da.

FATHER: All right, all right. (*Gives the cigar to Mother*) 'Ere, shove it down 'er throat.

MOTHER: (*Uncovers Granny's head. Her face is the face of death*) 'Ere's your cigar, Mumsie.

GRANNY: Da da da da.

FATHER: (*Lighting Granny's cigar*) Not only does she stay put, she smokes me cheroots, too.

MOTHER: It's up t'you to get rid o' 'er, if you 'ave a mind

to do it. But it's just as well. Ye ain't the man to raise up me boy.

FATHER: It could be a girl.

MOTHER: Wot? And 'ave 'er go through wot I gone through? No, ta.

FATHER: Mebbe she'd end up a film star in 'ollywood.

MOTHER: Mebbe she'd end up a tart on the streets.

FATHER: Surroundings ain't everything.

MOTHER: Are you or ain't you goin' to do the old woman in?

FATHER: I can't do it.

MOTHER: Fine man you are, ain't you? Make me talk like that duchess in that play, *Macbeth* or sump'n.

FATHER: What play?

MOTHER: Shikespeare. But just as well, for ye ain't a man. Ye jus' ain't.

FATHER: Yes, I am. I am a man. And if you don't believe me, ask them four Krauts.

MOTHER: What four Krauts?

FATHER: The four Krauts. Jes' ask 'em, only you can't, cause they're dead. I bumped them off and got the *Crocks de Gaire* for that.

MOTHER: Wot ye talkin' about?

FATHER: I done them Krauts in, in the war.

MOTHER: What war?

FATHER: 'Ow should I know wot war? I did'na make it, only fought in it. In some war. (*With nostalgia*) And some war it was, too.

MOTHER: I didn't know you was a soldier.

FATHER: What d'ye mean ye didn't know? Ye saw me in me uniform, didn't ye?

MOTHER: Yeah.

FATHER: Well?

MOTHER: I thought you was a bus conductor.

FATHER: Naw, I was a soldier. And them Krauts. . .

MOTHER: Aw, you and yer Krauts! Ye never saw a Kraut in the 'ole of yer life. Ye're dreamin'.

FATHER: It wasn't a dream, I tell ye. Wot wit' the ratatat

o' me tommygun an' the boombangbah o' me grenades and them Krauts who was about to die yellin' their 'eads off when they looked down and seen they'd no fingers or mebbe a 'ole limb torn off an' 'angin' on the window sill mebbe and their guts oozin' out o' their bellies like them tapes from stock exchange machines or their balls blown clear off. . .No, no man could 'a' dreamt such a nightmare. . .(*Nostalgically*) Ah, those was the days.

MOTHER: And you killed them four Krauts?

FATHER: What Krauts?

MOTHER: Them Krauts.

FATHER: Krauts? I'm sure it was darkies they was. We was in the jungle and the officer—bloody ass 'e was—sez, you boys shoot at anything that moves. Now in the jungle anything, but anythin' moves like. So before you could sneeze we each 'ave jus' five bullets in our Lee Enfields and we lyin' flat on the sof' ground too frightened even to move a couple o' yards for a quick shit. And the bugs and mosquitoes feeding on our blood and we 'urting somthin' awful, I can tell you that, yes, I can. (*Nostalgically*) Ah, them were the days. I can still 'ear the bugle. (*Bugle: Reveille, ending with a false note*) Never could end up properly, ol' Jimmy Logan. . .Well, mum, let's call it a day an' 'it the 'ay. (*Amorously*) Shall we. . . ?

MOTHER: Not before me baby comes. I'm goin' to keep meself pure for 'im. 'An anyway, no coward would touch me.

FATHER: I ain't a soldier anymore. I can't kill a defenseless old woman.

GRANNY: Da da da da.

FATHER: Wot she up to now?

MOTHER: She wants us to switch the wireless on for 'er.

GRANNY: Da da da da.

FATHER: Wot the 'ell for?

MOTHER: It's ten o'clock. There's a request program on. Mebbe she asked for a tune. That would be nice.

(*Switches the radio on*)

ANNOUNCER: Our next request is from a charming old lady . . .

GRANNY: Da da da da.

ANNOUNCER: Mrs. Granny Brown of 102, Great Short Street, Crockham. And here is the tune she wants us to play for her—*Fiesta.* (*Music: Bull-fight music*)

GRANNY: Da da da da.

MOTHER: Look, ain't she sweet? C'm'on, ask her to dance with you.

FATHER: Aw, bother.

MOTHER: C'm'on, don't be selfish.

(*Dance: A pas de trois in which Granny is the Bull, Father, the Matador, and Mother, the Picador*)

MOTHER: (*As Granny is about to charge*) It's now or never.

(*As Granny charges, Father stabs her forehead with the forefinger of his outstretched arm. She totters and falls behind the couch*)

FATHER: What 'ave I done? (*Picks up Granny's cigar, which he smokes nervously*) What 'ave I done?

MOTHER: (*From the couch, on which she has been crouching*) A boy. It's a baby boy!

(*Church bells*)

FATHER: It's a boy. Oh, what happiness!

MOTHER: I'm so happy. Call the neighbors.

FATHER: They're here already.

(*The lights change. Enter Two Men in black, carrying a coffin, followed by Two Women in black*)

MOTHER: (*Showing the baby*) Look, it's a boy!

(*The Men place the coffin on the floor. Funeral music*)

1ST WOMAN: (*Sadly*) It's a boy.

2ND WOMAN: (*Weeps*) It's a boy.

1ST WOMAN: It's such a lovely baby. (*Takes the baby from Mother*) May I dance with it, please?

MOTHER: Yes, do. Do.

(*1st Woman dances with the baby, then places it on the coffin, and prostrates herself on it. 2nd Woman then dances with the baby*)

2ND WOMAN: (*Sadly*) It has rosy cheeks and rosy fat buttocks. Just looking at him fills your heart with delight.

1ST MAN: Our—

2ND MAN: Hearts—

1ST MAN: Are full—

2ND MAN: Of—

ALL: De-light. De-light.

1ST WOMAN: Baby, dear, dearest baby.

2ND WOMAN: Be happy, little baby.

1ST MAN: And grow—

2ND MAN: To be—

1ST MAN: A happy—

2ND MAN: Young—

WOMEN: Man. Man. Man.

MOTHER: May I have my baby back, please?

1ST WOMAN: Just a minute, we want to play with him a little longer.

2ND WOMAN: Throwing babies about is good for them.

1ST MAN: It gives them strength.

ALL: Strength.

MOTHER: All right, do throw him about.

(*Music. They throw the baby from one to another as they recite*)

ALL: Baby, baby, we shall teach you.

1ST MAN: To eat.

1ST WOMAN: And sleep.

2ND MAN: And work.

2ND WOMAN: And love.

1ST MAN: And kill.

1ST WOMAN: And kill.

2ND MAN: And kill.

2ND WOMAN: And kill.

(*One of the Men throws it up and it rises, like a balloon, out of sight. Everybody looks up, at first pointing upward in unison. Then each one points in a different direction*)

1ST WOMAN: (*Joyfully*) It was such a beautiful baby. . . Oh, well.

2ND WOMAN: We are extremely sorry, aren't we?

ALL: Yes, very sorry.

1ST MAN: But then, there are by far too many babies in the world. (*The Men pick up the coffin and move away*)

1ST WOMAN: (*To Mother and Father*) Don't worry, we'll give Granny a jolly nice funeral, complete with brass band. What was her favorite tune?

FATHER: (*Trembling*) It was. . .

MOTHER: *Fiesta.*

1ST WOMAN: We'll speak to the conductor. He's a second cousin.

(*The Men and Women exit*)

MOTHER: (*With feeling*) My baby. My poor ten-minute-old baby.

FATHER: The bloody bastards, playing wiv'me baby as if 'e was a football!

MOTHER: They meant well.

FATHER: I wish it was the good ol' days. I'd shoot them like the dogs they are.

MOTHER: I'll never see my baby again.

ADOLPHUS: (*Enters*) Hullo, here I am.

MOTHER: (*Change of accent*) 'Beg your pardon?

ADOLPHUS: I am Adolphus, your baby.

MOTHER: (*In her church bazaar best*) But of course, you are. . .er?. . .er?

ADOLPHUS: Adolphus.

MOTHER: Well, don't stand on the threshold like a stranger. Come in and meet your father.

ADOLPHUS: How do you do, father?

FATHER: (*Change of accent*) How do you do, old chap? (*They shake hands*)

MOTHER: How *do* you do, *Adolphus dear?*

ADOLPHUS: O.K.

MOTHER: Pardon?

ADOLPHUS: O.K. It means all right, roughly.

FATHER: Must be a—humph—an American expression.

MOTHER: Yes, ra-ather.

ADOLPHUS: I picked it up on the underground—

MOTHER: Oh, how divine.

ADOLPHUS: —from the chap who picked me up.

MOTHER: How charming?

FATHER: Did he?

ADOLPHUS: Ra-ather.

FATHER: Oh.

MOTHER: What are you talking about?

FATHER: It's. . .it's. . .something between men.

MOTHER: Oh. I'll go into the library then, while you discuss it here like two old friends.

FATHER: No, *we* shall go into the library. We might need some literature. Come, son. (*Father and Adolphus exit*)

MOTHER: Sweet. Oh, I am so happy I want to talk to someone. I wish Angela were here. (*Angela enters*)

ANGELA: Good afternoon, my dear.

MOTHER: (*They kiss*) Angela dear, you don't know what—

ANGELA: I do.

MOTHER: Do you?

ANGELA: Yes.

MOTHER: Isn't it divine?

ANGELA: Yes, isn't it?

MOTHER: And do you know what he said?

ANGELA: Yes.

MOTHER: Don't you agree it's too wonderful?

ANGELA: I do.

MOTHER: And his father—

ANGELA: Yes.

MOTHER: Well, isn't it?

ANGELA: It is, isn't it? (*Adolphus and Father appear in the doorway. The women rise*)

ADOLPHUS: Yes, Father, I promise.

FATHER: Assert yourself. Project your manhood.

ADOLPHUS: Yes, but how?

FATHER: Well. . .(*Sees the women*) Let's go back into the library. (*Adolphus and Father exit. The women sit down*)

MOTHER: Well?

ANGELA: Nice.

MOTHER: Rather.

ANGELA: Very much so.

MOTHER: I agree.

ANGELA: Do you?

MOTHER: Yes.

ANGELA: Yes. Absolutely?

MOTHER: Positively.

ANGELA: Very nice.

MOTHER: Nice.

ANGELA: Nice.

MOTHER: Goody goody.

ANGELA: What do you want him to be when he's grown up?

MOTHER: I want him to be true to his own self. This above all. But just below, I have a glorious career laid out for him.

ANGELA: (*Sings*) Lawyer? Doctor? Engineer?

MOTHER: No.

ANGELA: Artist? Writer? Columnist?

MOTHER: No.

ANGELA: Captain? Major? Admiral?

MOTHER: No.

ANGELA: Buyer? Broker? Cartoonist?

MOTHER: No, no, no. I want him to be a plumber's mate.

ANGELA: Nice. (*Adolphus and Father appear in the doorway. The women rise*)

ADOLPHUS: And if I do get that feeling?

FATHER: No ifs about it, my boy. As soon as you get it—charge.

ADOLPHUS: Charge? What do you mean, exactly, by "charge"?

FATHER: Back into the library. (*Adolphus and Father exit. The women sit.*)

MOTHER: He will go to the best plumbing studio and study with the best master-plumbers and finish up a most plumboyant plumber's mate. He will know all about. . .(*Duet*)

MOTHER: (*Sings*) Tape and sinks and pipes and
Sockets, Cast Iron or plain
Spiggots and sockets for the drain

ANGELA: (*Sings*) Subject to low pressures

MOTHER: The pipes shall be true

ANGELA: True

MOTHER: Smooth

ANGELA: Smooth

MOTHER: Cylindrical and reasonably straight

ANGELA and MOTHER: And their inner and outer surfaces shall be. . .

MOTHER: As nearly as practicable concentric.

ANGELA: British standard cast iron drain pipes shall comply. . .

MOTHER: In every respect

ANGELA: With the requirements laid down in the specification. . .

MOTHER: The castings shall be. . .

ANGELA: Dark gray on fracture

MOTHER: And shall be such that they may be easily drilled, tapped, and filed.

ANGELA: Drilled, tapped, and filed.

MOTHER and ANGELA: Drilled, tapped, and filed.

ANGELA: (*Speaks*) Nice.

MOTHER: And after he has memorized the list of appliances, gadgets, spare parts, tools and sundries, he will design the most fabulously cheap and amazingly chic *you-know-what* in the world. And in every house in Europe, Australia, America, Africa, and Asia Major and Minor there will be an *un petit coin* that will be forever Adolphus', and every time I'll have to flush, I'll flush with excitement because it will be *Adolphus'* flush.

ANGELA: Quite.

MOTHER: Isn't it?

ANGELA: Isn't it?

MOTHER: And the United Nations will call on him to design the Assembly delegates' Men's Room, and it will be such a wonderful Men's Room that it will make them all, *all* those old diplomats, sit up and take notice.

ANGELA: Quite.

MOTHER: (*Although Angela has not budged*) *Must* you go?

ANGELA: Oh?

MOTHER: Oh.

ANGELA: Oh.

MOTHER: I'll ring the bell. (*Picks up a huge cattle bell, which she rings vigorously. Frieda, a cow, enters*)

FRIEDA: Moo-oo.

MOTHER: Frieda, please show madam to the door.

FRIEDA: (*Curtsying*) Moo-oo.

MOTHER: 'Bye my dear.

ANGELA: 'Bye. (*They kiss. Frieda leads Angela out. Father enters*)

FATHER: I left him in the library, engrossed in a book.

MOTHER: Shall I ask Frieda to show him up to his room?

FATHER: You know you can't ask her to do that.

MOTHER: Why not?

FATHER: She can't climb stairs.

MOTHER: Sometimes I forget she is a cow and not just a human. In a way, it is quite convenient, having a cow for a maid.

FATHER: Yes, in a sort of milky way.

(*Adolphus' head appears in the doorway*)

ADOLPHUS: I say, pater, I am through with the first chapter. Hot stuff, by Jimminy! I think I can spot the point now.

FATHER: Good boy. You can go on to the second chapter.

ADOLPHUS: Thanks awfully. (*Disappears*)

FATHER: I gave him one of Mother's books to read.

MOTHER: Oh, dear.

FATHER: I think it will do the trick.

MOTHER: What trick?

FATHER: You know.

MOTHER: Do I?

FATHER: What did you say "oh, dear" for then?

MOTHER: I was going to say "oh, dear, we'll have to reorganize our lives now. . ."

FATHER: Oh.

MOTHER: ". . .now that baby has arrived."

FATHER: Yes, I suppose you are right.

MOTHER: I shall have to change my coiffeur day from

Thursday to Friday, move my massage appointment to Thursday, go to Monsieur Laurent's French class on Mondays instead of Mme. Arselanne's class on Friday, see Angela on Thursdays, wash my hair on Wednesday and notify the Bel Canto Light Opera Company that I shall not be able to sing *Brunhilde* after all.

FATHER: I shall have to take the eight-thirty-five into town instead of the eight-twenty-three, which means that Frieda will have to call me at seven twenty-seven and I shall get to the office at nine-forty, have lunch at the quick service bar instead of at the restaurant, finish it at one fifty-two instead of forty-three, have tea at four-ten and take the six-six home instead of the five-fifty-seven.

MOTHER: This way you'll lose nine minutes a day.

FATHER: It's terrible, but it can't be helped.

MOTHER: No sacrifice is too great for our dear son's happiness.

FATHER: Well, at least we have our life beautifully reorganized, though at a price. We have turned a new leaf. Oh, dear!

MOTHER: What's the matter?

FATHER: You won't be able to come to town Mondays on the two-forty-two any more.

MOTHER: No.

FATHER: And I am so tired in the evenings.

MOTHER: I think we had better consider *that* side of our marriage a closed book.

FATHER: This is a blow, especially to my pride. What shall I do?

MOTHER: I suppose you will have to get yourself a three-thirty mistress. (*She goes out*)

ADOLPHUS: (*Putting his head through the door*) I say, father.

FATHER: Oh, go to hell.

ADOLPHUS: (*Hurt*) Father. . .

FATHER: Buzz off.

(*Adolphus' head disappears. Father looks very worried.*

A clock chimes the half hour. The Mistress enters. She is fat and wears an open dressing gown, underneath which a black slip can be seen)

MISTRESS: (*Welcoming Father*) Half-past three *precisely*. Come in, darling, take your jacket off. I've warmed my teeny-weeny room for you.

FATHER: (*Slumping heavily onto an armchair*) My wife doesn't understand me.

MISTRESS: But of course she doesn't, or you wouldn't be here, would you? Shall I play you a record? I've bought two this morning, with the money you had given me.

FATHER: No, sit in my lap.

MISTRESS: Like a little girl?

FATHER: Yes.

MISTRESS: And then you'll give your little girl a nice present?

FATHER: Yes.

MISTRESS: What will you give her?

FATHER: Hurry up. I have to catch the four-five. (*The Mistress sits in Father's lap. Adolphus enters*)

ADOLPHUS: I say. . .Oh, I am awfully sorry. (*Stands staring and gaping at the Mistress*)

MISTRESS: Who are *you*, young man?

FATHER: (*Sees Adolphus and jumps to his feet. Change of accent*) Oh, me blessed God!

MISTRESS: Who is it?

FATHER: It's me own flesh an' blood, the issue of me thighs.

MISTRESS: Who?

FATHER: Me son, you hignorant slut! Now that 'e's seen 'is ol' man in the cheap hembraces of a common *puteen*—

MISTRESS: What was that you called me?

FATHER: *Puteen*, that's French for 'ore.

MISTRESS: (*Calms down*) Oh, French—? I thought it was something real bad. In Irish.

FATHER: 'Cor. Now 'e's seen 'is own dad with a woman that ain't 'is ma, an' not knowing about all them circumstances that led me into this 'ere place, 'e will start gettin' all sorts of complexes.

MISTRESS: What?

FATHER: *Complexes.* That's when you can't do things you imagine or do things you can't imagine. Ol' Freud eskplained it all in 's famous hintroduction.

MISTRESS: What Freud?

FATHER: *Sigmund,* fer Gawd's sake! (*To the audience*) That one's real hignorant!. . .Oh, oi'm a lost man! Oi'm a bunch of failures: as a father, as a business man, as a sportsman—

MISTRESS: As a lover.

FATHER: Oi'm all frustrated like.

MISTRESS: Maybe you have an inverted Oedipus complex?

FATHER: Yeah, mebee oi 'ave. 'Ere, who taught you that?

MISTRESS: Nobody. I made it up meself a minute ago.

FATHER: Did ye?

MISTRESS: Honest to God.

FATHER: That's a remarkable feat. What the French call a *feat o complee.*

MISTRESS: Them Frenchies have a word for everything.

ADOLPHUS: Please.

MISTRESS: Pardon?

FATHER: Careful now. 'Es dangerous. There's no telling what 'e might do. 'E ain't normal no more, now that 'e's seen me wit' you. 'E just ain't normal.

MISTRESS: And what can I do for you, young man?

ADOLPHUS: May I have your telephone number, please?

MISTRESS: Ha ha. And you saying he ain't normal? He's all right, he is!

FATHER: Blimey. 'E takes after 'is granny!

MISTRESS: The age of 'eredity isn't passed yet. Come into the next room and I'll give it to you, sonny boy. (*The mistress leads Adolphus out*)

FATHER: Adolphus.

ADOLPHUS: (*Reappearing*) Yes, Father?

FATHER: (*In his "cultured" accent, nonchalantly*) Don't be late for dinner.

ADOLPHUS: Right-o, Father. (*He exits*)

(*Father sits down, dejected. A horn sounds, off. Mother enters*)

MOTHER: Dinner is served. (*Calls*) We'll have it in here, if you don't mind, Frieda. (*Frieda enters. One of her horns is in her mouth. She blows it*) Thank you, Frieda. (*She starts milking Frieda while Father sharpens a big knife*) She's such a honey, overflowing with milk.

FATHER: You know, my dear, I cut such a tragic figure.

MOTHER: Now that you mention it, I believe you do.

FATHER: But then, aren't we *all* tragic figures?

MOTHER: Or comic ones, as the case may be?

FATHER: Such is life.

MOTHER: Yes, it is.

FATHER: Isn't it?

(*Mother starts pouring milk from a pail into Father's saucer as the lights fade on them*)

(*Adolphus and the Mistress enter, wearing training suits*)

ADOLPHUS: At last, I am a man!

MISTRESS: Yes.

ADOLPHUS: Thanks to your training.

MISTRESS: You've been a very obedient trainee.

ADOLPHUS: It feels wonderful.

MISTRESS: What does?

ADOLPHUS: To be sportsman of the year.

MISTRESS: (*In a trainer's voice*) Come on, no time for daydreams now. You haven't done your daily dozen today.

ADOLPHUS: Yes, ma'am. (*Running round the stage*) Ah, I feel exhilarated.

MISTRESS: Up-up-up.

ADOLPHUS: I can feel every limb tuning up.

MISTRESS: Up-up-up.

ADOLPHUS: Every muscle.

MISTRESS: Up-up-up.

ADOLPHUS: This is wonderful! (*Stops running*) Sheer physical delight. Do you think I'll win the table-tennis championship tonight?

MISTRESS: Not if you don't go on training. (*She runs round the stage while Adolphus remains standing as if in a daze*) Up-up-up! (*She continues her exercises in the background*)

ADOLPHUS: The grace, the lightness. (*Plays imaginary ping-pong*) The ball Ping-Ponging sharply from one end of the tennis table to the other. The balletic, acrobatic, precise movements of the champion. Ping-Pong. The physical delight. The applause of the admiring onlookers, held back by the unyielding concentrations of the players. The white ball shooting like a clever butterfly, just avoiding the enemy's envy-green net.

MISTRESS: Adolphus!

ADOLPHUS: Sorry, I was thinking.

MISTRESS: The doubles! (*They perform a short Ping-Pong ballet*)

ADOLPHUS: Ping Pong. Ping Pong. Ping Pong. Victory! I'm the champ!

MISTRESS: Not bad.

ADOLPHUS: Gosh, I was wonderful, wonderful.

MISTRESS: Not at all bad.

ADOLPHUS: And my last ball. . .did you see how it volleyed to the very corner and completely foxed them? (*Takes a Ping-Pong ball out of his pocket*) Thank you, my little mascot.

MISTRESS: Remember, Adolphus, you're not the champion yet.

ADOLPHUS: No, but tonight's the night—

MISTRESS: Yes, tonight's the night—

ADOLPHUS: —of the Ping-Pong championship.

MISTRESS: —of the big fight.

ADOLPHUS: No, no, I wouldn't like to call it "a fight." It's a contest. A gentlemanly encounter. Cricket.

MISTRESS: Call it what you will, Adolphus, but the (*change of accent*) timekeeper says it's time for the fight.

ADOLPHUS: Is it?

MISTRESS: Come on, sit in your corner.

ADOLPHUS: Sit? But surely I have to—?

MISTRESS: C'm'on.

ADOLPHUS: What's *he* doing here?

MISTRESS: That's your opponent. (*She massages Adolphus' neck*)

ADOLPHUS: "Bear Face Killer" Thompson—?

MISTRESS: (*Recognizing him*) So he is.

ADOLPHUS: I didn't know he was a Ping-Pong player?

MISTRESS: What are you talking about?

ADOLPHUS: He has gloves on.

MISTRESS: Off it, Adolphus, don't play the goon! I told you it was a *fight*. Look, we're in an arena. Touch the ropes. Blink at the TV lights. Scowl at "Killer." Smile at the press boys. Do a dance for the audience. (*Adolphus obeys her orders*)

ADOLPHUS: (*Pleading*) But I was trained to play *Ping-Pong,* not to *box*.

MISTRESS: What does it matter what it is? IT'S ALL SPORT!

ADOLPHUS: Oh, I'm afraid. . . ! (*He buries his head in the Mistress' bosom*)

MISTRESS: You said you were a man! Get up and fight!!

(*A gong is struck. Adolphus' moves are described by a Commentator's voice over the loudspeaker*)

COMMENTATOR'S VOICE: The big fight's on! Killer hooks one to the left and—and Adolphus is down. Onetwothreefourfive-sixseveneightnine t–e–en! And it's a knockout! It's all over, after one-point-two-seconds, the shortest fight on record. The referee lifts up the arm of the new champion. Let's hear what the old champ has to say. Adolphus. . .Hey, Adolphus, what are your plans, if any? For the future, if any?

ADOLPHUS: (*He takes a broken Ping-Pong ball out of his pocket*) Look, he's broken my mascot! I want to die. . .

Blackout

Scene Two

A few bars of solemn "modern" music before the lights come up again. The stage represents an artist's studio. Can-

vases everywhere; on the floor, on stands, on the walls, hanging from the ceiling. Some are blank, others covered with geometrical shapes: triangles, squares, oblongs—but not circles. On one side: a screen, behind which sits a Model. She is visible to the audience but not to the painter in the other corner of the studio. It is Adolphus, looking quite neatly bohemian in corduroy trousers, turtle-neck sweater and a thin beard. He stands in front of a blank canvas, thinking.

MODEL: (*After a pause*) Can I strip now? Please. . .Adolphus. . .I am talking to you.

ADOLPHUS: I am not listening.

MODEL: Well, do listen.

ADOLPHUS: I am busy.

MODEL: I want to strip. . .I want to undress. . .Did you hear?

ADOLPHUS: Yes.

MODEL: Well?

ADOLPHUS: Don't.

MODEL: But why not? Why, Adolphus? I *am* your model, aren't I?

ADOLPHUS: Yes, you are. But, damn you, I'm doing a non-representational.

MODEL: Oh, you and your geometrical forms! I'm coming out.

ADOLPHUS: (*Almost hysterical, covering his eyes with his hands*) Don't you dare!

MODEL: All right, all right. I am sorry. I'll stay here at your pleasure, dear knight, and fully dressed, too. I hope at least you let me sleep with you tonight.

ADOLPHUS: No.

MODEL: Oh, well. . .

ADOLPHUS: I must not be contaminated by the voluptuous non-angles of your unartificial body.

MODEL: Thanks for the compliment.

ADOLPHUS: We must keep away from each other until the painting's done.

MODEL: Is it nearly finished?

ADOLPHUS: (*Looking sadly at the blank, white canvas*) No.

MODEL: Well, how do you like that? Here I am, a recluse from a recluse. Feeding him, humoring him, untouched by him, helping him to shut himself from the outer world, sending away callers, paying his bills, washing his dirty laundry, sewing up his torn clothes, pushing his food to him under the screen so that his *too* sensitive eyes would not spot my skin, unable even to see him, hidden as he is in the dark recesses of his straight limbed paintings. Adolphus, I wouldn't have minded all this had I not been in love with you. But I *am* and I can't stand it any longer! I'm leaving you.

ADOLPHUS: Silence.

MODEL: What?

ADOLPHUS: I think—

MODEL: What?

ADOLPHUS: That this—

MODEL: Is it?

ADOLPHUS: Is *it*. (*Looks at his hands*) Write everything down, for the record, for posterity. (*He dictates. She writes*) Inspiration. Like an attack of epilepsy on a thirsty man in a desert—it starts from one pinpoint—the nape of the neck—spreads out, sickeningly, meaninglessly, overpowering, sweet, intoxicating, goosepimpling you all over with excitement—ripples in a pool of vacuum—attacking now the eyes—now the ears—now the knees—my sex—I feel womby—coming up to my back—the shoulders—now it touches my. . .

MODEL: Your what?

ADOLPHUS: It can't be, but it is. *My wings!*

ANGEL: (*The Angel enters. He is carrying a walkie-talkie*) Anybody mention my name? (*Taking the situation in*) Oh, I'm sorry.

MODEL: Did you say "sorry"?

ADOLPHUS: . . .the hands. . .eager, itching, like a sailor on shore leave. . .head swimming. . .like a sailor after shore leave . . .It's come. (*He paints furiously*)

ANGEL: (*Sits on one side and talks into the walkie-talkie*) Hello, Gabriel?. . .*Wings* here. . .Yes, I am at the plumberchappie's, only he is an *artist* now. Has a studio. . .Yes, there *is* a model here, but she's all dressed. . .Where do I go from here?. . .You don't say. . . ? Do you mean *no* angel has visited the *Prime Minister* in the last quarter of a century? Right. . . 'Bye-bye. . .*Wings* signing off.

ADOLPHUS: (*Tired, sweating, but happy*) Darling. . . (*Shouts*) Darling!

MODEL: I didn't strip, honestly.

ADOLPHUS: Come out here.

MODEL: Do you mean it?

ADOLPHUS: Come here. (*She obeys*) Look at this. . .No, don't step back, this is one of those paintings you admire from close quarters.

MODEL: (*Not paying the slightest attention to the painting*) You are sweating. Are you in pain?

ADOLPHUS: (*Happily*) Yes! Yes!

MODEL: Would you like an aspirin?

ADOLPHUS: No. It is a *pleasant* pain! It is the companion pain of art. Art is painful. As painful as passion, as passionate as truth, as true as life, as lively as the ocean, as deep as the soul, as soul-tearing as a child's tears. Art is all, but all is not art. Please, angel of my inspiration, juxtapose my vision and pain and passion and truth and life and soul and depth and tears; combine them in this work of art. Admire it! It's done.

(*The canvas looks quite untouched*)

MODEL: But it isn't.

ADOLPHUS: Have a closer look.

MODEL: I can't see anything.

ADOLPHUS: It is a perfectly minute perfect circle.

MODEL: You. . .are not serious?

ANGEL: 'Trouble is—he is.

MODEL: I can't see *anything!*

ADOLPHUS: It's very small. You have to look at it through a magnifying glass. (*Adolphus takes out a magnifying glass. Through it a perfect circle can be seen*)

MODEL: (*Delighted*) Why, it's *perfect.* (*She kisses Adolphus*) You *are* wonderful!

ADOLPHUS: Ring up everybody. Spread the news. Get the critics.

(*The Critic enters, carrying a doctor's case*)

CRITIC: What is it I hear? Is it *true?*

MODEL: Of course, it's true!

ADOLPHUS: A perfect circle!

CRITIC: You are joking?

ADOLPHUS: Look! (*He holds the magnifying glass in front of the canvas*)

CRITIC: It *looks* perfect. But is it?

ANGEL: The bastard.

CRITIC: Your eyes are only the eyes of an artist. You have too much red blood in your veins. It rosifies your view. It looks a perfect circle to *you.* But is it, really? Will it stand up to my criteria?

ADOLPHUS: *Your* criteria?

CRITIC: My critic's criteria. Let's have a closer, better look at this. . .thing. (*He takes a huge magnifying glass from his case and holds it in front of the canvas. The "circle" now appears crooked*)

MODEL: It *isn't* perfect!

ANGEL: The bastard.

CRITIC: Do you see what I see?

(*Adolphus is too sick to answer. He groans, holds his stomach and rushes out*)

MODEL: Adolphus, what's the matter? (*She follows Adolphus*)

CRITIC: Here we go again. (*He picks up his case and follows them*)

ANGEL: Ah well, time to go. Oh, dear. I've sat on something wet! (*He rises and holds up a canvas that he has been sitting on. It bears the imprint of his bare bottom*) If Gabriel sees *this,* he'll laugh his head off!

(*Hearing voices, he rushes behind the screen, still clutching the canvas*)

CRITIC'S VOICE: (*Off*) I have given him an exceptionally strong sedative.

MODEL'S VOICE: (*Off*) Thank you, doctor.

CRITIC'S VOICE: (*Off*) Take his temperature every four hours and chart it.

MODEL'S VOICE: (*Off*) Yes, doctor.

(*The Critic and the Model return. He has a stethoscope round his neck and wears a white smock. She is dressed as a nurse*)

CRITIC: I should keep him on a diet of carrots, for at least a week.

MODEL: Yes, doctor.

CRITIC: Very good for the eyes.

MODEL: Certainly, doctor.

CRITIC: And then, shall we say, a couple of months in the South of France?

MODEL: We shall say so, doctor.

CRITIC: The South of France has always done a hell of a lot of good for artists. Picasso, Matisse, Johnny Schultz. . .

MODEL: Who's he, Doctor?

CRITIC: A Spaniard. As for an operation. . .

MODEL: (*Alarmed*) Operation?

CRITIC: It won't be necessary.

MODEL: (*Relieved*) Thank you, doctor.

CRITIC: You don't operate for a tummy upset. Anyway, that's what doctors tell me.

MODEL: Yes, doctor.

CRITIC: I wish you would stop calling me "Doctor." I am a *critic.*

MODEL: Sorry, it's the stethoscope and the smock.

CRITIC: I always carry them around with me. Artists are so easily upset.

MODEL: They are so sensitive.

CRITIC: Delicate.

MODEL: Selfish.

CRITIC: Where can I wash my hands?

MODEL: There's water behind the screen.

(*The Critic goes behind the screen, just as the Angel emerges from the other side. The Angel steps for-*

ward and pinches the Model's bottom, then goes out)

MODEL: Ouch! (*She looks around, mystified*)

CRITIC: (*Behind the screen*) Did you say something?

MODEL: No.

CRITIC: (*Ditto*) You are a cute kid, d'you know that?

MODEL: How could I? Adolphus never says such things to me.

CRITIC: You poor dear. . .

MODEL: I am so lonely!

CRITIC: I want to tell you something. But please don't think it's just a line. . .

MODEL: What line?

CRITIC: Marlowe's.

MODEL: All right, I'll *come* and live with you.

CRITIC: *Hullo, what's that?!*

(*He emerges from behind the screen, holding the canvas left there by the Angel*)

MODEL: I have never seen this mess before.

CRITIC: Mess? It's great! It's Adolphus in a new style. It's a wonderful re-creation, in color, of the. . .the chaos of our modern world. Call the press! Wake Adolphus up! Give him a reviver! Sound the horns!

(*Sound effects: sirens, noises, etc. Two bearded Beatniks, a beautiful Girl, a lady Gossip Writer and her Photographer appear*)

CRITIC: Ladies and Gentlemen, friends. You have seen the picture, now here is its *creator!* (*The Model brings in Adolphus, still under the influence of the sedative*)

BEATNIK I: Dig that, he's high! Marijuana.

BEATNIK II: You're flipping, that's morphine. I know, my gal takes it.

ADOLPHUS: Wh-wh-at's the matter?

CRITIC: These good people have come to look at your latest.

GOSSIP: May we take a picture of the artist?

CRITIC: Go right ahead. (*He poses in front of Adolphus. A flash from photographer's camera*)

GOSSIP: Can we have one with some "cheese," please?

(*The Model poses, exposing some leg. The Critic holds her by the waist*)

GOSSIP: Anything to say? Any good line for my column?

MODEL: Yes, Marlowe's line. We are going to live together.

GOSSIP: (*Writes on her pad*) The famous critic has asked the model to marry him and she blushingly gave her consent. . . Will it be a *white* wedding?

MODEL: I don't know, but I hope we spend many *white nights* together.

CRITIC: Ladies and Gentlemen, friends. Thank you all for coming tonight to this old, dark, airless attic. It is going to loom prominently in the art of our century. You have heard of critics finding great paintings in old attics. My claim to distinction is that *I* have found in an old attic not only a superb painting, but also a great *artist.*

MODEL: And a great love!

CRITIC: Adolphus! Speech.

ADOLPHUS: (*Rises uncertainly*) Me?

GIRL: Isn't he wonderful?

ADOLPHUS: What's going on? Who *are* these people?

CRITIC: Friends. A circle of admirers.

ADOLPHUS: Have they come to admire the circle?

CRITIC: They have come to see *this.*

ADOLPHUS: (*Seeing the canvas for the first time*) What is it?

CRITIC: Art!

ADOLPHUS: (*Still a little hazy*) Art is pain—art is all. . .I never saw this painting in my whole life.

BEATNIK I: He's real high. . .

GIRL: He's wonderful. . .

GOSSIP: Does the painting have a title?

BEATNIK II: What artist *isn't* high?

ADOLPHUS: I don't know. I never saw it in my whole life. . .

BEATNIK I: Yeah, all artists are goof—

BEATNIK II: Flip.

BEATNIK I: Creep.

CRITIC: Aren't you going to give it a *title?*

BEATNIK II: I don't dig their beards.

ADOLPHUS: If I must give it one, then I call it "Self-portrait."

GIRL: He's wonderful!

BEATNIK I: I don't dig *your* beard.

ADOLPHUS: "Self-portrait" because it was done all by its little self.

BEATNIK II: You hear that? The man's real goof.

BEATNIK I: A commercial whoretist!

(*A nouveau-riche Millionaire enters*)

MILLIONAIRE: Mr. Adolphus, allow me to introduce m'self. I've become an "instant" millionaire and I buy this 'ere picture for. . .fifty thousand pounds!

BEATNIK I: See what I mean?

BEATNIK II: Yeah, a square.

MILLIONAIRE: (*Giving Adolphus a check and taking the painting*) It's a square deal. (*He exits*)

GOSSIP: Goodnight, Adolphus. . . .Oh, surely, I may call you "Adolphus," mayn't I? Come, Gaston.

(*She exits with Photographer*)

BEATNIK I: (*To Adolphus*) Sorry, man.

BEATNIK II: About the check.

BEATNIK I: You may be too goof to know, but money's square.

BEATNIK II: Yeah, it creeps everything.

BEATNIK I: I should dig. I once had money.

BEATNIK II: Yeah, I remember I saw it.

BEATNIK I: Go, man, go. (*He goes out*)

BEATNIK II: Real square. I don't share his flips, only his flat. Why'd he say you're a whoretist? Dig this, he's right, but why hurt a man's feelings just because you ain't in his shoes? Crazy, man, crazy. (*He goes out*)

MODEL: Well, Adolphus, it's goodbye. We're. . .getting married. . .in June. . .that's what the papers say. . .I know what you're thinking. . .but you should have asked me. . .*he did*. . . sorry.

CRITIC: You'll be our best man, of course.

ADOLPHUS: Of course.

(*The Model and the Critic exit*)

GIRL: (*Approaches Adolphus*) Please, may I have your autograph?

ADOLPHUS: What would you do with it?

GIRL: Collect it. I have many autographs of the great. Even one of ex-King Farouk.

ADOLPHUS: I'll give you something better than a mere autograph.

(*He gives her a small red notebook*)

GIRL: It's so small. Is it your secret diary?

ADOLPHUS: It is my heart.

GIRL: Sorry.

ADOLPHUS: What for?

GIRL: Saying it was so small. I didn't know it was your heart, honestly.

ADOLPHUS: It *is* small, but it has sixty-four pages. I had to tear out one leaf, though.

GIRL: Was it some memory you could not bear to remember? A girl, perhaps? Oh, how romantic.

ADOLPHUS: No, it was nothing like that at all. You see, I once went into a toilet in Paris and there was no—

GIRL: That is very vulgar!

ADOLPHUS: I am sorry. That is the truth.

GIRL: I forgive you your vulgarity. You must be a very bitter man. Bitter men have no use for their hearts. Therefore, I'll take the notebook. I live in a suburb and am often short of reading matter on the bus. Goodbye. Shall I ever see you again?

ADOLPHUS: No. But please don't tear me out.

GIRL: I'll remember you. I can face the past. I have so little of it.

(*She goes out. Out of the shadows a figure emerges. It is dressed in a black gown, and veiled like a widow*)

ADOLPHUS: Mother! Oh, mother dear! I didn't know that father. . .Oh, my God, what you must have gone through! And I wasn't there when it happened—to hold your trembling hands, to press my head unto your sighing bosom, to stifle your screams of agony. Oh, Mother of my birth, forgive your sinful son.

FATHER: (*For the Figure is he*) Stop that nonsense!

ADOLPHUS: *Father!!*

FATHER: Yes, I am your father, and now your mother as well.

ADOLPHUS: Is mother. . .?

FATHER: She certainly is. Why else should I make a fool of myself wearing these silly clothes?. . .Ouch, my feet are killing me. (*He sits down and begins to rub his feet. He speaks rapidly and there is much bitterness in his voice*) She died and I didn't have one decent black suit to wear at her funeral. She never let me buy a black suit, but *she* had a closet full of mourning. "You'll die afore me," she would say. She was such an optimist, always. And do you know why she thought I'd go before she would? "Because our Adolphus is going to be a plumber's mate yet." Women *are* illogical.

ADOLPHUS: Poor mother.

FATHER: Poor mother he says. . .Why is it that people have always so much sympathy for the dead and none for the living? Because the dead don't eat, I suppose.

ADOLPHUS: I am sorry, father.

FATHER: Now you are sorry, after it's all over. Where were you when your mother was at the crossroads, when she uttered her last scream of protest, when she asked for quarter and was answered by the smile of death? When we needed you most, you deserted us. Your mother and myself were deserted by our son and heir.

ADOLPHUS: Forgive me, please.

FATHER: Heir, my foot! There's nothing left. All we had was spent on doctors, specialists, medicine, subsciptions to health journals, on wise women, faith healers and all the paraphernalia of the anti-death rear-guard. I even took your mother to Lourdes, on a cheap excursion ticket, that was exorbitantly expensive. We were so reduced we had to eat *Frieda*.

ADOLPHUS: Frieda?

FATHER: The maid, you know. She put on airs when she heard that. "I must say, Madam. . ." She always ignored me, the cow. . ."I must say I am most taken aback. You made me sweep floors—that was the price I had to pay for domestication. You gave me a home and in return I let you milk me dry, tit-for-tat. But *eat* me as well? Why, that is sheer cowibalism. Cowibalism." Neat little speech for a beast of burden, don't you think?

ADOLPHUS: What happened then?

FATHER: Come February, we were hungry again. And then. . .(*Breaks down*) Well, I'd better be off. . .

ADOLPHUS: Wait, father. . .(*He holds out the check*)

FATHER: What's this?

ADOLPHUS: A check.

FATHER: For how much?

ADOLPHUS: Fifty thousand.

FATHER: Did you sign on the back?

ADOLPHUS: Yes.

FATHER: Well, I guess this will help a little. I'll get me a new wife. I cannot live without love. Women like to count on men with money, and men can count on women who can count. It will do you good, too, to get married, son. Celibacy is selfish. Marry and be merry. There are countless unsuspected pleasures in the folds of matrimony, like bringing the little woman's morning coffee to her in bed. Ah, love, here I come.

ADOLPHUS: Love. . .! (*He exits*)

(*Blackout. The Calypso Singers appear downstage and sing:*)

CALYPSO OF LOVE

It is good to have
A little love.
Those who have had
Say it wasn't bad.

Calypso,
Calypso of love.

Oh, love, said He of Nazareth,
Love, ye sinners, by all the means,

For love in you will obliterate
All sins, all sins, all sins.

Love to have is very wise.
And, oh, so cheap, doesn't buy or sell.
It leads you straight to paradise
Not hell, not hell, not hell.

So love, my friends with lots of passion,
Love will give good cheer and health.
For of *life* it's the very foundation
Not death, not death, not death.

(The Calypso Singers exit. A Voice comes over the loudspeaker)

VOICE: Adolphus, disgusted by his own selfishness, resolved to put himself at the disposal of society and be of service to his fellow men and women.

(The lights come up. Adolphus, now dressed as a butler, is carrying a breakfast tray. On the stage are a few chairs, a couch, a table with a radio on it, a telephone and a screen with a bed behind it)

ADOLPHUS: This is my first day in service. I tried to become a plumber's mate, but no plumber would have me as a mate. I am employed by Mr. Smith, the famous multi-billionaire sheepowner, who also runs a few film companies. His films are very good indeed, and he loses a lot of money making them.

LORNA: *(In bed, behind the screen)* Man!

ADOLPHUS: Ma'am?

LORNA: You are late.

ADOLPHUS: That's Miss Smith, behind the screen, I am bringing her her breakfast in bed. She is very beautiful and I am trying desperately hard to fall in love with her. In my spare time I write: sonnets, greeting-cards verses and radio plays.

LORNA: Man!

ADOLPHUS: Coming. Shall I pour your coffee for you, ma'am?

LORNA: That's what you are here for, man, isn't it? To serve me, isn't it? So pour.

ADOLPHUS: Yes, ma'am.

LORNA: Break the eggs, man.

ADOLPHUS: At your service.

LORNA: Are you with us on approval?

ADOLPHUS: I'm afraid so, ma'am. I'll do my best to give satisfaction.

LORNA: We'll soon see about that. Hop in.

ADOLPHUS: In where?

(*Music: A few bars of noisy Wagner as Adolphus is dragged behind the screen. Then Lorna comes out from behind the screen, wearing a sumptuous negligee. She is beautiful, young, and a nymphomaniac*)

LORNA: No, no, stay where you are.

(*She folds the screen and Adolphus is discovered, lying in bed. Lorna comes to sit by his side*)

LORNA: More coffee?

ADOLPHUS: But. . .I am. . .

LORNA: You are my lover. I always do my lovers' work for them. Do you love me, lover?

ADOLPHUS: I hope so. Love never came easily to me. I am trying to follow my father's advice and find a true love. Not merely physical love.

LORNA: (*Astonished*) What's wrong with physical love?

ADOLPHUS: It doesn't endure.

LORNA: You are naive, aren't you? Tell me more about yourself.

ADOLPHUS: I have already told you.

LORNA: You are a man of many ideas.

ADOLPHUS: I have an ideology. Have you got one, Miss Smith?

LORNA: No. But, you see, I don't need one. I have a yacht.

ADOLPHUS: I unfold my ideology in a radio play I've written. Could you persuade your father to listen in to it? He might find it suitable for one of his money-losing films. I don't want anything for myself. If he buys the play, I'll give the money away, to some charity or other.

LORNA: You are very generous.

ADOLPHUS: (*Simply, without double-entendre*) So are you.

LORNA: They all say so. But you say it more nicely.

ADOLPHUS: Really?

LORNA: Yes. James, say that you love me.

ADOLPHUS: James? I am *Adolphus.*

LORNA: Sorry, you never introduced yourself.

ADOLPHUS: There was hardly time for that. Who is James?

LORNA: Our chauffeur. (*James, a big man in a chauffeur's uniform, enters*)

JAMES: The car is waiting.

LORNA: Thank you, James. (*To Adolphus*) Stay here and wait for father. (*To James, who is helping her into a mink coat*) I'll drive. (*Lorna and James exit. Smith enters*)

ADOLPHUS: Mr. Smith, about my radio play. . .sorry to be a nuisance. . .But, you see—

SMITH: The radio play. . .? Certainly. Is it on now?

ADOLPHUS: Yes, but your time must be precious.

SMITH: True, but there is precious little I wouldn't do to find new talent. Switch it on.

(*Adolphus switches on the radio*)

VOICE: (*Over loudspeaker*) Good evening. We take great pleasure in presenting an outstanding new play by a new dramatist, who has directed his own play, devised the sound effects, and composed the music. He also plays the part of *Adolphus, the Millionth,* the hero. Ladies and Gentlemen—*"What?"* a radio play by Adolphus.

(*Music: a few bars of musique concrète*)

VOICE: We take you into the distant future. As far into the future as there is past. . .

SMITH: Excellent. Science fiction. All the rage. That's what they all clamor for nowadays.

VOICE: . . .But before we take you into the future, here's

a thought about your *own* future! Your future depends on good teeth. And good teeth depend on *B A R T*. *Bart* your teeth, six times daily, with *Bart,* the only toothpaste that contains Teetheld.

SMITH: Excellent. Bart's commercials are always excellent radio.

VOICE: The future. . .Man has conquered new worlds. He has won Eternity, but he has lost *Touch*. You will say, perhaps, he could never *really* communicate. . .But around the year ten million, he *definitely* lost Touch.

SMITH: Ten million? That's laying it on a bit thick, isn't it?

VOICE: People began to talk like this. . .

(*Sound effect: Screeches*)

SMITH: What the hell is that?

VOICE: . . .People's brain-waves are now automatically translated into *Significant Sounds,* deciphered by the listener into brain waves of his own. But it is hardly *Touch*.

SMITH: I say, this is fascinating!

VOICE: As for love, it has disappeared. True, here and there, sex lingered on.

SMITH: Sex. That's capital!

VOICE: Let us visit the flat of our hero, *Adolphus the Millionth*. He is a presentable young man, with a decent job and a clean mind, and he has met a young girl. He is fond of her. Very fond. As a matter of fact, he is not quite sure that he is not falling in sex with her. Not unnaturally, he asks her to have dinner with him in his flat. . .

SMITH: Action at last!

VOICE: They have dined and wined and Adolphus says to her. . .

(*Effect: Screeches*)

VOICE: Meaning: "Shall we sit on the couch?" She replies. . .

(*Effect: Screeches*)

VOICE: "Thank you." He starts whispering sweet nothings in her ear. . .

(*Effect: Screeches*)

VOICE: To which she responds with. . .

(*Effect: Screeches*)

VOICE: And then they. . .

(*Effect: Everything is drowned in screeches, whistles, etc.*)

SMITH: We can't have that on the screen! The censor will never pass it.

ADOLPHUS: That's not in the play at all. I think it's atmospherics. Or, maybe there's something wrong with the set?

SMITH: Something wrong with the set? Do you realize, young man, that this set is a *Fortunello Sixty-Eight?* You just have a bad play on your hands and are trying to put the blame on *science.* I know your sort! Always blaming *something.* Art is bad—the age is too scientific. Food's no good. *Why?* Because kitchens are too antiseptic. Families break up, divorces are a dozen a penny, adultery's committed every day. The reason?: Cars run faster! The weather's bad: it's the Bomb. Do you know that if it *weren't* for science, you wouldn't be here at all; child mortality would be absolutely prohibitive? We would have had the Black Death all over again if it weren't for *science!*

ADOLPHUS: Mr. Smith, if you will only—

SMITH: Out of the question!

(*He makes for the door, almost bumping into Lorna, who enters dressed in dirty brown overalls*)

LORNA: Hello, dad.

SMITH: Busy. (*He goes out*)

LORNA: What's corroding *him?*

ADOLPHUS: We were listening to my play and your father got infuriated over some static.

LORNA: How like Dad. He's such a stickler for perfection.

ADOLPHUS: Where have you been?

LORNA: Under the car, with James. Don't look so worried, I'll get you into films yet. I'll speak with Reggie.

ADOLPHUS: (*Tenderly*) Oh, Lorna, why do you do all this—?

LORNA: Reggie's a film director and quite a dear. Do what?

ADOLPHUS: Nothing.

LORNA: (*Into phone*) Hello, Reggie. . .? I have someone with me that I feel you ought to gaze at. *And* he has a profile. . .

(*Reggie enters with Goetz, his cameraman, Lolly, a clapper boy, and a few "Yesmen"*)

REGGIE: Let's see if you have a profile. So few actors nowadays have any profiles at all.

LORNA: Yes, so few. . .

REGGIE: Let's have a look at your other profile. (*Adolphus turns his head*) He has got quite a good profile.

LORNA: I am sure you'll agree. . .

REGGIE: Don't you agree?

YESMEN: Yes. Excellent profile. . .

REGGIE: Not so fast, boys.

YESMEN: Yes. Not so fast, boys. . .

LORNA: (*Still into the phone*) Why not give him a film test, Reggie?

REGGIE: We'd better film-test him first.

YESMEN: Yes. Bright idea. . .

(*Camera, lights, etc. are lined up for shooting*)

GOETZ: All set for test.

LORNA: (*Hangs up*) Hullo, Reggie, glad you could manage.

CLAPPER BOY: Scene one of film test, take one.

(*Pause*)

REGGIE: Cut. That was pretty good.

YESMEN: Yes, oh, yes. Very good. . .

REGGIE: But not good enough.

YESMEN: Yes, hardly good enough. . .

REGGIE: Take two.

GOETZ: All set.

CLAPPER BOY: Scene one, film test, take two.

(*Pause*)

REGGIE: Cut. Perfect. Magnifico.

YESMEN: Yes. Magnificent. . .

REGGIE: We'll make a super star out of you, man!

LORNA: Oh, how wonderful.

REGGIE: What's your moniker?

ADOLPHUS: Pardon?

LORNA: Adolphus.

ADOLPHUS: Too long. *Adol.* Much better! I can see the *Variety* headline: *Adol the Idol with Plenty of Id.* But in my films it's not star value that counts, it's the story. The idea.

GOETZ: I'm all set, Reggie. B & W or color?

REGGIE: B & W, Wide S, fifty-five mm, SS sound. It's an adult intellectual, psychological fictional documentary. . .

GOETZ: Ready for rehearsal.

REGGIE: (*To Adolphus; quietly, man to man*) Man, this is a film about *suffering*. About a man's quest. For what? For happiness? Why, this man could be happy, if he wanted to. But he soon realizes that there is something mysteriously unhappy about *being* happy. Does he want to be unhappy, then? Why, man, if happiness is hollow, so is unhappiness, if you see what I mean? So, what is this man looking for, then? Why, for something to look for. . .if you see what I mean?

ADOLPHUS: Not quite.

REGGIE: Good, you could wear a bewildered look on your face. Now, the plot. . .(*He goes on gesticulating in silence*)

LORNA: (*To Clapper Boy*) What's that you're holding?

REGGIE: All set for a rehearsal, then?

GOETZ: Just waiting for your "go."

REGGIE: Good. Well, Adol, what. . .(*He goes on in mime*)

CLAPPER BOY: These are clapper boards. I clap them together. It's on their account I'm called "clapper boy."

LORNA: Would you let me clap in your place?

REGGIE: Well, Adol, you sit here, on the couch and. . .

LORNA: How would you like to see my collection?

REGGIE: (*To Adolphus, who is watching Lorna*) Are you listening, man?

ADOLPHUS: Sorry.

REGGIE: Pay attention, man, this is serious. It's *art!*

CLAPPER BOY: *What collection?*

REGGIE: Now this is the love scene. The big one. You are holding. . .(*He mimes a couple of lines*)

LORNA: . . .of Baroque beds.

REGGIE: . . .for many years. At last, the great day has come and you. . .

CLAPPER BOY: Beds?

REGGIE: Are you listening, man? Well, as she brings her lips to. . .

LORNA: Certainly. They were normal in *those* days. C'm'on.

CLAPPER BOY: But, Mr. Reggie—

LORNA: Don't worry, *I* am the boss's daughter!

REGGIE: Pay attention, please, Adol!. . .Listen, Lorna, do me a favor, will you? You are distracting glamor man.

LORNA: Don't worry, Reggie, I am making myself scarce. (*To Clapper Boy*) C'm'on.

ADOLPHUS: Lorna!

LORNA: (*To Adolphus*) No, I mustn't stay. You go on with your good work. (*Lorna and the Clapper Boy exit*)

REGGIE: You are holding her in your arms, then. Right?

ADOLPHUS: Right. Where is she?

REGGIE: Who?

ADOLPHUS: The girl I love. The Countess Mona Lisa.

REGGIE: Oh, we don't know yet who's going to play her, but you can rest assured it'll be a Name. A big name.

ADOLPHUS: But how can I play the love scene without the woman I love?

GOETZ: Montage.

REGGIE: We do your bits first, and then we do hers. Stuck together, it looks like the real thing. If you see what I mean?

ADOLPHUS: Well, quite frankly, I. . .

REGGIE: (*Suspiciously*) You aren't *Actors' Studio* by any chance? Not a Method man, I hope.

ADOLPHUS: I don't even know what you're talking about.

REGGIE: Good. Let's shoot. Right.

GOETZ: Right, ready to shoot.

YESMEN: Right, all ready to shoot.

REGGIE: Where's the clapper boy?

GOETZ: Oh, hell, where's that clapper boy?

YESMEN: Clapper boy!

LORNA: (*Lorna enters, holding clapper boards*) I promised I'd clap for him (*She does so*) Scene three-hundred-and-twenty-two, take one.

GOETZ: Camera!

REGGIE: Action!

ADOLPHUS: (*To Lorna*) What have you done? Don't you see I love you and can't—

REGGIE: Cut—! That's grand, man, grand!

YESMEN: Grand, man. . .Yes!

REGGIE: But you were too emotional.

ADOLPHUS: But I suffer. . .

REGGIE: Yes, you do. And that's a good thing to remember. But you are *Adol the Idol.* You are a HERO. You can take your medicine like a man. Be dead pan, man. Dead pan.

YESMEN: Yes, dead pan. Like a man. . .

REGGIE: Silence!

LORNA: Scene three-hundred-and-twenty-two, take two.

ADOLPHUS: (*Very dead pan*) Yes. . .yes. . .no. . .yes. . . no. . .

REGGIE: Cut! Cut! Still too much emotion. Play it down, man. Play it down.

LORNA: Scene three-hundred-and-twenty-two, take three.

ADOLPHUS: (*Mechanically*) Yes. . .yes. . .yes. . .I love you, Juliet me honey. I am dying, Egypt. Behold, thou art fair, my love, behold, thou art fair. . .Stick 'em up, pardner. . .Thou hast doves' eyes within thy locks. . .Sorry to do this to you, Ghengis Khan, but I have a mission, a duty, to Western Civilization. Thy lips are like a thread of scarlet. . .A slut, that's what you are, but I'm crazy 'bout you babyohsocrazyIwannadie. Thy neck is like the tower of David. . .(*He shakes imaginary hands*) Boys, the whole nation—the whole world—looks upon you today. Drop it straight on the target and happy landing, and remember —your wives and sweethearts will be right here to welcome you back. And boys, look out for radiation. . .Thy two breasts are like two young roes that are twins. . .Rocket number one, ready! (*He breaks down*) I can't do it!. . .There are women and children there. . .and flowers. . .and babies. . .I just can't. . .forgive me! (*There is an icy silence. No one moves*)

LORNA: (*Quietly*) Adolphus, you must.

ADOLPHUS: I. . .I can't!

LORNA: But you are a *hero.*

ADOLPHUS: I am a *coward.*

LORNA: No, you are not. . .Look in my eyes. . .You can't do this to Reggie. He was counting on you.

REGGIE: (*Quietly*) He'll have us all in hot water.

LORNA: See? You've upset Reggie.

ADOLPHUS: But I just can't do it, Lorna!. . .Not with all the children and babies and flowers. . .and cats. . .

REGGIE: Cats?—He's mad!

LORNA: But, Adolphus, this is *only a film.*

REGGIE: What d'you mean "only a film"?

LORNA: Adolphus, please do it. . .for me. . .

ADOLPHUS: And if I do it. . .will you. . .?

LORNA: Yes.

ADOLPHUS: All right then. For you. For you.

REGGIE: Ready?

GOETZ: Ready.

YESMEN: Ready. . .

REGGIE: Right.

GOETZ: Camera.

REGGIE: Action.

LORNA: Good luck, love.

ADOLPHUS: Men, today is D Day. . .This thing is better than anything we've ever had on this planet! Better than the gas chambers. Better than the Rolls Royce. We'll show them that Rome isn't eternal, that although it wasn't built in a day it can be wiped out in a millionth of a split second. Down with the Pope, Muhammad, Jesus, Karl Marx, and Freud. . .Death to the niggers. . .*Juden raus. . .everyone!*. . .Rocket number two, ready!

A YESMAN: Rocket number two ready for firing, sir.

ADOLPHUS: Ten-nine-eight-seven-six-five-four-three-two-one-FIRE!

(*Pandemonium. Smith dashes in, very excited*)

SMITH: Terrific! Great! I've just seen the rushes.

REGGIE: He's had us all in tears. I even forgot to call "cut". . .*Cut!*

(*Lorna has gone out on the previous line*)

GOETZ: I couldn't keep my eye on the camera.

SMITH: Wonderful! True art. And such tension. You are a real star.

(*Music. People are shaking Adolphus' hand, taking pictures of him, etc.*)

PEOPLE: —Congratulations—You're stupendous—We've never seen anything quite—No, not quite—You're tops—You broke our hearts—Real catharsis—A great hero—A tragedy in blank prose—We love you, etc.

REGGIE: Silence, please! *Silence!* Mr. Smith has an important announcement to make.

(*There is an abrupt silence*)

SMITH: Ladies and gentlemen, I have great pleasure. . . (*Mimes a few words*)

(*Lorna enters and rushes to Adolphus, whom she hugs. She is wearing overalls and is holding a huge wrench*)

LORNA: Oh, my hero, my hero, my big silent tall dark and handsome so very virile and brave hero, oh my love, oh!

ADOLPHUS: Where have you been?

LORNA: Helping one of the men working upstairs.

ADOLPHUS: Helping *whom?*

LORNA: That man upstairs. One of the workmen.

ADOLPHUS: Oh, Lorna, you. . .(*He starts choking her. A woman screams. The others stand immobile, too frightened to move*) You. . .

LORNA: The plumber's mate.

ADOLPHUS: (*Lets go of her throat*) *The plumber's mate?*

LORNA: Yes. He let me be the plumber's mate's mate.

SMITH: (*Resumes his announcement*). . .in announcing that I have given my consent.

ADOLPHUS: What consent?

SMITH: To marry Lorna, of course.

ADOLPHUS: But I don't—

(*Thunderous applause. Music. A Woman brings in a long

white veil for Lorna. Lorna and Adolphus are pushed up-stage by the people who form a solid wall, with backs to the audience, hiding the young couple from view. A Priest hurries in and disappears in turn through the human wall)

PRIEST: (*Over loudspeaker*) We are here assembled in the presence of. . .

(*The rest fades under as background for the following scene:*

Lorna enters stage right, with Captain Rix. She is wearing a navy blue mackintosh and a captain's cap. She is holding a baby in her arms)

LORNA: Hurry up, Captain Rix.

RIX: This is mighty awkward, ma'am.

LORNA: C'm'on, skipper.

RIX: Are you sure your. . .he. . .won't mind?

LORNA: I left him a note.

PRIEST: (*From the background, over the loudspeaker*) Do you, Adolphus, take Lorna Smith. . .

LORNA: And you did promise to let me navigate the yacht through the Straits of Magellan, didn't you darling?

RIX: Yes, I did, but. . .the. . .baby. . .?

LORNA: Why, it's my baby.

ADOLPHUS: (*Adolphus enters*) My baby! Where are you *taking* my baby?

LORNA: Don't you dare lay a finger on me, Adolphus, don't you dare now! Captain Rix, sir, please protect me!

RIX: (*Salutes smartly*) Yes, ma'am. Sir, it's no use making a scene.

ADOLPHUS: Oh, dry up! Lorna, what are you doing with this jacktar?

LORNA: We're sailing today. To the Straits of Magellan, and it's no use chasing me.

ADOLPHUS: But the baby. . .the baby. . .

PRIEST: (*From the background*) Do you, Lorna Smith. . .

ADOLPHUS: My little, oh, so little, baby boy. . .(*He is in tears*)

LORNA: Baby boy? He doesn't even know it's a *girl*.

PRIEST: I pronounce you man and wife. . .

RIX: The judge said. . .

ADOLPHUS: *What* judge?

LORNA: The divorce judge.

ADOLPHUS: *What* divorce?

LORNA: He doesn't even remember that we were divorced!

ADOLPHUS: What did the judge—?

VOICE: (*Over loudspeaker, situated in the back of the auditorium*) Adolphus, you are a menace to your own child!

ADOLPHUS: But *why?*

LORNA: *Why?* He doesn't even know why! (*She goes out. Adolphus tries to stop her, but Rix prevents him from doing so*)

RIX: Because, sir, you are too often three sheets to the wind.

ADOLPHUS: What?

RIX: You're a drunk, old man, that's what.

ADOLPHUS: Drunk? Me? But I never. . .(*Suddenly, he is unsteady on his feet*). . .never. . .tou. . .touched a drop. . .ne . . .never. . .honest. . .(*He takes a bottle out of his pocket and swallows a gulp*) Ne. . .never drink. . .tha. . .thash me. . .honest to G- (*Hiccups*). . .'Xshuse me. (*The People in the Crowd now turn and face Adolphus*) I. . .I shwear I. . .I love my baby boy-girl. Lorna, where are you? Oh, Lorna, my love, my life, oh?

(*He exits, sobbing and rocking. Some of the characters we have seen earlier are now on the stage*)

GIRL: (*To the audience.*) He's wonderful.

BEATNIK I: He's high.

BEATNIKS II: He's goof.

SMITH: He's beastly to women. My daughter told me things about him I wouldn't care to repeat anywhere, even to a stranger in a bar.

MODEL: Was he beastly to her in bed?

SMITH: Where else?

MODEL: The beast! He was never beastly to me, damn him!

GOETZ: No talent whatsoever! Not even an iota of creativity.

REGGIE: Don't mention creativity, please, please!

GOETZ: Yeah, one day in the—

REGGIE: Yeah. Remember?

GOETZ: I remember all right.

REGGIE: Yeah, one day in the studio he made us all cry like babies, he exasperated us so. . .

GOETZ: I couldn't keep my eyes on the camera, honest!

SMITH: And I had to rush in in order to save the day, and the film. Had to say to him "You were great" and all that kind of malarkey. How I hated myself all that month!

CLAPPER BOY: And he was always so jealous.

YESMEN: Yeah.

GIRL: I sort of liked him. I thought he was great!

FATHER: (*Entering*) *Was?* Is he dead?

SMITH: As good as. . .

FATHER: *Drink?* Tell me please, I have a right to know, I'm his father.

SMITH: In that case, it is my sad duty to inform you. . .

DAUGHTER: (*The same actress who played Mother, rushes in, screaming*) No, no! Oh no no. . .!

FATHER: There now. . .

DAUGHTER: If only he had become a *plumber's mate!*

SMITH: Excuse me, ma'am, are you his dead mother?

DAUGHTER: (*Indignantly*) Certainly I am not his dead mother! I am his *daughter!*

SMITH: Granddaughter! What joy! (*He hugs her*) My granddaughter, at last!

LORNA: Captain Rix, I thought you had disposed of her in the Straits of Magellan, as arranged?

RIX: Sorry, Miss Smith, but I just couldn't, God, I couldn't do it.

DAUGHTER: Do what?

RIX: I handed her over to some friendly Patagonians who gave me their solemn word of honor never to let her leave the *Tierra del Fuego.*

LORNA: How embarrassing. Why, she looks older than I do.

DAUGHTER: That's because of my Spartan upbringing.

LORNA: Spartan? I thought you said Patagonia—?

MISTRESS: I had to chuck him out of my room. . .

BEATNIK II: Who?

MISTRESS: Adolphus.

FATHER: Yes, I remember it all, as if it were last night. . .

MISTRESS: But it was last night. . .

MILLIONAIRE: Remember that painting he sold me, the dud?

PEOPLE: Yes, yes. . .

MILLIONAIRE: Well, it turned out to be a dud! The imprint of some bum's "bum." Hung it over my bed, I did, then my doctor came to look me over, sighted the painting and roared himself sick. "Modern stuff," I explained. "More like Rumpostion," he said, "because, don't you see, it's some bum's *'bum'"!*

BEATNIK II: A queer, that's what he was. A queer.

BEATNIK I: Right you are, darling.

LORNA: I once said, quite by accident, "poothtick," and he said we were kindred souls. . .

JAMES: He had no driving license. . .

RIX: Every time we passed through the Straits of Messina or Bering, he would be sick all over "A" deck.

MODEL: Yes, he always suffered from claustrophobia and he had a hideous birthmark on his tootsee wootsie thumbie. . .

FATHER: He was a Shylock. Never gave me more than a measly fifty thousand.

DAUGHTER: He was rude. He never helped old ladies across the road. . .

LORNA: Look out, he's crossing the road.

SMITH: Careful, he might be dangerous!

(*They all steal away quietly, very much afraid. For a short time the stage is empty. Then Adolphus enters, led by a Boy Scout. Adolphus is now extremely old—a ragged, tattered tramp*)

BOY: Well, here's your bench, sir.

ADOLPHUS: Thank you, son.

BOY: I'll be off now. (*He salutes in Boy Scout fashion*) Be prepared.

ADOLPHUS: (*Salutes back*) To meet thy God. . .Wait, I want you to do me a great favor.

BOY: Sorry, sir, can't.

ADOLPHUS: Can't?

BOY: No, sir, not today. Not more than one good deed a day, that's the Scouts' motto. (*He walks away. To audience*) Dirty ol' man, ain't 'e? (*He goes out*)

ADOLPHUS: One good deed a day. . .(*After a long search through his many pockets, which contain all sorts of junk, he finally finds a cigarette butt and lights it*) Ah, the good life. (*He smokes contentedly*)

VOICE: (*Over loudspeaker*) At last it was time for Adolphus to turn to dust. . .

ADOLPHUS: (*A long pause. Then, suddenly, he gets down on his knees and whispers*) No. . .

VOICE: Yes.

ADOLPHUS: Please, no!

VOICE: Oh, yes!

ADOLPHUS: I was hoping. . .(*Change of accent*) 'opin' as that you 'ood gi' me mo' time to enjoy wot's lef'. Gi' a feller a chance to die properlike, wiv 'is face to the wall. There ain' no wall in this 'ere bloody park. Please, Guv, oh please. . .?

VOICE: Oh, go jump into the lake!

ADOLPHUS: Yes, sir!

(*Adolphus exits. A shadow appears and looks, off, after Adolphus. It is the Angel, all in black, wingless and grim*)

ANGEL: . . .There he is, standing on the edge of the water, preparing for the plunge. The water is as dark as the night and the stars hide their faces. Slowly, deliberately, he takes off his jacket; it is full of gaping holes. (*A hand, from the wings, hands him Adolphus' jacket*) Adolphus' jacket, no doubt about it! Indecent, that's what he was. . .indecent. . .(*Angrily*) But you can't be indecent without paying the penalty, sooner or later. If only I could burn his clothes. . .But not even I. . .(*He puts the jacket on the bench*) He has taken off his shoes and sock. One single, orphan sock you could almost fish with. Not that he is one-legged. . .One sock and it is stiff with the dirt and sweat of many weeks. His feet are filthy and the water is so cold. It tickles him and he giggles. How dare he! He has taken off his shirt. (*The shirt is produced from the wings*) Patches! (*Angrily*) Who the—*did that?* It was decreed that he would have *nobody, not a soul in the whole wide world!* It was decided many years ago that he would be all alone, like a discarded lover in a big city. And yet *somebody* mended his shirt! (*Angrily*) There is no discipline! No discipline left in the world! Only anarchy. . . Never mind, it's too late to mend now. (*He places shirt on the bench and takes trousers from the wings*) There is nothing quite as silly as *this* garment. Only the human body they hide's more ridiculous! (*A top hat is produced from the wings*) A top hat. . . and he had nothing in the world. . .Is he up to his old tricks? (*Looking inside the hat*) No, not even a white rabbit. (*A splash is heard, off*) He is in the water! His head—a brief moment—a gasp—a shudder—a short struggle—water water all around—and under—and on top of him—finis—goodbye. (*A woman's scream is heard*) There is no respect for the dead. (*Angrily*) *Someone* cares! (*As he goes out*) Too late.

(*The Girl appears. She is almost naked in a brief swim suit. She is holding the notebook Adolphus gave her*)

GIRL: . . .I was bathing in the lake when he jumped in and drowned. He looked so young and naked. He gave me this book long ago and now there is nothing left, except the book and his old clothes and his memory in my heart. Adolphus darling, I shall *never* forget! Please let me unstrip into your clothes. (*She puts on Adolphus' shirt*) The touch of your shirt is like old wine that makes a swinging trapeze of all our *old concepts*. He wrote beautifully cruel verse, collected in this notebook under the title *O Four or Poems of a Self-Vampire*. (*She puts on Adolphus' vest*) There's still some blood on his vest. Of course, he would puncture his thumb and use his own blood for ink. Blood is thicker than water, but not as durable as ink. Already, not a trace is left of his life work. . .(*She puts on Adolphus' trousers. Out of one of the pockets, she takes a piece of paper and looks at it closely*) Blank. But his memory lingers on. In *me!* No one else remembers or cares. . .(*She puts on Adolphus' jacket*) Not even the old professors. They used infra-red on his manuscript. Just curiosity, they said. Nothing. Only his old clothes remain. I am his *only* disciple. His only inheritor. His daughter never really knew him. Only *I* understand and appreciate his soul, his ideology. . .and it is such a pity that I never came. . .(*She puts on Adolphus' hat*). . .round to actually reading his poems.

(*Fitzi, an overdressed gigolo-about-town, enters*)

FITZI: (*Laughs*) What the hell's this?

GIRL: I thought you said it was in fancy dress?

FITZI: Quite.

GIRL: Well, then?

FITZI: You look superb.

GIRL: I feel spiritual, Fitzi. Come, take me to the party.

FITZI: Have you got enough cash for a taxi?

GIRL: I am loaded tonight.

FITZI: Good. (*Pause*) You remind me of someone I knew years ago.

GIRL: Was she beautiful?

FITZI: It was a man. He was a tramp.

GIRL: Good. I *am* he, thank God.

(*They go out, as down comes the:*)

Curtain

Curtain Call
(*Entire Cast On Stage*)

The show is over, our play is done
A moral? There's absolutely none
But if the stuff with moral rife
Is what you want—there's always life!

John Cromwell

OPENING NIGHT

John Cromwell

John Cromwell first came to the theatre as an actor. Born in New York City and educated at Harvard, he appeared on the Broadway stage and with the national companies of many distinguished productions including *Saint Joan* (with Katharine Cornell, Maurice Evans); *Pygmalion* (Gertrude Lawrence, Raymond Massey); and *Macbeth* (Michael Redgrave, Flora Robson).

The production that was to hold the greatest significance for the author-actor, however, was a revival of *Outward Bound* starring the legendary Laurette Taylor. And, as close observers will note, it was Miss Taylor's own personal life and professional comeback that inspired the characterization of Fanny Ellis in Mr. Cromwell's extremely affecting drama.

Opening Night was first presented on the New York stage at the East End Theatre on October 2, 1963, with Peggy Wood as the pivotal character and Ruth Gates as her loyal dresser-companion.

Miss Wood's extraordinary performance as the actress who almost is thwarted by a bottle of brandy sent her by a sadistic drama critic on her crucial "comeback" opening night, engendered loud cheers and considerable press coverage, including a feature interview with this editor for the *Chicago Daily News'* weekend supplement, *Panorama.* Her acclaimed interpretation of the role perhaps can be best described in Peggy Wood's own words: "That bottle of brandy is the antagonist, the third person in the dressing room along with me and my maid. As it sits there on my make-up table and looms at me, I must play around it, against it, build with temptation, suspense and finally, with courageous resistance. That bottle of brandy is like a monster, staring at me menacingly and, though it doesn't say a word, it alone holds the fate of this woman. Will she or will she not open it?

"I tried to re-create Laurette's own special qualities, especially her laugh, the half-completed gestures she always made, the peculiar lift of the arms out of the kimono when she spoke. The slightly hesitant delivery, followed by the shatteringly direct line. You always felt as though she had never thought of the words before they were spoken."

How well Miss Wood succeeded in capturing the soul and spirit of the great star in *Opening Night* was mirrored in the high praise bestowed upon her: "I've been in the theatre for a good many years, half a century to be blunt, and I've been in many successes, yet I've never had a part like this, nor such extraordinary critical praise. But there's something else, very strange, that happened to me during the production. I actually felt *possessed* by Miss Taylor and suddenly. . .found myself. . . doing things. . .just as Laurette always did them. . ."

In addition to *Opening Night*—published here for the first time—Mr. Cromwell has had three other plays produced Off-Broadway: *A Matter of Like Life and Death, A Banquet for the Moon* (in collaboration with Jean Shepherd), and *A Breezy Fourth*. He also has published two novels: *Egan Rendy* and *A Grain of Sand*.

An international commuter, Mr. Cromwell divides his time between his East Side apartment in Manhattan, London, and his home in Positano, Italy, where he does most of his writing.

Characters

FANNY ELLIS *is a* star. *Never beautiful, getting older now—sixty on the street; forty-five onstage, if she keeps thin—she retains all of whatever it takes to make an actress a star. She is a woman of infinite sensibility, almost too high-strung to survive. Despite numerous misfortunes, survive she has. Her voice sounds strangely unsure of itself. Her movements seem tentative. This is an illusion. She knows exactly what she is doing. Although she "comes over" all feeling, she is an intellectual actress.*

HECKY, *Fanny's maid, dresser, and companion of many years, is fearfully old but most expert at her job. While cherishing Fanny, she takes no nonsense from her.*

Scene:

The Star dressing room of a Broadway theatre.

Time:

A half-hour before the opening night curtain of a revival of The Sea Gull.

The dressing room, although it has been chintzed up, remains bleak. It is bare of flowers. Naked bulbs provide a cruel light. The enamel of the washbasin is chipped. The only window gives onto a wall a few feet away. Dampness pervades the room. At intervals, the radiator clanks. A dressing table stands against the fourth wall. When Fanny Ellis sits at it, she is facing the audience. The mirror frame is empty.

At the moment, the dressing room is in almost complete darkness. A thin shaft of light from the door, slightly ajar, penetrates the shadows. Somewhere nearby—jarring sounds of a piano being tuned.

Fanny Ellis gets up from the window seat where she has been trying to rest, turns on the lights over her dressing table, goes to the door and slams it. She comes back to the table, sits at it and goes over a speech from her role: Madame Arkadin in The Sea Gull. *She is wearing a dressing gown—once a treasure of satin and lace. The dressing gown has endured hundreds of repairs and dry cleanings. She wears it because it is lucky.*

On the dressing table, besides her makeup box and tray, is a silver-framed photograph.

FANNY: "There are six country houses on the shore of the lake. I remember laughter, noise, shooting and love affairs without end. Music and singing used to float across that lake. . ." (*Hecky comes in and turns on a light over the sink*)

HECKY: It's almost half-hour.

FANNY: They couldn't have tuned that piano earlier, could they? Try to get forty winks with *that* going on. (*Fanny starts cold-creaming her face. Hecky puts up an ironing board. She is plugging in the iron when there is a knock at the door. A second knock.*)

HECKY: All right! All right! (*Hecky goes to the door, gets into a whispered argument with a delivery boy who is on the other side of it.*)

FANNY: What is it? (*The whispering continues. A package is shoved into Hecky's hands*)

HECKY: (*To Fanny*) I told Tim you wanted nothing brought into the dressing room—(*She tries to return the package. Fanny decides on direct action, gets up, takes the package from Hecky, pushes the door shut*)—no flowers, no telegrams. . .

(*Fanny takes a card out of an envelope which has come with the package. Her mood of irritation vanishes, she is evidently pleased. Returning to the dressing table, she opens the package. It contains a bottle of brandy*)

FANNY: Damn his soul! *Damn his soul!* (*Hecky attempts to take the bottle away.*) No. Leave it. It wasn't sent by an enemy. See—it says, "From an admirer." (*Hecky examines the card. She is shocked*)

HECKY: Why would he want to do a thing like that?

FANNY: It's a dare. He *dares* me to drink it. . .It's meant kindly. What he's daring me to do is *not* to take a drink. I haven't! It will be four weeks tomorrow. You know I haven't!

I got rid of the bottles. There was still the cooking sherry and the brandied peaches. I haven't touched them.

HECKY: But a dramatic critic, to send a bottle of brandy—?

FANNY: He is the most dramatic of the critics. He can't know what it's like!—Screw him! (*Again Hecky starts to remove the bottle*) No, leave—leave it! Let it remain there. . . looming at me. . .(*She sits to finish cold-creaming her face. Hecky starts pressing a blouse*) Did he laugh when he sent it? Is the joke already making the rounds? "I sent Fanny Ellis a bottle of her favorite sauce for an opening night present". . .I know he didn't do it in that spirit. I know he did it—for my good. Screw him, does he think I've forgotten? (*With relish*) That management *never* had another success. Pulling the curtain on me!

(*The Callboy knocks*)

CALLBOY: Half-hour, Miss Ellis.

FANNY: Thank you. In the middle of a performance! How dared they! *Anyone* can blow a line.

HECKY: You're—

FANNY: And lying about me!

HECKY: You're going to make a sensation tonight.

FANNY: Don't give me a lot of that crap, Hecky. (*She wipes her face clean and pats the bottle of brandy*) After the performance, you and I have a date! (*Then, withdrawing her hand*) No. Not until the end of the run. (*A brief, harsh laugh*) It's in my contract. . .Getting through this afternoon was like when I pick my way over the light cables—through the narrow alley to where I make my entrance. I dread that narrow alley! Trying to keep from brushing against the whitewashed wall with the *No Drinking* sign on it. (*She is startled into laughter*) Did you hear me, Hecky? I said "No Drinking—No Drinking sign!" Instead of *No Smoking*.

HECKY: I was thinking I miss Grisbie. What a stage-struck dog! He never got over that he couldn't be in all your plays.

FANNY: Get down, get down, Grisbie. He loved the smell of greasepaint.

HECKY: He loved you.

FANNY: He did not. I loved him. There's a difference.

HECKY: He'd always be quiet in the dressing room.

FANNY: He was a self-centered dog.

HECKY: Oh, he knew everything that was going on, that mutt did. He was smarter than some humans. When Mr. George won him in the raffle, just a puppy he was. . .Well, he couldn't last forever.

FANNY: Who couldn't last forever? Grisbie or Mr. George?—

HECKY: I was referring to Grisbie.

(*Fanny looks at the photograph framed on the dressing table*)

FANNY: Do you suppose he knows his plays are *still* being performed? It would please him if he knew. The revival I saw of *The Almond Tree*—Off-Broadway—what would he make of that? The girl playing my part was clever,—truthful. Not as *exciting* as I was, of course. (*She touches the frame*) I did enjoy being "Mrs. Herbert George." The *wife,* not the widow. A tricky role, if there ever was one. Mrs. Herbert George, received in the stateliest homes of England. I used to always carry a book with me. So they'd think I was worthy of him intellectually. (*A slight pause*) Sometimes it was awkward managing a purse and a parasol and a fan and a book all at once. . .I chose books with bindings to match the color of my dresses. . .(*This confession makes Fanny blush, she hides her face*)

HECKY: When we were invited to Gloucester Hall, I was seated in the place of honor—at the right of the butler.

FANNY: It turned your head. You've never been the same since. . .(*Indicating the photograph in the silver frame*) He'd say to me, "You're a thoroughbred." That's how he used to take care of me. As if I were a thoroughbred racehorse. . .The casts—the fine actors—he surrounded me with! He wouldn't have allowed that old ham who's playing Trigorin past the stage door! I'd like to cut his face in little pieces. I must tell him so, "I'd like to cut your great ham face in little pieces."

HECKY: You wouldn't do that.

FANNY: Wouldn't I, though! That line he has in the

scene with Nina, "I've never cared for myself." I feel like shouting from the wings, "And nobody else has either!" Nothing goes through his head except, is he advantageously lit—? The only advantageous lighting for *him* would be a—a moonless night! Acting demands involvement. (*She shuts her eyes*) Involvement! (*She opens them and reapplies herself to her makeup*) People speak of personality—what's that! I have no personality, not offstage I haven't. . .The old ham has made Trigorin over to suit himself. The spats, the cane, the monocle—the *monocle!* Does he imagine spats and a monocle add up to a *human being?*

HECKY: He's still a fine figure of a man.

FANNY: He "characterizes" Trigorin. . .How can he do that to Chekhov? Well, he did it to Hamlet thirty seasons ago. Was his Hamlet ever melancholy! Everything he does is false and artificial, everything I do—

HECKY: God made you a great actress.

FANNY: Would he want me to be modest about it? When Stanislavsky asked me to Russia—long before his books had been translated—invited me to play there in English, assuring me I'd be understood—(*She lets the sentence trail off unfinished*) He invited me because he *knew* I knew. Knew instinctively what he was driving at. Knew that acting requires *total involvement*. . . (*She raises her voice*) Not that I can't be heard!

HECKY: Oh, you can be heard.

FANNY: I'm quite conscious that there's an audience to be appeased. I'm aware there's no fourth wall. (*She quiets down and makes up in silence*) The day before rehearsals began I took the bottles to the incinerator myself. Some of them with a goodly quantity left in them. Well, perhaps not too goodly a quantity—(*She measures it with her fingers*)—and listened to them rolling down into purgatory. (*To the photograph*) Are you proud of me? Be proud of me. (*She opens a box of gumdrops and takes one*) *Ethel Barrymore,* older and more established though she was, was not given a warmer reception—was not more fêted—in London than I. The stagedoor Johnnies! Earls. I counted young earls among my. . .They called me *Molly*. The little colleen I played was more real to them than I was. . .Acting means giving up your identity. That's why actors weren't buried in consecrated ground. Not because we're an immoral lot—but because actors were thought to have lost their souls. . .Playing other people, we lose our own identities.

HECKY: God doesn't like to hear you talking that way.

FANNY: (*Continues gleefully; to tease Hecky*) Heathens, heretics, suicides, and actors were denied the blessings of the church. . .I have a soul, the *remnant* of a soul. They'll bury me in the plot on that hillside in Brooklyn. Next to him. It gets cold over there in winter. . .(*To Hecky, irritably*) Stop pressing that blouse. It's pressed enough. (*Hecky ignores her*) Belted earls flirted with me. Knowing I had a husband. Thinking he was too thin-lipped to care. *He cared.* (*Laughs*) Being married to a jealous man waters the ego. "Champagne for Miss Ellis!" How I used to adore champagne. It puts you in the mood to accept compliments. Now it only gives me indigestion. Without a drink, the world is as shabby as this room! (*She gets up and goes to the window*) Imagine a window that doesn't look out on anything. Except that wall.

HECKY: And the pigeons.

FANNY: It's a prison. I'm in *prison!* (*Hecky leaves her ironing to go to her*) Leave me alone!

HECKY: God love you! (*After a moment's hesitation, Hecky returns to her iron*)

FANNY: Stop pressing that blouse, that blouse is pressed.

HECKY: I'm just finishing. (*Observing how near the breaking point Fanny Ellis is*) I'll hang it up. (*She does so. Fanny sits again at the dressing table*)

FANNY: There are plenty of telegrams, aren't there?

HECKY: You said you didn't want to see them.

FANNY: Flowers?

HECKY: Masses. Masses of flowers. Care to see a bunch? (*Hecky starts toward door*)

FANNY: *No!* I don't want this dressing room smelling like a mortuary chapel.

HECKY: (*Returning*) Would you like me to give you a massage? Just between your shoulder blades.

FANNY: I couldn't bear to be touched!

HECKY: To relax you a little. (*Fanny yields. Hecky lightly massages the back of her neck*)

FANNY: I wasn't so nervous before I had my teeth capped. I spent thirty-six hours, that whole spring in the dentist's chair. A whole spring is a long time for anyone to spend in a dentist's chair.

HECKY: Hollywood! You had such beautiful teeth. Why they had to do them over! To look just the same as—(*Hecky sniffs*) *Hollywood!*

FANNY: They were after people who could speak. They were willing to pay.

HECKY: You'll never get me to admit one good thing about that place. A godless place! I never liked it and I never liked *him*.

FANNY: (*Smiles in pleasurable, if shamefaced, reminiscence*) The great cowboy star. You've never forgiven me, have you, Hecky? (*She indicates the photograph*) Jealous as he was, *he* forgave me. But you couldn't. He couldn't very well *not* forgive me. He was unable to accompany me to Hollywood, quote: because of previous commitments here in New York, unquote. Commitments including the oh-so-statuesque Miss Diana Cleveland of the *Ziegfeld Follies.*

HECKY: Your cowboy star. . .

FANNY: He was cute.

HECKY: . . .taught you to drink. (*Fanny cannot suppress a cry of dismay*) I didn't mean to say it!

FANNY: (*Recovering herself*) I'd had a good many lessons *before* I met *Cowboy.* When I was barely ten years old, my father would look across the dinner table at me. "You look peaked," he'd say. "You need red blood," and he'd pour me a glass of wine. Red wine—red blood. I'd get up from the table reeling. Those dinners are among my happiest if haziest recollections. Speaking of *la vie en rose. . .*!(*Hecky's face is a study in disapproval. Fanny bursts out laughing*) If you could see what you look like, Hecky! . .*Cowboy* was a student drinker, not a teacher. Sometimes he functioned as an object lesson. Gazing into those bloodshot pools—"Close your eyes, darling, or you'll bleed to death"—I'd promise myself to swear off and I would, I'd refuse the next round. . .I *never* drank on the set! Well, hardly ever. . .Poor *Cowboy*. Poor golden *Cowboy*. His biceps—he was so proud of his biceps—were stronger than his liver. Why does everyone have to be dead! If it weren't for you, Hecky. . .*I'm lonely!* The frightening thing is I'm going to keep on that way. (*An attempt to cheer herself up*) Or shall I buy myself a young man? Shall I do that, Hecky? The young man who plays my son? Konstantin? I think he's normal. Don't look so shocked. Your affair with God is an open scandal. That's enough. (*She shrugs off Hecky's massaging hands*) I won't put on my wig yet. It itches me. (*Suddenly, she seems confused. Then, in a plaintive voice*) *Where are they all—?* (*After a moment; briskly*) Go see if there's a telegram from Helen. Look through my telegrams, see if there's one from Helen. (*Hecky starts*) *No!* I don't want to know if there isn't. (*Hecky, having made an exaggerated gesture of "What next?" fusses around the room*) I had to conceal my children, it was the custom then. My children. Helen and Richard. I saw to it they had every advantage. I sent them to the best boarding schools. . .Stars weren't supposed to have offspring. The studio wouldn't allow them around me—on the entirely accurate theory that children make a woman seem—*bourgeois*. Today's movie stars and television stars are prototypes, the more typical the better. *We* were exotic. . .

HECKY: You were like nobody.

FANNY: Those pudding-faces on television, those television women, those mistresses of ceremonies! Mistresses of not much else *except* ceremonies. They can have as many babies as they like. In public, if they like! They owe their curious celebrity to the fact that they could be your next-door neighbors, God forbid. . .(*A second*) Helen must have sent a telegram. She relents from time to time. A telegram wishing me good luck. (*Another second*) How peculiar of Richard to marry a woman "old enough to be his mother," as they said at the time. In order to have a mother he had to marry one? I wrote his wife a friendly letter when I lent them the money to start their damn art school. She didn't answer. He told her not to answer. They cashed the check all right!. . .Helen was always precocious. I had to explain the situation ever so carefully: "You know and I know I'm your mother. To other people you'll be my niece. You'll call me Aunt Fanny. Won't that be a funny game? A secret between us?" We laughed about it together. I *thought* we laughed about it together. . .I sent her to Bryn Mawr, one of the very best women's colleges. That was when she began writing. Remember that first story she had published, Hecky? *The Clown*. . .(*Another second*) The children *never* blamed their father for anything. He took them on trips, gave them presents. I gave them *birth*. That's what they don't appreciate! Giving someone birth is no joke. Except for having my teeth capped by that sadist, I can't bring to mind two more *painful* ordeals. (*To Hecky*) Why are you standing there with your hands clasped? Go out and exert your charms on the stage doorman, why don't you. (*Hecky doesn't budge*) "There are six country houses on the shore of the lake. I remember laughter, noise, shooting and love affairs without end." Are you afraid I'll *sneak* a drink if you leave me alone?

HECKY: If you want a drink you'll have one whether I'm here or not.

FANNY: I'm glad you're clear on that, got that through your thick head. You're not my keeper! Oh, Hecky—! (*Hecky goes to her. The two women cling together*) *How am I going to get through it?* I have no reserve of strength. (*She turns to the mirror*) Look at her mouth. It used to curl up at the corners. I barely recognize that woman. . .I feel cold! I know it's not cold in here. . .

HECKY: It's damp. The rain.

FANNY: I feel cold. . .Haven't I had all the fame I need, the glory—? *Why must I prove myself again?* At my age, when I have so little ammunition in the way of looks or charm, to try to sell what's left. An old whore would retire gracefully. I'm scared to death, Hecky! Suppose I find there's nothing left to give?

HECKY: You never had a failure yet. (*Fanny makes a grimace of disagreement*) None that was your fault.

FANNY: *The Almond Tree* ran a thousand performances—between here and London.

HECKY: A thousand and *eleven* performances.

FANNY: That was long ago. The young people don't know me, except as some kind of dark legend. Where have I been these last years? If I haven't exactly risen from the dead, I'm coming back from very far. . .One drink would steady me. It would *steady* me. . .They think it's so *easy!* You just say, "No, I won't"—that's all there is to it. "Use your strength of character, Fanny"—*Job's comforters!* They'll be sitting out there wondering: "Is she all right?" "How does she seem?" Give a dog a bad name. . .(*She is trembling. To control her nerves, she stiffens her body*) "Fie, my Lord! A soldier and afeared!" It's unlucky to quote *Macbeth* on an opening night!

HECKY: They'll be rooting for you.

FANNY: People aren't as generous as you think. I've been arrogant in my time. There are plenty would be glad to see me go under. Ha! Ha! If they imagine I'm going to give them the satisfaction—! *One drink,* that's all. . .(*Taking the bottle, she rises and goes to the washbasin. She sets the bottle down on the edge of the basin and turns on the cold water. She tests it with her finger*) One drink to steady me, that's all. (*When it is cold enough, she runs a little of the water into a glass and drinks it*) Ha! Ha! (*She shows the unopened bottle to Hecky*) I didn't, you see! I drank a glass of water. I did it to tease you, Hecky. Wipe that stricken look off your face. I was teasing—teasing you. Ha! Ha! Did I tell you the joke that was told me once, by no less a person than he who sent this bottle? (*Lapsing into it*) Seems there was this drunk. Drank all day. Gin before breakfast, out of a bottle in the medicine chest. Gin all morning. Gin all afternoon. Gin until he fell into bed at night. Someone asked him, "How do you feel, how does drinking so much make you feel?" He answered, "I feel swell, I feel great. Except for that little moment when I wake up in the morning before I get to the bottle in the medicine chest in my bathroom. Sometimes during that moment I go *'Aaagh!'*" (*She screams the Aaagh!*) It doesn't make you laugh? (*The Callboy knocks*)

CALLBOY: Fifteen minutes, Miss Ellis.

FANNY: Thank you. You don't think he heard me? (*She covers her mouth to stifle her laughter. Her amusement is short-lived*) *Fifteen minutes!* (*Hurriedly, she sits down to finish her makeup*) Where are my eyelashes? (*Hecky hands her the box*) Between these things and that wig, I look. . .(*Hecky tries to assist her*) No, not like that! You can't do it, *I've* got to do it. . .you'll put my eye out—(*Gluing on the lashes*) The eyelashes and the wig make me look like *Grendel's mother*. But then, as I take it, there's a lot of Grendel's mother in Madame Arkadin. Irina Nikolayevna Arkadin. "There are six country houses on the edge of the lake. . ."

HECKY: Who would Grendel's mother be when she's at home?

FANNY: (*Makes a sound of disgust at the glue*) You wouldn't know if I told you. Grendel's mother was a monster. I mean a real monster. I don't speak metaphorically. . .People imagine I'm uneducated. I read when I was a child. I hadn't much schooling but I read. . .*Grendel's mother was the mother of Grendel*—does that clear it up? A character in an epic, an early English epic called *Beowulf*. . ."There are six country houses on the shore of the lake. I remember laughter, noise, shooting and love affairs without end"—I am Madame Irina Nikolayevna Arkadin, described behind my back by my son Konstantin as "a psychological freak. Unmistakably talented, intelligent, capable of sobbing over a book." (*She continues quoting from Konstantin's speech about his mother, transposing the pronoun "she" to "I"*) As a sick nurse I'm an angel. But just try praising Duse in my presence. No one must be praised but me! I must be written about, made a fuss over. To score a hit with me, mention how thrilled you were by my performance as Camille. Living in the country bores me, it makes me cross. I'm superstitious—fearful of the number thirteen—and I'm stingy. I have seventy thousand rubles in the bank at Odessa, but ask me to lend you money and I'll burst into tears. (*She sums up Mme. Arkadin's ambition*) I want and will have my way. . .I despise the new art forms. Modern plays—decadent. . .If I'm selfish—

well—an actress is by definition selfish. She has to be. If she doesn't take care of her interests, who will? . . .(*Mme. Arkadin addresses her lover*) "Trigorin, my wonderful splendid darling. You are the last page of my life.". . .I will *not* let Nina have him! (*The eyelashes are on, making her eyes even larger, more luminous than before*) There. They look all right, don't they. I can barely see out from under them. (*Hecky hands her the wig. Fanny puts it on. Its dyed redness coarsens her. She guffaws*) *Dainty little dandelion!* "Fanny, your fun-loving five-year-old favorite, will now oblige with her rendition of. . ." (*She sings*) *"Dain-ty lit-tul dan-de-li-on."* I never left an amateur night without *first prize. "Dain-ty lit-tul dan-de-li-on, sit-ting in the sun."* Isn't she a darling! I didn't know what stagefright *was* in those days. People imagine opening nights get easier as you go along. They get harder! They get more and more terrifying! You know the dangers, the pitfalls. . . .I wore a yellow poke bonnet. My mother would stand in the wings, rapture on her face. She made all my costumes. . .Incredible for me to be older than my mother was when she died. . .She didn't witness my disgrace. I needed her then more than I'd ever needed her. I was glad she was dead. She never saw me except going up. . .I gave her a pair of long white glacé gloves to wear to the opening of *The Almond Tree*. She sat in the right hand box. During the curtain calls, I bowed to her. She was clapping—white gloves over her head!

HECKY: Hold still!

FANNY: You couldn't take the airplane then. When I got word in London that she was dying it was too late. . .Her death made me realize, for the first time—nobody wins. You may think you're ahead—you may be ahead—but nobody wins in the long run. . .Except the saints. I wish I had *your* faith, Hecky. You're —good. Sometimes, "thou almost persuadeth me."

HECKY: (*Sharply*) Hold still!

FANNY: My father turned up after how many years? To drown his sorrows at her wake. He was in his grave soon after. . .All gone. All gone. All gone. (*Abruptly, she shakes off this mood*) I'm maudlin sober. . .That's enough, Hecky. Stop fussing. (*Hecky stops fussing with the wig. Fanny takes a gum-drop*) Did Madame Arkadin take a nip of vodka ever before she went on stage? My Camille—(*Fanny looks at "Madame Arkadin" in the mirror and gives a tiny tubercular cough*)—not a dry seat in the house either in Moscow or on tour in Kiev and Omsk. (*Suddenly suspicious*) Do you suppose—why did it never occur to me *before?* Was I *typecast* for this part! Is that why they hired me? Do they believe I *am* Madame Arkadin? A monster of vanity? A grotesque living on the memory of her past triumphs? (*She calms down and considers*) Well, if that *is* why they hired me, they're quite clever! Clever young producers, swooning at the sight of me. . .(*She lisps*) "Miss Ellis, Miss Ellis!" Which didn't prevent their being hardboiled when it came to a question of *salary!* (*A knock on the door. Fanny is startled. Another knock. Hecky goes to open it*) Don't let anyone in. I won't have it! (*The Producer's Voice On the other side of the door*) May I come in?

FANNY: No.

HECKY: (*At the door*) No visitors! Miss Ellis doesn't want to see anyone. (*The door opens slightly, not enough to reveal the visitor*)

VOICE: Mind if *I* come in?

FANNY: Yes, I do.

HECKY: I'm sorry. No one is allowed in the dressing room before a performance.

VOICE: I didn't mean to bother her.

FANNY: Go away! I don't care if you *are* the producer, I don't care *who you are!* Tell him to leave me alone!

VOICE: (*Apologetically*) I was just going to wish her good luck. I didn't mean to upset her.

FANNY: (*Screams*) I'm all right, if that's what you want to know! *I'm all right!* (*In a frenzy she goes to the basin and tears the foil from around the neck of the brandy bottle. Hecky closes the door*) I can't have everybody sneaking around suspecting me! (*Her body sags. The frenzy is over*) Take this, will you? (*She hands Hecky the bottle*) Don't try to hide it. . .I have to concentrate. (*She covers her eyes. After a moment she straightens up*) You may not think so, Hecky, but that's what I've been doing. *Concentrating!* "There are six country houses on the shore of the lake. . ." (*Hecky sets the bottle down on the dressing table*)

HECKY: (*Tenderly*) I know you. I know you, my lovey, my dearie.

FANNY: (*Mocking herself*) "There's nobody home but Hazel and she's a nut."

HECKY: You could never stand anyone in the dressing room on opening night, but me. Not even Mr. George.

FANNY: He knew enough to keep from underfoot.

HECKY: Grisbie and me.

FANNY: (*Picks up a ring from the dressing table*) My engagement ring was nearly as big as that. It paid the rent for two years. . .Who's wearing it now? (*She sits on chaise longue*) Dreams go by contraries, don't they?

HECKY: Put it out of your mind!

FANNY: The skulls. Otherwise it was all quite normal. They were applauding. I could just see the first rows through the blaze of the spots. A fashionably dressed audience. Their faces were skulls. I curtsied, as I plan to do at the curtain call, to keep in character—and this voice, I can hear it now, this thin chirrupy voice from the balcony, calling out. . .(*She imitates the voice*) "Every day has a number." I could feel my throat constrict. I woke up choking.

HECKY: The audience will applaud tonight.

FANNY: But they won't be skulls—?

HECKY: They may be numbskulls—

FANNY: Hecky, you've made a joke! (*Returns to the mood of the dream*) Did he mean my days are numbered?

HECKY: You'll be playing when you're ninety.

FANNY: I think this is my last appearance. When the run of *The Sea Gull* is over, *I'll* be over.

HECKY: God doesn't like to hear you talk that way.

FANNY: (*Impatiently*) God can't hear me, he's deaf. . .

Hecky, please don't look like that. I know I've insulted your best friend.

HECKY: You'll be playing when you're a hundred.

FANNY: And you'll be dressing me, I suppose. (*Hecky shrugs*) What will I be playing? *King Lear?*

HECKY: I wouldn't put it past you!

FANNY: (*Amused*) I wouldn't put it past me either. I always wanted to play *Hamlet.* A *Hamlet* whose native disposition, before he got swept into the sea of trouble, was *cheerful,* why not? But I never had the *figure* for *Hamlet.* Still, neither did the Divine Sarah. Her wooden leg! (*She limps around on a wooden leg quoting Hamlet in the closet scene*)

"Mother for the love of grace
Lay not that flattering unction to your tongue
That not your trespass but my madness speak."

(*She stops limping and answers herself as Gertrude*) "Oh Hamlet, thou hast cleft my heart in twain"—(*Then, in a Southern accent*)—all I've been doing is trying to keep the family together! (*She roars with laughter*) How do you bear with me, Hecky?

HECKY: I don't know!

FANNY: You were the only one didn't pretend there was nothing wrong. The others all ran away—"You'll be fine, Fanny. Just use your strength of character." (*Hecky takes down Fanny's costume*) You're the only one who stayed—to mop up the vomit. . .

HECKY: You best put on your costume.

FANNY: (*Takes off her dressing gown and with Hecky's assistance gets into costume*) Haven't you ever thought you might like a drink, Hecky?

HECKY: I don't know why, it never tempted me.

FANNY: You're a dull woman, do you know it? That soldier-boy of yours killed in the trenches in the First War—how could you have been faithful to his memory all these years? All those years? What was his name? Charlie? "Charlie, my darlin'." (*Hecky is impervious to this*) You have not led what could be called by any stretch of the imagination a *full* life.

HECKY: I've had you. That was enough, thank you.

FANNY: (*Laughs*) Enough and more than enough. (*The Callboy knocks*)

CALLBOY: Five minutes, Miss Ellis. (*The announcement jolts Fanny back to the present*)

FANNY: Thank you. . .Oh God! What's missing? There's something missing, something I haven't done. Give me my shawl. (*Hecky starts to do so*) No, no! The necklace first. I asked for a full-length mirror.

HECKY: Now don't get excited. You have plenty of time.

FANNY: Wouldn't you think the cheapskates could afford a full-length mirror? Nothing that I ask gets done around here! . .What are you up to? (*Hecky is fastening the necklace*)

HECKY: It's caught in the wig. Hold still! There. (*Fanny appraises her reflection, bending over the mirror of the dressing table*)

FANNY: Madame Arkadin wouldn't have let herself get as fat as I am.

HECKY: (*Fastening on a bracelet*) You're not fat.

FANNY: Look at this.

HECKY: You've kept to your diet and you're not fat.

FANNY: She probably had to watch her weight. Was her Camille a trifle plump? (*She reaches toward the bottle. Hecky quickly takes her hand and puts the ring on it*) There wouldn't be time for me to have more than *one!* One doesn't affect me. It would just calm my nerves.

HECKY: Sit down a minute.

FANNY: (*Glances upward*) That old ham is looking in the mirror, preening his molting feathers, thinking about the time he *didn't* make Pola Negri!

HECKY: You're in love with him.

FANNY: You're right, Hecky, I should be. Don't think I haven't worked on it. Irina Nikolayevna Arkadin is in love with him. Within the bounds of her self-love, she is in love with the famous author, Trigorin. (*She quotes from the play*) "My joy, my pride, my bliss—if you forsake me even for one hour I shall not survive." It turns my stomach!

HECKY: You are in love with him.

FANNY: It's not my best scene, is it?

HECKY: It could be—

FANNY: —if I were in love with him? (*She quotes*) "You are mine, mine. This forehead is mine and these eyes and this lovely silky hair." It's too preposterous! Besides he smells of cigars.

HECKY: Try.

FANNY: (*Mockingly*) "You are so gifted, so clever." (*She repeats the words, with sincerity*) ". . .so gifted—so clever." She isn't as sincere as all that!

HECKY: She doesn't want to lose him, she wants to keep him. (*Fanny considers this*)

FANNY: (*Truthfully*) "My marvelous, my magnificent one, my master. You are the last page of my life."

HECKY: That's the ticket!

FANNY: (*Smiles*) That's the ticket. . . .(*She feels the back of her neck*) I'm getting a crick.

HECKY: It will go away once you've—

FANNY: Tell me it's psychosomatic! Such a help to be told that, when you're in agony. . .(*As she lowers her hand*) I haven't taken the red off my nails! Give me the stuff. (*Hecky hands her the nail polish remover. She applies it lavishly*) What a smell! Something to combat the smell of his cigars. . .Helen surely would have sent a telegram, *I'm positive!* She and I never really had a break, you know. We just drifted apart. The way parents and children do, unfortunately. I'm going to write her a letter tomorrow. Thanking her for the telegram. That will be the *excuse*. Invite her for dinner, Sunday dinner. Columbia Heights isn't so far away. It isn't as if she lived in another city. She used to like Jello for dessert with slices of banana imprisoned in it. I don't suppose she still would. To be an instructor at Columbia is very distinguished. . .I wish I could ask Richard—and his wife—to Sunday dinner. New Mexico is far away. Art schools in Taos must be as thick as thrift shops along Third Avenue. . .*Cowboy* came from New Mexico. . .Some dusty little pueblo. He'd say to me. . .(*She mimics Cowboy*). . .

"My mother was a lady." (*Hecky wipes off the nailpolish remover*). . ."Someday you're going to tell me your mother wore shoes!" *Cowboy* didn't like it when I said that. The next morning he couldn't remember the quarrels of the night before. We'd go to the ocean. He'd dive through the waves and dive through the waves. To get rid of his head, as he put it. He'd come up snorting. Like a porpoise with a profile. . .*Pray for me, Hecky!*

HECKY: I pray for you all the time.

FANNY: What do you call the prayers when you're doing something else, when you're not on your knees? Ejaculations toward God?. . .Call me your lovey.

HECKY: My lovey.

FANNY: You and he. . .(*She touches the frame of the photograph*). . .are going to be proud of me tonight! (*Without warning, she goes to the basin and retches. Hecky holds her head*) Nothing came up. (*She staggers to the dressing table and wipes her mouth with a paper tissue*) I might as well be drunk as the way I am. (*The Callboy knocks*)

CALLBOY: Places, please. *Places!*

(*Hecky puts a shawl around Fanny's shoulders. Fanny starts for the stage*)

FANNY: Now to maneuver that narrow alley. . .(*She turns back to give Hecky a quick pat on the behind*) Pray for me.

(*She goes out. Hecky begins to straighten up the dressing table as the curtain starts to descend*)

Curtain

Norman Holland

THE SMALL, PRIVATE WORLD OF MICHAEL MARSTON

Norman Holland

With *The Small, Private World of Michael Marston,* published here for the first time, Norman Holland celebrates his "diamond jubilee" as a playwright for it is his sixtieth play to appear in print.

A prominent British dramatist, he has published at least forty individual works and two collections of short plays, one with a foreword by Sir Ralph Richardson. His plays have been translated into a dozen languages, three have been filmed, eleven broadcast on radio, and eight televised, including an American network presentation of *Chair for a Lady* as adapted by Paul Slocumb and starring Angela Lansbury.

In February, 1968, the author's full-length drama, *Years of the Locust* (dealing with Oscar Wilde's two-year imprisonment in Reading Gaol), was given its world premiere by the Trinity Square Repertory Company in Providence, Rhode Island. The occasion was hailed in the press with such encomiums as "profoundly moving, intensely absorbing and quite unforgettable" (*Boston Herald Traveler*) and "a play of considerable sensitivity and dramatic value. . .the sort of thing a regional theatre should do more frequently. Cheers!" (*The Providence Journal*).

In reply to a request for biographical data, the author, a recipient of eight major playwriting awards, reflected: "I was born in 1910, son and grandson of high-ranking police officers. I have been a press officer, advertising copywriter, scriptwriter and now am employed in the British Government Service, being principally engaged in the promotion of British participation in overseas trade fairs.

"I served in World War II for six years, two months and ten days without distinction. Ended by lecturing in Drama at an Army school. Got no decoration for this!

"I've written a book on playwriting and lectured for seven years on the subject at London's City Literary Institute. Also have acted with amateur and professional repertory companies and, in off-moments, have directed some productions. That seems to cover my past, except perhaps something quite unaligned and not previously disclosed: I had an early ambition to be a heavyweight boxing champion and won thirty-eight fights as an amateur—twenty-six inside the distance."

Mr. Holland is no stranger to *The Best Short Plays* annuals: three of his works have appeared in previous editions including *Farewell Appearance,* in collaboration with this editor.

His newest work is *The Militants!* described by the author as "a manifesto in three acts, set against the background of the 1908 by-election in North Manchester when Winston Churchill, then President of the Board of Trade, was defeated as a direct result of the suffragette intervention."

Norman Holland lives in Chiswick, a suburb of London, with his wife and son whom he describes as being "beautifully balanced as fans and family."

Characters

MICHAEL MARSTON

PRISON OFFICER

SARAH

JOE

FELICE

STEPHEN

A WOMAN

and

OURSELVES: THE PRISON VISITOR

Place:

The small, private world of Michael Marston.

Time:

The troubled present.

Since we are to inhabit, however briefly, the small, private world of Michael Marston, it is well that we should explore it. This world of his is an unhappy marriage of his physical surroundings and fantasies of his own creation.

He is in prison, so the dominating feature is the prison gate which is sited centrally: forbidding, apparently of metal construction and designed, it seems, to be kept locked, bolted and barred forever. The gate and the four other small sets are all sited in front of a curtained background which, since it is never lit directly, provides a shadowy surrounding to the little world.

To the right of the prison gate is a couch, with a standard lamp behind it, and behind that a screen—all to indicate a setting suggestive of a corner of a room in a cozy flat. Further downstage from this is a nondescript door with a single step and a short rail running beside the step. This is the kind of door which serves as a barrier to a house which is not a home. To the left of the prison gate, there is an executive's desk with blotter, papers, telephone, and intercom on it and with an executive's chair behind it. A visitor's chair is to the right of the desk. Further left, beyond the desk, is a brightly painted door with a knocker and letterbox and with well-tended dwarf shrubs on either side of it. These shrubs are separated by a single step—one more symmetrical than that below the nondescript door. This, in contrast to the other door, is the welcoming entrance to a house which is certainly a home. Beside the door, to the left of it, is a garden seat.

At rise, the little world is in darkness. In the dark, Tchaikovsky's "Hamlet Overture" is heard. In a few moments, when the music has plaintively reminded us of life's impermanence, its sadness and insecurity, light breaks on the prison gate and, momentarily, the music swells in volume. Michael Marston is beating on the prison gate with his fists. The music stops and we hear Michael shouting.

MICHAEL: Let me out! Let me out! I've had enough! For God's sake, let me out! (*He beats desperately on the gate and collapses at the foot of it. Then, he laboriously hauls himself to his feet and drags himself over to a stool which is placed just in front of the gate and well within the circle of light. Spent by his outburst, he sinks onto the stool and sits hunched and staring vacantly before him. There is the reverberating clang of a heavy metal door closing. A second later, the uniformed Prison Officer comes into the lighted area. He looks outward, into the auditorium, where we are*)

PRISON OFFICER: That was him. Michael Marston. The man you've come to visit. Better give him a minute or two to settle down. He's just where you left him, and he'll be glad to see you. Nobody else visits him any more. At first, he had lots of visitors; but, one by one, they fell away. You can't expect people to keep it up, month after month, year after year. Besides, it isn't exactly a social asset to have a friend or relative in prison—especially one serving a sentence for robbery with violence. And then, this place. . .Doesn't it give you the bends? Why, I've known people take two months to get over the depression brought on by spending two hours in here. (*Nodding toward Michael*) What about men like him—in here for years? How do you think it affects them? I can tell you. They all crack sooner or later. He's cracked now: experiencing withdrawal symptoms. Oh, yes, that's the prison service today. We study the prisoners as cases and try to diagnose their states of mind. 5270 Marston has reached a stage where he can't bear any longer the monotony and the loneliness. . .the future stretching away, down a long corridor of empty days. He lives a life of his own. I know. I've heard him describing things I can't see and talking to people who aren't there. (*He contemplates Michael*) Seems quiet enough now. Look at him. Where is he now, do you think? (*He raises his voice and calls*) Marston! (*Michael remains impassive*) You see. Dead to the world. (*He moves closer to Michael, shouts*) MARSTON! (*Startled, Michael leaps to his feet and stands facing the Prison Officer. He is tense, wary, frightened*)

MICHAEL: What is it? What do you want?

PRISON OFFICER: You have a visitor. (*Indicating, to us*) In here, please. (*Quietly, as we pass him*) I'll be back presently.

(*The Prison Officer goes out through the exit behind the prison gate. Michael turns to us and an expression of joy gradually replaces one of incredulity*)

MICHAEL: You're here! Here at last. It's been so long. Yes, I know. I know. You've been ill. Are you better? You certainly look well enough now. Here, sit down. No, I insist. I can get another stool if I want it. I've been sitting all day. (*As he speaks, he is shepherding us to the stool. When we are seated, he stands off from us, surveying us, smiling almost affectionately. Then, suddenly, he springs toward us in a fury*) What did he say? What did he say to you? Oh, I can guess! He watches me all the time. Day and night. Watches me and takes notes. As if I were an animal undergoing some sort of test. That's almost the worst of this place—the absence of privacy. You're utterly lonely, but never alone. Always somebody peering at you—every moment of the day's twenty-four mortal hours. Or so it seems, and what "seems" is real in here. (*He moves in front of the prison *gate*) Did you notice the prison gate as you came in? You did? But, then, you could hardly miss it, could you? Isn't it impressive. . .implacable? The bolts, the bars, the locks, those great studs and the massive hinges which move it reluctantly. . . slowly as doom when, very occasionally, it opens. Opens only to shut again. Did you hear it close behind you? You didn't notice? Oh, I did. I heard it all those years ago when they shut me in. A reverberating clang, awakening echoes of doomsday. I've heard it every day since then. I hear it now. (*His listening attitude and haunted expression persuade us that we, too, hear a reverberating metallic clang and continuing echoes, diminishing gradually to silence. When the ghost of the sound has died away, he shrugs off its effects and assumes a resolute air*) But you're not to pity me. I don't have to stay in this hole—not all the time. I have my refuges. In here. In here! (*He strikes his forehead with his clenched fist*) It's all inside. All in the mind. Look, I'll show you! (*He moves up to the brightly painted door, as it becomes spotlit and the light goes down on the prison gate. He mimes putting his finger on a doorbell. Instantly, there is a strident ringing, and he stands waiting*) I always call on my wife first. (*Pause*) I suppose I should refer to Sarah as my *ex-wife*. Not that it matters here and now. . .(*The door opens and on the threshold stands Sarah, a youngish woman, vaguely pretty and with the bearing and dress of a harassed housewife. She regards Michael doubtfully for a moment, then rushes into his arms. They kiss hungrily and, afterward, remain happily embraced*)

SARAH: Michael! It's so good to see you.

MICHAEL: So good to be home, Sarah.

SARAH: You've come to stay? To stay for good?

MICHAEL: (*Releasing her and moving away*) Not this time. They've let me out for an hour or so on parole, as a sort of preparation for release.

SARAH: "On parole". . .that means they trust you. "Preparation for release". . .that means you'll be coming out soon.

MICHAEL: Quite soon.

SARAH: How marvelous! I can hardly believe it. What shall we do when. . .when you come home forever and always?

MICHAEL: Here, sit down. (*He goes to the seat and pulls it forward. She sits, and he eases himself beside her*) First of all. . .

SARAH: Yes?

MICHAEL: First of all, we'll spend a day or two at home, while I get to know Janet again. Just so she can get used to calling me "Daddy."

SARAH: Oh, I'm sure that's best—a day or two at home. And then?

MICHAEL: We'll go to the coast for a long holiday. All three of us. We'll stay a month. . .six weeks. . .as long as we like.

SARAH: But we won't be able to afford it.

MICHAEL: You're forgetting! There's the *special fund.*

SARAH: Of course! The special fund! It will be the most fabulous holiday. We can start looking forward to it now. (*She rises and hauls Michael to his feet*) Janet's asleep. Come in and see her.

MICHAEL: No. Not this time. If she woke up and saw me. . .You *do* understand, Sarah?

SARAH: I understand, darling.

MICHAEL: I'll be a free man when next I see her. Besides. . .

SARAH: Yes?

MICHAEL: I ought to be going. I ought to be getting back.

SARAH: So soon? You've only just arrived.

MICHAEL: I mustn't be late. Not at this stage of the game.

SARAH: It won't be long, will it?

MICHAEL: (*Taking her in his arms*) Not long. (*He kisses her and then moves away*) And then I shall be home.

SARAH: Forever and always.

MICHAEL: Forever and always. Goodbye, Sarah.

SARAH: Goodbye, darling. Be careful. Keep well. (*Near to tears, she hurries into the house and closes the door. Michael watches her for a moment, then restores the garden seat to its former position. As the lights fade, he strolls into the central area*)

MICHAEL: Corny, wasn't it? Sentimental to the point of

nausea! I hope you weren't embarrassed by the wish-fulfillment, the evasions, the distortions, and the contradictions of reality. Did you notice—I ignored the existence of her present husband . . .the possibility that she has other children. . .the probability that she is happily married? And I couldn't go into the house to see Janet because I couldn't imagine what she looked like. . . not after all these years. You must have noticed the pathetic reference to the *special fund*. It doesn't exist. Merely a figment of the imagination. . .(*Suddenly, shouting*) None of that. . . (*Pointing to the brightly painted door*). . .none of that has a basis in fact! (*Deeply troubled, he turns his back on us momentarily; then, after a moment, he turns to observe us again. Quietly*) More's the pity. . .(*He reflects sadly, then recovers sufficiently to smile at us*) But I mustn't depress you or you won't come to see me again. (*Starting toward the desk*) Let's try . . .once more. Over here.

(*The light in the central area, surrounding the stool, fades and comes up above the desk. JOE, an easy-going tycoon, is seated at the desk. As Michael approaches, he looks up, peers at him in disbelief, then, recognizing him, springs to his feet and comes around the desk in an ecstasy of greeting*)

JOE: Michael! Mike! (*Vigorously shaking Michael's hand*) This *is* a pleasant surprise! How are you?

MICHAEL: Fine, Joe. Fine. (*A tiny pause*) All things considered.

JOE: You've had it tough, boy. Very tough indeed. But we're going to make it up to you. Here. Sit down. (*He conducts Michael to the visitor's chair, then crosses to his own side of the desk. He sits, mimes the opening of a drawer, the lifting out of a box of cigars and the raising of the lid. This done, he proffers the invisible box to Michael*) Have a cigar. (*Michael goes through the motions of making a selection*)

MICHAEL: Thank you.

JOE: Let me give you a light. (*He mimes the striking of a match and holds the light until Michael apparently has availed himself of it. Joe shakes out the unseen match, tosses it into the *ashtray on the desk and sits back in his imposing chair. Michael goes through the motions of withdrawing the cigar from his lips and exhaling luxuriously*) Okay, Mike?

MICHAEL: Superb. Just superb. But then, you always had taste.

JOE: That's a Perfecto from the box I keep for myself.

MICHAEL: (*Looking about him*) Snug layout you've got here, Joe.

JOE: It'll do. Thanks to you.

MICHAEL: (*Incredulously*) *Me?*

JOE: If you'd opened your mouth, before *or* after your trial, I'd have been inside there, along with you. But you kept me out of it, and I'm very grateful.

MICHAEL: No need to be. There was no point in involving you.

JOE: That's not the way I see it. You took the rap. I got clear away, and it meant that I was able to work for *both of us!*

MICHAEL: Both of us?

JOE: That's what I said. (*He stoops again to a lower drawer in his desk, mimes the unlocking of it and lifts an invisible wad of money onto his desk before pushing it across to Michael*) There you are! *Your* share of the original haul.

MICHAEL: (*Skeptically*) Mine? This lot?

JOE: All yours. It's not in the original notes so you needn't be afraid of spending it. (*Michael is still staring at it, transfixed*) Well, go on. Aren't you going to count it?

MICHAEL: I. . .I don't have to, Joe. I know it's right if you say so.

JOE: Why, thanks, Mike. Thanks. (*A slight pause*) Well, put it away. Put it away! We don't want it lying about if somebody should come in. (*Michael mimes the stowing away of a considerable stack of currency notes. He apparently has filled all his pockets by the time he has finished*) And that isn't all you've got coming to you!

MICHAEL: No?

JOE: Not by a long chalk. (*He unlocks another drawer—this time on the other side of the desk—and tosses several im-*

perceptible stacks of something onto the desk) There! Do you know what they are?

MICHAEL: (*After a quick glance*) They look like share certificates.

JOE: Right first time. *And*. . .they're all yours.

MICHAEL: Mine?

JOE: You heard me! They represent your share of the profits *I* invested for you each half year. We've been lucky, Mike. I'd say you were quite comfortably off.

MICHAEL: You've done all this for me?

JOE: (*With a gesture of dismissal*) Nothing. Nothing as to what you did for me. (*Raising a hand as Michael is about to speak*) Now, don't thank me! The debt is all mine. I'll just put this lot in an envelope for you. (*He mimes the taking of a big envelope from another drawer, gathers up the unseen share certificates, thrusts them into the invisible envelope and licks the imaginary flap*) There you are.

MICHAEL: (*Taking the envelope*) I've got to say it! Thanks, Joe. Thanks for everything. I didn't think such loyalty existed.

JOE: Forget it. Just one thing! We'd better not be seen together for a bit, or the police might connect us. (*He rises and holds out his hand*) Be seeing you though, boy.

MICHAEL: (*Rising, shaking hands*) Yes, Joe. Be seeing you.

(*He turns away from the desk as the lights fade on Joe and come up again on the central area. When he has moved back into the light, Michael faces us and displays his empty hands*)

MICHAEL: Look! No money, no shares, nothing! All a fabrication! But there is some foundation for this one. Yes, this one! Joe was in on the job. . .same one that landed me in here. He got clean away with most of the take. I've heard that he's prospered and turned his back on his old life. But he wouldn't forget an old friend. Not Joe. He'll see I'm all right when I get out. So, perhaps, I *have* got a special fund, after all. Where next—? (*A second*) Well, if you were embarrassed by my visit to Sarah, I'm covered with confusion about the approaching encounter. (*Another second*) I've been doing my best to show myself as a faithful husband and a doting father. A man can be *both* and still be. . .interested in Felice. . . .What is she like?. . . Attractive, certainly. Sympathetic, yes. She makes you feel good . . .important. . .necessary. . .fulfilled! Here, see for yourself!

(*He moves toward the couch, as the lights brighten, and the central area dims out. Felice, an attractive young woman who wears a dress in close harmony with her personality, is seated on the couch. She peers beyond the lighted area and calls, invitingly, in a seductive voice*)

FELICE: I hear you. I hear you out there. Come along in, lover boy. (*Michael appears in the lighted area*) There you are. (*Patting the couch*) Come and sit here. . .beside me. (*Michael does so*) Now, I can really look at you. (*She takes his face between her hands and inspects him closer*) Yes, you do look grim. What's wrong with you, darling? What is it? (*Without waiting for a reply, she leans forward and kisses him*) That better?

MICHAEL: A whole world better. (*He kisses her more passionately than she had kissed him, but she responds only tentatively. Freeing herself, she taps his lips lightly with an admonitory finger*)

FELICE: That will be all for now, Bob!

MICHAEL: (*Springing up*) *Bob?!* My name's not Bob!

FELICE: I know. But Bob suits you best. I *always* think of you as Bob. Now, come on, love, I want to hear where you've been. . .what you've been up to. . .

MICHAEL: (*Sitting again*) That's soon told.

FELICE: Is it now—?

MICHAEL: I've been nowhere in particular and I've done nothing worth discussing.

FELICE: Aren't you in a mood, though—? Not that I mind, really. I'm sick to death of hearing men blabber about how important they are just about everywhere on God's crust. (*A pause: she contemplates him*) Something's really troubling you, isn't it? What is it, love—?

MICHAEL: Just about everything, I suppose. But to take

just two items: I see you so rarely, and when I do, it's for such a brief while.

FELICE: (*Soothingly*) Then why not make the most of it while you're here? God knows, we'll all be converted to dust soon enough, once they push that bloody button. . .(*Shuddering slightly*) Sends cold shivers up m'spine. (*Then, changing her tone*) Well, never mind all this apprehension. This is *your* night, love. (*She kisses him lightly. Michael responds by putting his arm around her and drawing her closer*) You brood too much. Take things easy for a while. Let others do the worrying for a change. You owe it to yourself to have a bit of fun and relaxation.

MICHAEL: But I don't brood when I'm here with you. When I leave you, I'm soothed. . .stimulated. . .refreshed. . .and renewed.

FELICE: Get on with you! You make me sound like a welfare officer or a head-shrinker.

MICHAEL: Sorry if it came through that way. I simply wanted to say—you're just about the most marvelous person I know.

FELICE: More, please. Absolutely more! That's the sort of stuff benefits my ego. (*She sighs contentedly*) Nice to have you all to myself. What time do you have to leave in the morning—?

MICHAEL: I can't stay, Felice. Not this time.

FELICE: Can't stay—? (*Drawing away from him*) Can't stay, Bob—?

MICHAEL: No, I have to be back. I promised. I should be in trouble if I was late. You know how it is.

FELICE: I wish I had known. I passed up a date with Humphrey and you're off again almost as soon as you get here.

MICHAEL: I am sorry, darling. You know how much I want to stay. Next time. . .

FELICE: If there is a next time. . .

MICHAEL: Don't say that. It's worse for me. Please try to understand.

FELICE: I do. I do understand. I know how bravely you've borne all this—this bad luck. It's just that I miss you very much and want to keep you near me.

MICHAEL: That's exactly where I want to be—near you. And it won't be long now. I'll be back.

FELICE: Hurry, then. Hurry. (*He takes her in his arms and kisses her. A clock nearby strikes the hour. Startled, Michael releases her*)

MICHAEL: I must go. Goodbye, darling. See you. . .soon! (*He moves away as Felice watches his departure. The lights fade and come up in the central area. Michael stands looking back toward the couch for a moment, as Felice's voice echoes out of the darkness*)

FELICE: Yes. . .soon, Bob. Do come back soon. . .

(*Michael turns to face us again*)

MICHAEL: That wasn't fair to Felice. There's more to her than you saw. A great deal more! She's kinder, wittier, more sophisticated, more understanding, than she appeared then. It's my fault that you didn't see her as she really is. I was inhibited because I knew you were watching. But one thing *was* very clear, wasn't it? She's desperately fond of me, that girl! You did notice that, didn't you?. . .Well, that's the lot. The only three people I visit. There were more, but they've dwindled away, one by one. These are all I have left besides you and it's been such a long time since you came to see me. Don't, please, let it be as long again, or I shall be lost! Promise me that you'll be here next week. . .and the week after. . .and the week after that. . .Promise me! Promise me!

(*Michael slowly turns away from us. The Prison Officer enters from beside the prison gate and pauses, as if listening outside the cell door. Then, he mimes the unlocking of the door and his gesture indicates that we are to leave. When it appears that we have left the cell, he closes and re-locks the door. Michael notices that we have gone. He crosses to the stool and sits, almost numbly*)

PRISON OFFICER: You see, it was just as I told you. But don't let it get you down. Remember that he has a lot to bear. Come along. . .(*He leads the way and goes out beyond the prison gate. Michael sits, motionlessly. The music is heard again, quietly at first, then builds to full volume and fades as the Prison*

Officer returns) Your time is measured in terms of sharing happiness, making love, hearing music, watching sunsets, smelling roses, spending money, eating hearty, drinking deep, sleeping dreamless. . .You are living and time fleets by on a tide of happening, a swell of incident. You live in your varied world with senses responsive to each flicker of chance and change. In prison, it is otherwise—far otherwise— Here, there's only monotony, grayness, shadow, regret, ache of loneliness, the numbness, the despair. . .Time goes slowly by. . .then, seems to stop altogether. But at last, the sentence comes to an end and, incredibly, comes that order of release. . .(*He mimes the opening of the cell door, steps in and calls*) 5270 Marston! (*Michael gives no indication of having heard*) *Marston! Wake up, man!*

MICHAEL: (*Springing to his feet*) What is it? What have I done now—?

PRISON OFFICER: Good news! Your release has come through!

MICHAEL: (*Dazedly*) Release—?

PRISON OFFICER: A week earlier than expected.

MICHAEL: A week early—?

PRISON OFFICER: Your time's up, old chap. So you'd better get cracking!

MICHAEL: (*Incredulously*) Today? I'm to be released today. . .? (*He sinks down on to the stool*)

PRISON OFFICER: Bit overwhelming at first, but you'll get used to it. Of course, there are certain formalities still. . .

MICHAEL: . . .Certain formalities. Of course. Where would we be without them? (*He rises*) Shall we. . .shall we get them over?

PRISON OFFICER: The sooner the better. (*He picks up the stool and leads Michael out of the cell. They disappear behind the prison gate. Music. As it fades, the echoing clang of the prison gate is heard. Michael reappears in the central lighted area*)

MICHAEL: What a different sound when it closes behind you. . .from the outside! Now, I'm—doubtful. . .apprehensive. How much of all that was real? True? Too often, reality contradicts illusions. . . .Still, one must chance the gamble. . .(*The lights come up on the brightly painted door and as Michael moves toward it, the central area darkens. After a second of hesitation, he presses the doorbell. He listens eagerly, at the door; then turns, smiling confidently*) Someone's rushing down the stairs! It's very much as I thought it would be. . .(*The door opens and Sarah appears. She is better groomed, more smartly dressed than when we last saw her. There is an awkward moment of silence, as they confront one another*)

MICHAEL: (*Breaking the strained silence*) Sarah! Darling!

SARAH: (*Tensely*) Leave! Leave, before he catches sight of you!

MICHAEL: It's Michael! Don't you recognize me—?

SARAH: I recognize you, all too well! (*Stephen appears in the doorway. He is a large man with an air of deserved prosperity. He takes in Michael, then turns to Sarah for an explanation*)

SARAH: It's him. Michael.

STEPHEN: Oh, is it, now—? (*His disapproving glance ranges Michael from head to foot*) What do you want? What are you doing here?

MICHAEL: I've come to see Sarah. And Janet. Just to see them. That's all.

STEPHEN: Damned impertinence! After all the trouble you've brought them—?

MICHAEL: I wrote to Sarah—many times—begging her forgiveness. . .

STEPHEN: Your letters went unread, I assure you!

SARAH: The miserable situation you'd left us in. . .

MICHAEL: It was only to provide for both of you that I. . .

STEPHEN: Don't give me that, now! Or try to justify yourself! It'd be a waste of breath. All you've ever been concerned with is "Number One". . .

MICHAEL: No!

STEPHEN: You were out for easy money, to pursue your own pleasures. And you made a mess of it, as you've always done with everything you've ever touched!. . .Well, I'm glad I've laid eyes on you at last. I've always been curious to know what a born-loser looked like. . .

MICHAEL: You're not hurting me. No. You couldn't. Because you really don't know me. (*A second*) Perhaps, you're afraid of me. . .

STEPHEN: I'll show you whether or not I'm afraid of you! (*Michael quickly lifts a restraining hand as Stephen makes a movement toward him*)

MICHAEL: I wouldn't if I were you. . .

SARAH: (*Grasping his arm*) Stephen! They're all like uncaged animals. . .

MICHAEL: (*To Stephen*) If you'd just leave us alone for a few minutes. . .

STEPHEN: My wife doesn't wish to be alone with you!

SARAH: Quite right! (*Facing Michael*) It makes me violently ill even to look at you! Your presence only stirs up a parcel of dreadful memories. . . .We're divorced. And that's that! So, push on and don't ever bother us again!

MICHAEL: If I could see Janet. . .for a second or two. . .

STEPHEN: You'd better be on your way!

SARAH: We told her you were dead!

MICHAEL: (*Incredulously*) Dead. . .?

SARAH: You heard me!

STEPHEN: *I* am the only father she knows.

MICHAEL: (*A pause*) I was supposed to've squared accounts. . .by serving my sentence. It seems I haven't. . .

STEPHEN: Bloody right, you haven't! If you lived to be a hundred-and-two, you couldn't possibly make it up to Sarah and Janet for what they suffered. Now, once and for all, you'd better take my kind advice and start down that road. . .

SARAH: It'll lead you directly to the "underground". . .

MICHAEL: (*Quietly*) Yes. . .

(*Michael slowly moves out of sight. Stephen puts his arm protectively about Sarah and they disappear into the house. The lights fade in that area and come up again in the central area, as Michael approaches*)

MICHAEL: . . .Self-deception, wasn't it, on my part—? The way she stared at me when she opened that door. . .the bitterness. . .the eyes raging with combined hatred and fear. . . How I wish I'd seen Janet. . .just a glimpse of her. . .even for a moment. Oh, well!. . .(*Pause*) I could go along and visit Felice. . .she always managed to "'soothe and refresh". . .but perhaps I ought to collect a bit of what's due me first. . .

(*The lights fade as Michael approaches the desk area, now brightened. Joe is at the desk, occupied with a flood of papers and smoking his customary cigar. Suddenly, he glances up, in surprise and irritation, at Michael, standing beside the desk*)

JOE: Yes, yes. What is it? You have an appointment?

MICHAEL: I didn't think I needed one, Joe. It's *Mike*. . .

JOE: Mike? Mike? Mike who—?

MICHAEL: Marston. I've just been—released. . .

JOE: (*A second*) Oh! Oh, that's it. Well, what do you want?

MICHAEL: I just thought I'd pop 'round and see you, Joe.

JOE: (*Curtly*) I've nothing for you, so you'd better head for the lift at the end of the corridor. . .

MICHAEL: (*Sincerely*) Joe, I've had a bad time. Very bad.

JOE: I've heard that rot before! Too many like you floating in here, attempting to put the bite on. But I've laid down the law. . .*my own!*

MICHAEL: I've got nothing, Joe, except perhaps a few guineas. And nobody, really. . .nowhere to stay. . .I could do with a bit of help.

JOE: Why should I help you? Come on, you tell me.

MICHAEL: You ask *why—?* Joe, we were in the thing together. I had the bad luck to get caught. . .

JOE: Your misfortune.

MICHAEL: Yet, I—I kept my mouth shut, didn't I? You walked off with the spoils while I. . .

JOE: Now, be careful. . .

MICHAEL: You've done well for yourself. I'm flat broke, Joe.

JOE: That could be construed as, shall we say, blackmail? And that, my lad, could fetch you back to where you've just emerged. . .

MICHAEL: No, no, Joe, please! I'm not threatening you.

JOE: (*Rising: firmly*) Now, let's get this straight. . .(*He comes forward*) Not being the lying sort, I'm not denying that I once had a "passing" acquaintance with you. I knew a lot of odd characters during a certain—and now, forgotten—period of my life. But things are vastly different today. I'm respected in all quarters. . .family, business, community. . .

MICHAEL: I didn't come here with the intention of stirring up trouble for you, Joe. But if you could possibly spare me a little. . .to give me a start again. . .

JOE: (*Tapping the desk*) Notice this desk? Rectangular, eh? Four straight edges, no curves, no devious corners. Well, this rectangular piece of carved mahogany represents something the likes of you wouldn't understand. Lawful boundaries. . .and solidity. . .(*A pause*) Get the picture—?

MICHAEL: (*Quietly*) Yes. . .I get the picture. Unfortunately. . .

(*Michael turns and quietly leaves. Joe gazes after him; then, assured that he has left the premises, returns to his desk and resumes his paper work. The lights fade. A moment later, they come up on Michael, now standing in the central area*)

MICHAEL: I whined. . .crawled to him! I let him walk over me!. . .And he owed me something! Yes! I could easily have betrayed him. . .then, there'd have been no chance afterward for that *sterling citizen. . .respected in all quarters!* No! (*A second*) Well, let him keep the lot! I know where I'm going now—perhaps I should have gone there first of all. . .

(*The lights fade and come up on Felice, who is half-sitting, half-lying, in a somewhat ungainly position, on her couch. She appears older and wears unbecoming spectacles. Her hair is tousled, her dress is bedraggled and about her shoulders is a stole of sorts. She rouses herself as Michael approaches the couch*)

FELICE: (*Popping up*) Here, what are you doing? You've no business in here! Invading a lady's private flat. . .

MICHAEL: Felice! Don't you remember—? *Michael!*

FELICE: Michael—? (*She continues to stare at him, rather curiously and without recognition*)

MICHAEL: You've got to remember! We meant such a good deal to each other. . .

FELICE: (*After a moment; reflectively*) I meant a good deal. . .to many. . .yes. . .*many!* Often, I recall faces. . .bodies . . .embraces. . .words that would charm the wings off a butterfly. . .(*She laughs*) Precious nonsense! (*She gazes doubtfully at Michael*) But I don't remember. . .I can't recall a face as tired and worn. . .

MICHAEL: I was younger then. So were you, Felice. Time does strange things to us. . .

FELICE: (*Moving slightly away*) In many ways. . .

MICHAEL: You used to call me Bob.

FELICE: (*Turning back to him*) I called every man I'd touched *Bob.*

MICHAEL: I like to believe that I. . .

FELICE: . . .He was the only man ever meant anything to me. I didn't mean much to him, though. Went off and married above him. After that, it was easy for me to be loving and tender as long as I could call the man who shared my bed. . .Bob. . .

MICHAEL: Then, I never meant anything to you? As an individual—?

FELICE: No more, no less than any of the others.

MICHAEL: At least, then, you *do* remember me—?

FELICE: You're all lumped together in memory. One big, heaping lump. . .

MICHAEL: Try, Felice. . .try to disassociate me from the others. . .

FELICE: No, no damnable use anymore! It was different when I had m'looks. Now, I stare steadily into my mirror, for minutes at a time, when I'm feeling particularly brave. It's a chastening experience.

MICHAEL: I've had a rather—chastening experience, too. . .

FELICE: My whole life changed patterns that. . .that day. . .

MICHAEL: When, Felice? What day?

FELICE: That day I saw him stepping into the Grosvenor, her linked tightly to his arm. . .

MICHAEL: But—that was the past.

FELICE: I said to m'self then: Bob belongs to her—lock, stock, and barrel—for now and always—and no other "Bob" in this ruddy world would ever touch me again! I've kept m'word!

MICHAEL: Felice! This is *today*. . .the *present*. . .

FELICE: Likely good it does me!

MICHAEL: You're not the only one trying to overcome the past.

FELICE: I've given up *trying!* A waste of energy.

MICHAEL: Even for *us*. . .there's *still* the future. . .

FELICE: There's a laugh for you: the *future!*

MICHAEL: The Felice I recalled. . .in my loneliest moments. . .

FELICE: She's nothing more than an empty shell now. . .

MICHAEL: Yes, you *have* changed!

FELICE: Partially by fear and partially by drink, if you want to know the truth.

MICHAEL: (*Gazing at her*) What are you afraid of—?

FELICE: The bloody bomb, that's what! Don't you dream of it, alone in your bed. . .wake up screaming in the pitch-blackness. . .

MICHAEL: No, no, I don't dream of it. . .

FELICE: Sets you to drink, believe me! It'd be different maybe if life gave you a better turn. But when you're completely alone. . .and nothing and no one's really a part of you. . .

MICHAEL: I can sympathize with you there.

FELICE: (*Turning on him*) Bah! What d'you know and what d'you care? All too soon, someday, somebody—there or there. . .(*She points east, then west*). . .is going to press the button! And we'll all be one with the lava, the dust, clouds of ashes. . .

MICHAEL: It won't happen, Felice. It can't.

FELICE: Can't it? We'll be gone—poof! Not that I care about the others. It's *me* I'm concerned about! Being blown to bits without contributing anything special to the world. . .

MICHAEL: There are treaties, agreements, safeguards. . .

FELICE: (*As before*). . .and going out *alone,* that's the frightening part! (*She shudders and tightens the stole about her*) Have you got a drop of the hard stuff on you? A flask, maybe—?

MICHAEL: No, I don't drink very much any more.

FELICE: If you're a thinking man, you'll soon start up again. (*A sudden thought*) There's a wine-and-spirit shop, just across the road.

MICHAEL: I—have very little money on me.

FELICE: (*Flaring up again*) What kind of a man are you, coming here, without even enough to treat a lady to a bit of drink—?!

MICHAEL: I'm sorry. Perhaps, I shouldn't have come, after all. (*He makes a move to leave*)

FELICE: Yes, you do that! Take yourself off! To the *Rowton House* for "down-and-outs"!

(*Michael is backing away, out of the lighted area, as she continues, shouting after him, more uncontrolled*)

FELICE: . . .and you can give all those poor bastards a personal message from me! There's no more bloody use in *trying* . . .for soon there'll be no more life on earth! *No life on earth whatsoever. . .*!

(*Sudden darkness and silence. A moment later, the lights come up in the central area, illumining Michael, still and distressed*)

MICHAEL: I'm afraid myself now—mortally afraid. I wish I'd never seen her! If she's right, then sooner or later, this world will be a cratered cinder whirling endlessly through space. . . and there's little use in *trying* any more. . .(*A moment*) Ah, she was crazy! Poor Felice. Madness through fear and drink. . .even admitted it, didn't she—? (*Then*) Strange, to her I was neither a *name* or *number*. . .

(*As he slowly moves away from the central area, the lights fade and come up at the far right. A Woman, dressed in drab garments, stands firmly in front of the door, a suitcase beside her on the ground. Michael approaches, about to enter the house. The Woman bars his way*)

MICHAEL: (*Attempting to pass her*) Excuse me.

WOMAN: (*Sternly*) Who says you've any right to go prancing in there—?

MICHAEL: I live here. Engaged a room. Yesterday. . .

WOMAN: Not from me, you didn't!

MICHAEL: The young lady settled everything. Ask her. Mr. Marston.

WOMAN: Oh, so it's *Mister* Marston, is it? How long is it since you had a *number,* Mr. Marston—? (*Michael remains silent*) I'm not surprised at your keeping your mouth shut! Hardly something to boast about, is it?

MICHAEL: All right! I didn't mention it to her! I didn't see the necessity. It's the past. . .over and done with!

WOMAN: The past and present go hand in hand!

MICHAEL: The young lady, your household assistant, she accepted me for what I *am*. . .not what I *was*. . .

WOMAN: Easy enough to beguile that bit of puff-pastry! But I happen to be made of sterner stuff and I have my own method of digging into things. . .

MICHAEL: If I told you, I've already paid—heavily—for. . .

WOMAN: (*Resolutely*) I'm the proprietress of a clean-and-respectable establishment; not one of your prison social workers! And my first and foremost obligation is to my lodgers. With the likes of you in the house, hardly one of us would get a decent night's rest!. . .There's your bag! You'll find all your worthless bits and pieces there. I packed 'em myself!

MICHAEL: (*A moment*) Couldn't you just let me stay, until—?

WOMAN: Go on, now! Let me see the back of you! Before I summon the police. . .

(*She turns and goes swiftly into the house, slamming the door behind her. Michael stands looking after her for a second*)

MICHAEL: People! Humanity!! The world!!! Frightened,

self-indulgent, self-advancing, self-righteous. . .self-destructive! How I wish I could hide away somewhere, not gaze upon another human being till the day I die! But where. . .*where* can one hide—? (*He picks up his suitcase*) We're *all* shut in. . .behind or beyond those walls. . .and none of us knows who's got the proper key. . .or, whether there ever will be a true order of release. . .(*He starts to leave as the lights gradually fade. The lights come up slowly from dim to full on the prison gate which appears as formidable, intractable and dominating as ever. Michael wearily approaches and surveys it. Then, thrusting his suitcase aside as a useless burden, he rushes at the gate and strikes it with his fists, shouting*) Let me in! Let me in!! (*He bruises his hands on the gate's unyielding surface as he collapses to his knees, still beating at the massive, barred and studded barrier*) For God's sake, let me in! I've had enough out here! *Let me back in. . .!*

Curtain

Patrick O'Connor

THE WOODEN BOX

Patrick O'Connor

According to Patrick O'Connor, he was "the last of a large Irish family and the first to be born in Scotland, where the clan had emigrated because of religious riots and unemployment. Therefore, I claim to be an Irishman forced to carry a British passport."

Mr. O'Connor served in the Merchant Navy during the Second World War and was on an ammunition ship "which blew itself to pieces off Halifax, Nova Scotia." He was brought ashore "clad in a sweatrag and a pack of cards," ringing down the curtain on his active service.

After the war, he became an actor and toured Ireland before moving on to London where he organized an experimental theatre group with Frank Marcus who, later, was to gain international fame with his "dark comedy," *The Killing of Sister George*. During this period, Mr. O'Connor performed the leading role in Mr. Marcus' first play, *Minuet for Stuffed Birds* at London's smallest theatre, The Torch, and also, at intervals, managed to squeeze in some television work and a part as a comic Telegraph Boy in the film *Treasure Hunt*.

"My performance in that epic inspired two fan letters, both from Telegraph Boys," relates the author, "and with this recognition and success, I decided to terminate my acting career and concentrate on writing for the public. Until then, you see, I had been writing exclusively for myself—ever since I was first able to hold a pen."

The decision was a rewarding one for, in the past decade, he has had a goodly number of articles and short stories published in the United States, Britain, Ireland and Australia. His short plays have been performed extensively in Ireland and elsewhere and presently he is at work on two full-length dramas and a novel.

The past and present more or less taken care of, Mr. O'Connor's future ambition is "to explore the possibilities of marrying the avant-garde with the popular and trying to rescue some of the vast 'captured' audience for the theatre."

Patrick O'Connor's *The Wooden Box* appears for the first time in book form in this anthology.

Characters

JOE
BLACKSMITH
FRUITERER
FISHMONGER
SHOP ASSISTANT
SHOP MANAGER
THREE SHOPPERS
FOUR PUB LOCALS
BARMAN
BANK MANAGER
LOCAL GOVERNMENT OFFICIAL
UNDERTAKER
SCHOOLMASTER
POLICE SERGEANT
JOE'S WIFE
POLICE SUPERINTENDENT
CONSTABLE
REPORTER
HOT GOSPELLER

Scene 1:

Dunderville, morning

Scene 2:

Joe's shack, afternoon and evening

Author's Note

I visualize this play set and performed in a stylized fashion.

Sets should be of the simplest on an otherwise bare stage. A wooden frame for the entrance to the chain store. Also for the shack. Upended barrels for the pub. Benches for merchant's stalls. Simple wooden tables, chairs, etc.

Rhythmic grouping of the cast is important. Most of the characters can be doubled or trebled. That is, five males can take all male characters except Joe. They can also do the three female shoppers if they are versatile enough. Joe's wife can double the shop assistant. This gives a basic cast of seven: six male, one female.

Scene One

Early morning, just before sunrise. A man appears from wings, left, pushing a wheelbarrow before him. The wheelbarrow is a rough, homemade type, a series of flat, wooden slats nailed together, no sides, two shafts for handles and one wheel knocked into the front. The man is "colored" (according to the whim of the director; the author's preference inclines towards green), not "white." There is a chorus of birds from a nearby wood.

The man turns backstage, pushes his barrow as far back as he can, then turns right, stops and rests. A spotlight illuminates a signpost which says "Dunderville, Town Center 200 yards." There is a seagull perched on top of the signpost. The man looks up. Then he picks up the shafts of his barrow and continues toward the center of the stage. After a little way he puts his barrow down again and a spotlight illuminates a blacksmith who looks up from his anvil.

SMITH: Good morning, Joe.

JOE: (*Smiles; he speaks halting English*) Good morning. (*He waits*)

SMITH: Ah, you want your spade, don't you, of course. (*He picks up a spade*) Here it is. . .That's it. I did the best I could with it. Welded this across here, see. . .And I hammered that part in all right. . .Yes. . .I think you'll find that will last you for a good while yet. . .Yes. . .(*Joe makes a gesture with hand in his pocket*)

JOE: How. . .How much?

SMITH: Oh, I don't know. . .You haven't been long here from Abaracay, have you? (*Joe nods*) Having a struggle, I'll bet. . .It wasn't a big job. Pay me some other time. . .

(*He waves him away and his spotlight goes out. Joe places the spade on the barrow, picks up the shafts and carries on. Spotlight on fruit stall. Joe stops. He selects some apples here, some oranges there. The Stall Man takes them, puts them in a bag. Joe pays him*)

JOE: Excuse. . .I. . .I. . .am. . .

FRUITERER: Yes.

JOE: I am wanting. . .want. . .Ah. . .

FRUITERER: Yes.

JOE: Wanting. . .A box. . .box. . .Am wanting. . .

FRUITERER: What sort of a box?

JOE: A box. . .Ah. . .(*He gestures with his hands*)

FRUITERER: This? (*He picks up an orange box. Joe shakes his head*) This? (*An apple box*)

JOE: No. . .No. . .Big box. This. . .This. . .(*He measures with his hands*)

FRUITERER: No, I haven't got one that size. Next please . . .(*Joe gestures again*) No, I'm sorry. . .(*Joe picks up barrow and pushes on. Spotlight on Fish Stall. He stops again, selects a fish, has it wrapped in newspaper, pays for it. He says something to Fishmonger*)

FISHMONGER: What, a box? What size? What do you want it for?

JOE: I want. . .It is. . .

FISHMONGER: Come on, chum. I haven't got all day. I've got other people to serve. They've been here a lot longer than you have. . .

JOE: It is. . .I want. . .This long. . .

FISHMONGER: I haven't got what you want. (*Joe picks up barrow*) Can't keep my customers waiting all day, can I? These Abaracayns! Come over here. . .I don't know. Can't even speak the bleedin' language. . .Yes, mum? 'Alf a pound, mum?

(*Spotlight out. Joe should have reached limit of backstage right. He turns left again and proceeds towards footlights. He stops, still holding the shafts of his barrow. He looks to right and left as different voices shout at him. The sun comes up slowly*)

VOICES: No, sorry. . .What kind of a box?. . .Short box . . .A long box. . .Big box?. . .Little box?. . .It is a wooden box you want. . . .No, sorry chum. . . .Look, d'you mind, I'm busy. . . .What do you want?. . .No. . .Why don't you go to the joiners. . . .We don't sell boxes here. . . .What do you think I am, a carpenter?. . .No. . .Cor Blimey. . . .These Abaracayns would drive you up the pole. . . .What?. . .Look, you brought your interpreter with you?. . .No, I ain't got a box. . . .

(*Joe pushes on. He should be downstage now and just turned slightly towards centre. A neon sign flashes on: "Mortum and Facies Supermarket." Joe stops, rests his barrow, hesitates for some time, then slowly enters through a wooden frame, gazing all around him awesomely. Simultaneously is illuminated a counter with a prim Shop Assistant behind. Joe walks up to her*)

JOE: Bean? Bean?

ASST: I *beg* your pardon.

JOE: Bean, bean, bean.

ASST: Been where?

JOE: Bean, bean. . .bean. . .*backed* bean. . . .

ASST: Huh?

JOE: Backed bean, backed bean. . . .

ASST: Oh. . .*baked* beans. (*Three ladies who have been wandering about in the haze now form a queue behind Joe*) Why don't you say what you mean? (*She gestures to the ladies, throwing her eyes up to heaven. Hands over a tin of beans*) One and twopence halfpenny, please.

JOE: Have you. . .You have. . .a. . .a. . .box, yes?

ASST: Pardon?

JOE: A box. . .A box. . .

ASST: A box of what?

JOE: No. . .No. . .Not box of. . .a box. . .*wooden box*. . . .

ASST: *Wooden* box? . . .What sort of a wooden box?

JOE: Yes. . .Yes. . .*Empty* wooden box. . . .

ASST: You want an empty wooden box?

JOE: . . .Ah. . .Yes. . .Please. . . .(*Suddenly, Joe sees high on a shelf at the other side of the shop, the exact size and shape of box that he requires*) Ah. . .There is box. . .That is box . . .I want. . .I. . .I want you should give me. . . .(*He gets very excited and begins to gesticulate wildly*)

ASST: *That* is not my department. *I* cannot get it for you. . .Besides, I think there is something *in* those boxes. . .I have all these *customers* to serve. . .(*The customers are getting impatient and beginning to sniff openly at Joe, saying "These Abaracayns" and turning their eyes up to heaven*) Next, please! (*She turns to next customer*)

JOE: Please. . .Please. . .The box, the box. . . .

1ST CUSTOMER: She said you couldn't have the box. Come along, now, buckle under, young man. . . .

2ND CUSTOMER: I say! Move along, there.

3RD CUSTOMER: Hear, hear!

JOE: The box. . .The box!

ASST: *Next,* please. . . .

(*The Manager appears, spick and span, a glint in his eye, filled with an after-elevenses confidence. He makes a split second appraisal of Joe's clothes, appearance, background and antecedents*)

MANAGER: Now, what can I do for *you?*

ASST: He wants a *box. . . .*(*She points*) *Empty.*

MANAGER: A box? I see. . .

JOE: Wooden box.

MANAGER: A wooden box. . .Yes. . .The size of that one up there. . .Yes. . . .

JOE: Empty.

MANGER: Yes. . .empty. . *.Empty?*. . .H'mm. . . .What did you want the box for?

JOE: The box. . .The box. . .I am wanting. . .

MANAGER: Yes. . .

JOE: This box. . .Little girl. . .

MANAGER: You want to give it to a little girl?

JOE: No. . .No. . .Little girl is going. . .

MANAGER: Going where?

JOE: Going in box. . .

MANAGER: I see, she wants to make a little house. (*He smiles a frosty smile*)

JOE: Ha, ha, little house. . .

MANAGER: To play in the box. . .

JOE: To lay in the box.

MANAGER: To play in the box.

JOE: Not play. . .*Lay*. . .She is lying in box. . . .Lying in box. . . .

MANAGER: In bed, eh? Go sleep, eh? (*He puts his head on hands in sleep motion*)

JOE: Yes. . .Yes. . .Go sleep. (*He repeats motion*) She is dead. . . .

MANAGER: I see. . .(*He is grinning*) She is dead. . . . (*Grin disappears from face*) She is *dead?* (*The mention of death arouses the immediate interest of the other shoppers*)

JOE: She dead. . .I am. . .putting in box. . . .How say? . . .burying her. . .My little girl. . . .My poor little girl. . .Two days sick. . .Yesterday gone. . . .I am burying her. . .my plot of ground. . .need box. . . .(*The Manager's jaw has been steadily dropping during this speech. . .He now stares stupidly—in his life as a store manager he has not come up against anything like this before. However, he sees by the women customers who are pointing and whispering among themselves that scandal is in the air and, sensing ridicule, draws himself up valiantly and looks at Joe suspiciously*)

MANAGER: Look here, my man. I don't know whether this is some kind of a joke. But I would remind you that Mortum and Facies, although we sell almost anything, is *not* a funeral parlour. . . .I don't think you will find what you want in *this* store. . . .

JOE: But. . .but. . .but (*He points again to the boxes*)

MANAGER: (*Putting all his authority into it. He wants to get rid of this character as soon as possible*) I'm sorry.

JOE: But. . .but. . .

(*Manager with absolute finality, points dramatically to the door. Joe walks out disconsolately with his tin of beans. He stands outside with his barrow, looking about him from right to left, peering into the distance, wondering where next to go.*

After he has left the shop, the customers begin to talk among themselves while the Manager hovers around, now trying to catch a glimpse of Joe through the window, now listening to what the customers are saying)

1ST CUSTOMER: Did you hear what he said?

2ND CUSTOMER: He did. . .I heard him. . . .

3RD CUSTOMER: He didn't.

2ND CUSTOMER: He did say that.

1ST CUSTOMER: He said he *wanted to bury his little girl in his plot of ground.*

2ND CUSTOMER: Yes, I heard him.

3RD CUSTOMER: No.

2ND CUSTOMER: That's right.

1ST CUSTOMER: Did you ever hear of such a thing?

3RD CUSTOMER: Was he an Abaracayn?

2ND CUSTOMER: Yes, works in the mines.

1ST CUSTOMER: Fit for nothing else. It shouldn't be allowed if you ask me, burying a little girl in a wooden box.

3RD CUSTOMER: Fair gives you the shudders, doesn't it?

2ND CUSTOMER: Somebody should stop it. It might be all right for Abaracay, but it's not all right for here.

1ST CUSTOMER: I wouldn't be surprised if there was some dirty work afoot.

3RD CUSTOMER: No, surely not.

1ST CUSTOMER: Why not? He's a foreigner, isn't he?

2ND CUSTOMER: That's right, you know.

(Blackout on store scene. Joe picks up his barrow again, makes a turn with it until he is facing the way he came and then slowly trundles it back. When he reaches backstage left, he carries straight on and off. Light fades slowly. Stage left, light up. Interior Inn. Sign saying "Public" over four barrels standing on end with pump handles jutting from behind. At this bar stand four "locals" named Fred, 'arry, Les, Ron.

Adjoining, nearer stage right, are four shorter barrels upended with pump handles and sign saying "Saloon." Rising from between the bars is a tall pole suspending an Inn Sign: "Pack and Hound."

The four "locals" stand at public bar facing backstage and a good three paces apart. They all wear the same type of dingy overcoat, a muffler and a cap. No one speaks.

Enter Barman. Dialect not "Zummerzet" but present day working class London)

BARMAN: Evening, Fred.

FRED: Evening. Pint bitter.

BARMAN: Evening, 'arry.

'ARRY: Evening. Pint bitter.

(*Barman draws two pints*)

BARMAN: Evening, Les.

LES: Evening. Pint bitter.

BARMAN: Evening, Ron.

RON: Evening. Pint bitter.

(*Barman serves up two pints and begins to draw two more*)

BARMAN: What do you think of this Abaracay lark?

(*Silence. Four long drinks. More silence*)

FRED: Ay?

'ARRY: This what's-er-name. . .Abaracayn. . . .

(*Silence. Drink*)

LES: Not right, *reely,* is it?

RON: No, not *reely.* (*Silence. Drink*)

FRED: Shouldn't be allowed really, ay? Should it?

RON: No, shouldn't be allowed.

'ARRY: These 'ere Abaracayns. . .

LES: Cor! (*Silence*)

FRED: Got no sense of what's proper.

'ARRY: You wouldn't bury your little girl in a box, would you, would you?

RON: No. . .

LES: Shouldn't be allowed. . .(*Silence. They continue to stand in same position. Blackout.*

Furtively, from different directions enter four men into Saloon. They wear the same type of dingy overcoat but with bowler hats and no mufflers. Each one has a large card suspended around his neck with the following inscriptions:

"THE BANK MANAGER"

"THE SCHOOLMASTER"

"THE UNDERTAKER"
"THE LOCAL GOVERNMENT OFFICIAL"
The Bank Manager sidles up to the bar)

BARMAN: Evening, Fred, what's it to be?

B. MANAGER: Good evening, small bitter please. (*The Undertaker sidles up to the bar*)

BARMAN: Evening, 'arry.

UNDERTAKER: Good evening. Bitter please, a small one. (*Barman pulls up drinks; Undertaker takes his, drinks some*) Oh hullo, Fred, didn't see you there.

B. MANAGER: Hullo, Harry; how are you, all right?

UNDERTAKER: Mustn't grumble. (*Schoolmaster sidles up to bar*)

SHOOLMASTER: Small bitter, please.

BARMAN: Good evening, Sir.

SCHOOLMASTER: Good evening. (*Local Government Official sidles up to bar*)

BARMAN: Good evening, Les.

L. G. OFFICIAL: Good evening, small bitter, please. (*He turns to Schoolmaster*) Hello, Ron.

SCHOOLMASTER: Hullo, Les.

B. MANAGER: Hullo, Ron, Les.

SCHOOLMASTER, L. G. OFFICIAL: (*Together*) Hullo, Fred, Harry. . . .(*They all drink*)

B. MANAGER: Well, what do you think of this Abaracayn business? What do you think, Ron?

SCHOOLMASTER: Oh, I think it is barbaric, Fred, simply barbaric! Into the cold earth without rites or a proper burial. It goes against all traditions, all human dignity. What do you say, Harry?

UNDERTAKER: I agree. It's not as if he couldn't have a reasonable funeral for very little. My fees are not high. He needn't have worried about having anything elaborate. It's possible to have a simple, inexpensive funeral. Everything laid on for very little. Easy payments too, if required. That right, Fred?

B. MANAGER: He can't be so poor. I understand they make

quite good money in the mines now. This would undermine our entire economy.

L. G. OFFICIAL: How would it be if everyone started burying their loved ones in their own plot of land?

SCHOOLMASTER: The country would be strewn with corpses, if you'll forgive the expression.

ALL: (*Together*) It oughtn't to be allowed.

(*Blackout. Inn. Light up table with three ladies sitting at tea: This morning's three customers in Mortum & Facies*)

1ST LADY: It makes your heart bleed to think of that poor little girl being put in a box—a wooden box, mind you—and dumped into the earth.

2ND LADY: Whatever would become of us all.

3RD LADY: How could he be so cruel?

1ST LADY: Would you dream of doing such a thing?

2ND LADY: When I think. . .My little Betty—may she rest in peace—was buried in a little, white, satin coffin. There were flowers everywhere. A great many mourners, too. We tried to do our best for her. Well, it's all you can do, isn't it? We had nothing to be ashamed of over her funeral. The neighbors all said what a nice turnout it was. She was laid to rest in our cemetery and we had a little stone as well.

1ST LADY: It's only right, isn't it?

3RD LADY: I've never heard of anything like this before. They must be queer people, these Abaracayns.

1ST LADY: I think the whole business is shocking.

2ND LADY: There he was in Mortum and Facies, this morning, asking for this wooden box as bold as brass.

1ST LADY: I am going to speak to my husband about it.

2ND LADY: So am I.

3RD LADY: So am I.

ALL: (*Together*) It ought not to be allowed.

(*Blackout. Short Pause. Light up Police Sergeant on phone*)

SERGEANT: The Manager of Mortum and Facies? Yes, Sir.

(*He writes in a book*) This man had come into the shop this morning, yes. . .And he had asked for a box. . .Said he wanted to bury a little girl in it, did he?. . .What time was that?. . .I see. . .Yes, I can understand that it worried you afterwards. . . One of the Abaracayns, was it?. . .Yes. . .No, there might not be anything in it. . .But you never know. . .You did quite right . . .Thank you, I'll look into it. . .Yes. . . .

Fade out

Scene Two

Afternoon. A rough wooden shack somewhat to left of stage. A back door to a path which leads through a small plot of earth upstage to a newly dug grave under a little tree.

Right of shack, steps leading from front door to yard, which occupies rest of stage up to wings, where a fence bounds the yard. Inside the shack sit Joe and his Wife on each side of the fire, facing the footlights. Between them on a table is resting a rough wooden coffin which Joe has nailed together himself—his tools are still lying nearby. His daughter lies inside the coffin.

Joe rises and walks over to his Wife. He embraces her and comforts her, whispering in her ear. She pats his hand and remains brave, keeping her feelings in check. She is the same color as Joe. While they are together a Reporter enters the yard, crosses to the door and bangs loudly on it. He carries a camera with flash equipment. Joe crosses and opens door to him.

REPORTER: Ah, I'm from the *Dunderville Gazette.* May I come in? (*Joe admits him. He brushes past*) You haven't buried her yet, I hope. (*He catches sight of the coffin*) Ah, no. Only, I wanted to get some pictures, eh? Very good, very nice pictures, eh? (*Crosses to Wife*) There, you want your picture taken, don't you, dear? Very nice, eh? (*She stares mutely at him. He looks her up and down, muttering to himself*) I think we could have one of you by yourself for next week's follow-up story. Just sit as you are. Hold it. Cross your legs, dear. That's right, cross your legs. (*He crosses to her and raises her skirt*)

That's right. Very good follow-up next week, eh? Very good pin-up. "*Wooden Box Girl's Mother Speaks,*" eh? You might be in the money yet, Ducks, eh? (*He takes photo*) Oh, have you got any more kids, Joe? (*Joe shakes head*) Well, there's still time, eh? (*He nudges Joe*)

JOE: What is. . .What is all about?

REPORTER: Oh, don't you know? I expect you'll find out soon. You've made quite a stir, eh? Never mind, I just want some nice pictures, eh? Very good, eh? All free. I give you picture of yourself, eh? It's a custom, see?

JOE: Oh, custom. . .(*He nods to Wife, who nods back*)

REPORTER: Yes, we always do this here. I take one (*He crosses to coffin*) of little girl in coffin. (*He takes it*) Then I give you copy hang on wall, eh? Picture to hang on wall, eh?

JOE: Picture hang on wall, thank you. . .

REPORTER: Free. All free. No cost, no money. Just stand over here, would you, missus? (*He grabs her by the arm and makes her stand by coffin. He turns to Joe*) No cost, no money. . .

JOE: No money?

REPORTER: No. You on the other side of the coffin. That's right. (*He takes a picture of them standing one on each side of coffin*) Good. You take a nice picture, girlie. No kidding. Knock three times. Very good. Let's have another one of you, eh? Sitting down. (*She sits. He crosses and lifts her skirt this time as far as he dares. Turns to Joe over his back*) Custom, eh? (*Joe grins bewilderedly. Reporter crouches on floor in front of Joe's wife to take picture*) Yes, nice picture. (*He takes picture*) Lovely. (*Half to himself*) That's one for the boys. (*Aloud*) Very good, right. (*Takes out notebook*) When was doctor here last? Doctor here yesterday?

JOE: Yes, doctor here yesterday.

REPORTER: Give certificate? (*Writes on palm*) Certificate?

JOE: Oh, yes. (*Crosses to drawer*) Here. (*Takes out certificate and holds it up*)

REPORTER: Just hold it up beside you, will you? I'll just take a picture of that. (*Takes it*) Right. . ."*Joe Says Everything Above Board*". . .Good. . ." (*Knock on door*) When are you burying her, Joe?

JOE: Burying?

REPORTER: Yes. In ground. (*He makes gesture*)

JOE: Oh, this evening.

REPORTER: Right. Goodbye. (*Makes for door, reaches it, turns*) See you at the funeral. Bye, bye.

JOE and WIFE: (*Together*) Bye, bye. . .(*They see a man standing outside*) Good evening.

MAN: Good evening, I am Major Todhunter; may I come in? Thank you. (*He halts inside door and draws a thick black book from his pocket and clasps it in front of him*) There is still time to repent. . .In your ignorance, brother and sister, ye knew not. . .But let ye accept the way, all is won. . .Take my yoke upon thee. . .Only believe. . .Only believe. . .Oh, if only ye will accept tonight. . .Let love come into your hearts tonight. . .Before ye do this wicked thing. . .Consider what a seed ye will be sowing in the earth. . .Ye must be born again. . .Now. . .Tonight. . .Before it is too late. . .Come with me, brother and sister . . .Come with me tonight and be saved. . .Let love save you. . . Ask and ye shall receive. . .Seek and it will be given unto you . . .By the glorious action of love ye will be saved. . .Bathe yourself in it tonight. . .Do not delay. . .He is waiting for you. . . He calls out to you. . .He seeks you. . .It is simple. . .It is easy . . .Speak tonight. . .Ask love to come into your hearts tonight . . . Only be saved by it. . .Now. . .This minute. . .The hour is at hand!. . .Hallelujah! (*He walks over to Joe and his Wife, hands a small pamphlet to each, then moves towards the door. He turns*) Good evening, sister!. . .Good evening, brother! (*He exits. Joe and Wife have been listening with acute interest to the harangue, trying to get hold of some clue. They now stare stupidly at the pamphlets, then turn to each other helplessly. Joe takes his wife's pamphlet and together with his own, places them carefully on top of the dresser*)

JOE: I think it is time.

(*She nods. Joe picks up a hammer and some nails. He places the lid on the coffin and hammers four nails in, one at each corner. He walks to front door, opens it and peers out from right to left, then returns to table. It is now dusk. The Wife moves to the foot of the coffin and with himself taking the head, they walk slowly out the back door bearing the coffin between them. They descend the steps onto the path leading to the grave. As they go through the back door a kind of hum meets their ears. This increases as they go up the path until it begins to sound like the hum of distant voices. As they near the grave the noise has become steadily louder until, having rested the coffin beside grave, it is clearly the noise and clamor of a large crowd of people, including a number of dogs barking. Joe and his Wife look at each other, then turn and, leaving the coffin beside the grave, they go back into the house and out the front door to stand on the steps. At this there is a great shout from the crowd. The headlights of a car sweep across Joe and his Wife, to be followed by another pair as two cars draw up.*

The Local Government Official, the Bank Manager, the Undertaker and the Schoolmaster—in that order—now enter the yard, having alighted from one of the cars and still wearing the cards around their necks. They are followed by a Superintendent of Police and a Constable. The Superintendent details the Constable to keep his eye on things outside, then joins the other four who are entering the shack after Joe and his Wife.

The crowd is by no means an angry one. It sounds very excited and a trifle hilarious. They shout a little badinage at the Constable, who returns it good-naturedly.

Inside the shack, the Superintendent asks to see the death certificate, says "Death Certificate in order" and takes up a position at the door, while the four officials confer in a corner. Joe and his Wife stand awaiting the outcome of this new development. The Schoolmaster detaches himself from the group.)

SCHOOLMASTER: Good evening. . .I do hope we are not intruding. . .Please sit down. . .Mrs. . . .Mrs. . . .

JOE: Brown.

SCHOOLMASTER: Mrs. Brown. . .Seated. . .sit. . .sit. . .Asayeh Vous. (*He bends his knees slowly and gestures to her. She sits*) The fact is, with all respect to you, Mrs. Brown, we are somewhat chagrined at the manner of burial chosen by your spouse here for your dear, departed daughter, yourself no doubt concurring. We gather that it is the custom in Abaracay to inter deceased members of the family in this fashion. . .

L. G. OFFICIAL: (*Interrupting*) It's going to be difficult, Ron. She doesn't understand a word of English and he speaks very little himself. . .

SCHOOLMASTER: Oh. . .That is difficult. . .I felt I was *communicating* somehow. Shall I keep trying?

OTHERS: Yes, give it a go anyhow. Why not? You can only try, etc. . . .

SCHOOLMASTER: I don't suppose anyone speaks Abaracay? . . .No. . .Well, you see, Joe, we feel it is barbaric, *bar-bar-ic* to bury. . .bury child without rites. . .No funeral. . .See?. . .little girl. . .

JOE: Yes.

SCHOOLMASTER: Go in box. . .Coffin. . .Not your box. . .

JOE: No?

SCHOOLMASTER: No. . .White *satin*. . .*Silver* ornaments . . .Silk cords. . .

JOE: Yes?

SCHOOLMASTER: Yes. . .Go in big motor car. . .Beautiful glass windows. . .

JOE: Oh-h!

SCHOOLMASTER: Yes. . .Flowers everywhere. . .Masses of *beautiful* flowers. . .lovely grave marble stone. . .Yes. . . .

JOE: Oh-h. . .Why? (*Schoolmaster is speechless*)

UNDERTAKER: Let me try, Ron. . .Look, Joe, I know you're not rich. . .ha-ha. . .Not by a long shot, eh? Says you. Look, I can offer you easy terms. . .*easy terms*. . .you know, tally-man?. . .Never-never?

JOE: Yes, Never-never. . .Very good, Never-never.

UNDERTAKER: (*Looks proudly around for praise*) Yes, you like? And (*He lowers his voice*) I can do you a special price for the whole funeral: cars, coffin, dress—I'll throw in a little stone—if you will let me do the interment. (*He whispers in his ear*)

JOE: (*Pulls out lining of pockets*) No money.

UNDERTAKER: (*Turns to Bank Manager*) Fred! (*Fred reluctantly comes over while Undertaker takes himself out of it. The phrase: "No money" concluded things as far as he was concerned*)

B. MANAGER: Can I be of any assistance, Joe?

JOE: Yes?

B. MANAGER: Well, let's see. . .You have no money, eh? People start accounts for very small amounts, nowadays, you know. The bank is no longer only for privileged people, you know. The small man and all that. . .The small man. . .(*He looks around him*) I don't know *how* small we are prepared to go, these days. . .Um. . .(*He looks around him again*) You haven't got a mortgage, I suppose. . .No. . .Have you any insurance?. . .*in-sur-ance*. . . .

JOE: In-Sur-Ance?

B. MANAGER: Yes. . .Have you?

JOE: Me?

B. MANAGER: Yes.

JOE: In-Sur-Ance. . .Me. . .Yes. . . .

B. MANAGER: (*Pleased*) Good. Jolly good. They're thrifty, you know, these boys. . .They don't throw their money away like the Irish.

JOE: In-Sur-Ance. . .Yes. . .*Nat-Ion-Al* insurance. . .

B. MANAGER: You try him, Les.

L. G. OFFICIAL: Now, look here, Joe. . .I understand you're one of the people. . .Well, I'm one of the people myself. . .I always was for the little man. . .I'm a-telling you. . .I've lived in this town all my days. . .And I always did my best for the people. . .It's not easy, I know. . .I've had my struggle. . .But we must all pull together. . .Every cloud has a silver lining. . . This might turn out to be yours. . .There might be prospects that you wouldn't think in this town. . .You might not always have to go down a mine. . .A little co-operation goes a long way. . . .

JOE: Yes?

L. G. OFFICIAL: Yes.

(Joe's expression remains unchanged. They all drink tea, looking expectantly at Joe. He looks expectantly at them. Pause.

Mrs. Brown goes over to Joe. They whisper together, then start to make for back door)

L. G. OFFICIAL: Where are you going, Joe?

JOE: To bury little girl.

L. G. OFFICIAL: No, no, wait a minute. (*He throws up his hands in despair and motions to his confederates. They confer in a corner, then straighten up clearing their throats in the manner of an archbishop confronting a burglar who has broken into his silver cupboard*)

L. G. OFFICIAL: Well, it's like this, Joe. . .We've tried to make you see reason and see it our way. . .We know it's hard for you and we have requested your co-operation. . .Now, the fact is that we find ourselves forced to uphold the law. . .We haven't wanted to make this a legal case, but there *is* a law against this, you know.

We regret that we have to take charge of the burial ourselves. . .Understand?. . .*We* bury little girl. . .

JOE: *You* bury?

L. G. OFFICIAL: Yes.

JOE: Yes?

L. G. OFFICIAL: Yes. (*Joe confers with his Wife, who nods her head. He concurs*)

JOE: What do with her?

L. G. OFFICIAL: She will be taken to the mortuary tonight and tomorrow she will be buried under the auspices of the town council.

JOE: (*Inclines head towards garden*) *I* bury her? (*A final appeal*)

ALL: No. . . .

(Joe remains impassive. The four gentlemen confer with the Superintendent, who goes out and calls Constable. There is a murmur of expectation from the crowd. The Constable enters shack, and together with Superintendent goes out to plot of land at rear. Having reached the grave they lift coffin onto shoulders and slowly make their way back to house. The L. G. Official now leaves the shack after saying goodbye to Joe and his Wife, followed in their usual order of precedence by the Bank Manager, the Undertaker and the Schoolmaster who all say goodbye to Joe and his Wife in turn. In single file, they make their way slowly and respectfully across the yard followed by the Superintendent and the Constable carrying the coffin. As this funeral cortege moves slowly across the yard there are mixed comments from the crowd. Joe and his Wife stand watching from the door.)

CROWD: Isn't it a shame. . .That poor little dear. . .Well, I wouldn't like to go out like that. . .Nor would I. . .What a way to go. . .Thank goodness I'll be taken care of when I die . . .So will I. . .I'm paying every week for it. . .So am I. . .Mind you, I'll only be able to have a coffin without brass handles because of the television. . .Well, you've got to make sacrifices, haven't you. . .You do your best. . .I feel sorry for him and her. . .Who?. . .The Abaracayns, I wouldn't feel sorry for them . . .They should have given her a proper burial. . . .(*The coffin being so small, the Superintendent and the Constable have difficulty in avoiding each other's feet as they carry it*). . .Fancy doing a thing like that. . .Look at it. . .A rough old box it is, too. . .I don't know what I would have done (*The woman from the tea meeting earlier*) if my little Betty hadn't had a proper burial in her little white satin coffin. . .Yes, there were flowers everywhere. . .The neighbors said. . .

(The rest is mercifully lost in the increased noise of the crowd. The coffin having been laid in the Police Car, we hear it starting up and moving off at funeral pace, to be followed by the other car. The crowd now falls in behind the cars and we hear their feet beginning a slow funeral march. Someone begins to sing drunkenly until a voice yells, "Belt up, George." He belts up. A voice begins

shamefacedly "Nearer my God to Thee," falters and stops. Somebody else starts it again. He bravely continues. It is taken up. Then they all sing it quietly in unison as they walk behind the cars. The dogs begin to howl. Joe puts his arm around his Wife as they stand at the top of the steps of the shack. The sound of the funeral fades slowly into the distance. The light fades around the shack. . .Joe and his Wife silhouetted. There is a faint glow around the newly dug empty grave and the little tree beside it. . .)

Slow Curtain

Gary Gardner

A TRAIN GOING SOMEWHERE

Gary Gardner

Born in Danville, Illinois, on March 24, 1944, Gary Gardner attributes the genesis of his fascination with the drama to a number of contributing factors, notably his relentless passion for motion pictures. An advanced movie fan at an early age (four, to be precise), his devotion to the cinematic art came to rich fulfillment in 1967 when he was named co-winner of the first prize in the playwriting category of the annual *Story College Creative Awards* sponsored by the Four Winds Press and conducted by Whit and Hallie Burnett, two of the nation's prime and most indefatigable discoverers of outstanding new writing talents. Mr. Gardner's play was titled, naturally enough, *Just Like in the Movies.*

The youthful author graduated in 1966 from the University of Illinois where he majored in speech education and "carried spears" in numerous campus productions, as well as authoring three short plays, four musical revues, and two local television shows.

In September, 1966, he moved westward to continue his education at the University of California at Los Angeles where he presently is working for a MFA degree in playwriting under the guidance of Dr. George Savage and dramatist Robert E. Lee (co-author of *Inherit the Wind, Auntie Mame* and its musical variation, *Mame*).

Gary Gardner's prize-winning comedy was produced at U.C.L.A. in May, 1967, and its campus success reassured the author that talent and dedication sprinkled "wiv a little bit o' luck" indeed could make life "just like in the movies."

A Train Going Somewhere, published here for the first time, vividly reflects the versatility of the young author whose range runs from poignant drama to comedy to musical satires. The play is one of a quartet of short dramas collectively called *Purgatory on a Saturday Night.*

Mr. Gardner's immediate plans include fashioning the book and lyrics for a musical with John Rubinstein, a U.C.L.A. classmate and son of the pianist, Artur Rubinstein, and the completion of his graduate studies.

A pragmatist as well as a gifted creator, he also proposes to fortify himself against the vagaries of show business by planning a career in educational theatre on the university level.

Characters

EDDIE PRUITT

SAM

JOBY

LINDA LOU

THE SLEEPING MAN

Scene:

The waiting room of a small railroad station in a Southern town. The time is the present.

The waiting room of a railroad station in the worst section of a Southern town. And it is not even the first-class waiting room; it's one of those dingy little corner holes where the Negro passengers used to board. But the era of slavery has been officially over for a hundred years or so, and now the dregs of any color can wait here. There are backless benches; along the upstage wall is a particularly long bench on which The Sleeping Man, a bewhiskered old bum, lies prone throughout the play. Upstage left, there is a swinging door which leads to an immediate street entrance, although the logical way to enter would be through the information lobby, directly off right. Upstage right, a large bulletin board with only the following three lines:

TRAIN SCHEDULE

ARRIVING DEPARTING

ALL LISTINGS SUBJECT TO CHANGE

As the lights come up, Sam, an aging Negro with bent back and thinning gray hair, is sweeping the floor upstage right. Eddie Pruitt is sitting on one of the benches, cigarette in hand, legs spread over the numerous butts he's stamped into the floor. Eddie is a "folk singer" of sorts; tall, rugged, virile, a "man's man." He finishes his ciga-

rette, stamps it out; then sits, hands on his knees and head bowed, staring at the butt menagerie. After a moment, he throws back his head and begins to sing.

EDDIE: *"Gone are the days*
When my heart was young and gay
Gone are my friends
To the cottonfields away. . ."

(*With a sad little laugh*) Hey, Sam. 'Djever hear such a voice? Bing Crosby, Pat Boone, and Eddie Pruitt! The triumvirate of musical manure. *"Gone are the days—"* Isn't that one of your songs, Sam? Hey, aren't you part of that Southland that gave "birth to the blues"?

SAM: Not mine, no, sir. None of those ethnic songs for me.

EDDIE: (*The bemused philosophy of alcohol*)
The opposite of black is bright.
The opposite of bright is dumb.
So anyone who's black is dumb. . .
But they sure can hum.
Who said that? I've got a feeling I'm quoting one of the great late philosophers.

SAM: Mebbe it was Governor Wallace.

EDDIE: Mebbe it *was* Governor Wallace. Or Sammy Davis' manager.

SAM: Or Sammy Davis' manager.

EDDIE: Did I ever tell you I was a great singer, Sam?

SAM: Many times. Many times.

EDDIE: I was always gonna be a singer. A *great* singer. That's what Reverend Bennett told me the first time he ever heard me in the choir. The *a cappella* choir of the Ninth Street Church of Christ. 'Djever sing in church, Sam?

SAM: Sure I did. And I polished the preacher's shoes on the streetcorner six days a week so's I'd have enough money to put in the collection plate on Sundays. Somehow, at the time it seemed logical.

EDDIE: You would've loved Reverend Bennett, Sam. He

used to rehearse those sermons of his for hours. Ev'ry pause, ev'ry gesture down just perfect. Ev'ry second he wasn't behind the pulpit he was in front of the mirror. A regular *Barrymore,* that man. And he sang. Tenor. Not a bad tenor, really, but he insisted on singin' solos ev'ry Sunday with the whole goddamned choir Alleluhahing *sotto voce* in the background. Huh. Anyway, he told me once that I had a golden voice, yeah, *a golden voice.* Me. My talent from the *Good Man,* he called it. And he asked me maybe would I like to do a duet of *Whispering Hope* with him some Sunday. *Whispering Hope,* hell! When I went over to his place to rehearse, he kept grabbin' for my crotch. Huh. Poor old Reverend Bennett. You know, Sam, you just can't trust a man of God who sings tenor. (*A very long pause*) What time does the train get in?

SAM: Supposed to be here by now. Sometimes it's early and sometimes it's late. Way late.

EDDIE: What the hell kind of schedule is that?

SAM: The schedule it runs on, man. You never can tell.

EDDIE: (*Restlessly*) I wish to hell it'd hurry. I'm so damned tired of just waitin'!

SAM: An' where you goin'?

EDDIE: I don't know. Anywhere. Where there's some beer joint cheap enough to hire on a *has-been baritone* to draw the boozers in.

SAM: That all?

EDDIE: Well, there should be a woman there, too. You know, a real woman. With big ones and long soft hair. And plenty of liquor. And heat in the "john." And, and all good things. (*Sings*) *"Gone are the days. . ."*

SAM: (*Indicating The Sleeping Man*) You're gonna wake up the whole waitin' room with your golden voice, Mister Eddie. Mebbe a little more *sotto voce,* huh?

EDDIE: Sam, you're a real card! Whaddya mean the whole waitin' room? One lousy drunk. What's he sleepin' off, anyway?

SAM: Don't know. Said he was goin' to Greenville on the next train. Said he was goin'—had to go—'cause the biggest deal of his life was waitin' for him there, and he told me to wake him up when the train come in. So if I'm not aroun', give him a shove, huh? I'd hate for him to keep some Jay Gould-type waitin'.

EDDIE: The biggest deal of his life, huh? Who do ya reckon it is, Sam? Johnson, maybe? Or Elizabeth Taylor. Yeah, I bet that scroungy drunk is havin' a thing with Elizabeth Taylor. I bet—

SAM: (*Looking off right*) You're gettin' company, Mister Eddie. Comin' in now.

EDDIE: (*A moment's pause*) Joby?

SAM: Yeah. I'll, uh, I'll go finish up in yonder. (*He starts his broom off right*)

(*Joby hurries in, obviously looking for Eddie. He is thin, tired, older-looking than his late twenties, all of which enhances his self-image of a lost poet. As soon as he sees Eddie, he gives a sigh and finally notices Sam*)

JOBY: Hi, Sam.

SAM: Hi, Mister Joby. How's the cold? Better?

JOBY: Oh, yeah. How's everything with you, Sam?

SAM: Oh, 'bout the same. Nothin' ever changes.

JOBY: (*Gestures toward The Sleeping Man*) Drunk?

SAM: I don't know. You never can tell. (*Sam exits right*)

JOBY: (*Moves slowly downstage; checking his steps*) Hi . . .I thought you were comin' over around eleven.

EDDIE: (*Curtly*) You thought wrong.

JOBY: It's not the first time. (*A long silence*) I. . .I'd ordered a pizza. (*Pause*) Pepperoni. . .(*Pause*) It wasn't very good. Too many chunks. (*Finally asking the question*) Going traveling?

EDDIE: Yeah, I thought I'd see America first.

JOBY: By train?

EDDIE: Yeah, by train. I was gonna fly now and pay later, but TWA was showin' a movie I'd already seen, so. . .yeah, by train.

JOBY: (*Uncertain of what to say or how to say it. Then, after a moment's hesitation*) I'm sorry about the club. (*Pause*) You could at least've told me. (*Silence*) I didn't know what happened until tonight when I went in and heard that throaty dyke. . .Well, anyway, you could at least have told me. (*Pause*) I'm sorry.

EDDIE: Okay, you're sorry! I'm glad you're sorry. Thank you for being sorry. Is that enough? I'm goddam glad you're sorry! I'm grateful. Now go walk the streets.

JOBY: (*A sigh; it's been worse before*) Read any good books lately?

EDDIE: What the hell is all this? Are you tryin' to be cute, Joby? Are you gonna give me your cute routine? No, I *haven't* ready any good books lately. And I haven't seen any good movies lately. And I haven't heard any good jokes lately. And it's been even longer since I've had a good piece of ass!

JOBY: Oh, that was good, Eddie. That was real good. You've got a touch of the poet in you. And a touch of the coarse and a touch of the common and a touch of the vulgar. (*Silence; Eddie chooses not to combat*) What the hell are you doin' at the train station at two in the morning?

EDDIE: I told you. I'm waitin' for the train.

JOBY: What train?

EDDIE: (*Exploding*) Any train, dammit, any train! I walked outta that club tonight and I felt so, so really low and rotten and—

JOBY: (*Moving closer*) I know, Eddie, I know—

EDDIE: No, you *don't* know! Quit playin' the tea-and-sympathy social worker. You don't know a damn thing! I felt tonight like, like—well, have *you* ever been fired? That's what he called it. That was the word he used—*fired!* He was firin' me, he said, because I just didn't draw customer-interest anymore. How d'ya like that? Nobody wants to pinch your butt when, when. . .I decided to get out of it. Out of all of it! To just get away from the whole damn mess! From Harry, the club and you and—oh, especially you! You and your neat little room with the linen you call napkins and your marble statuettes and your Garland albums. I just wanted—

JOBY: Eddie, for God's sake—

EDDIE: I just wanted to get the hell out of there!

JOBY: Eddie, I—

EDDIE: Just don't start. Don't sympathize. Don't empathize. Don't. . .don't talk. Just shut up or go back home and leave me alone! Just let's not play *psych-out-Eddie* and get him back into bed. *Okay?*

JOBY: (*A long pause*) I think I'll take a trip, too.

EDDIE: Oh, hell.

JOBY: Okay, oh hell. I *still* think I'll take a trip, too. (*Pause; no reaction*) Where do you think I should go? (*Meaningful silence*) Well, I didn't have any place particular in mind. There're a lotta places I'd like to see. I thought maybe Oz. Or maybe Kansas. (*Still no response*) You ever been to Kansas?

EDDIE: (*Snapping*) No, and I've never been to Oz!

JOBY: No, I don't suppose you have. What time does the train come in?

EDDIE: Which one? *Oz* or *Kansas?*

JOBY: Either.

EDDIE: (*Turning away*) I don't know.

JOBY: When does *any* train come in?

EDDIE: I don't know. . .

JOBY: (*Cheerfully*) You don't know much. Maybe the Wizard could give you a brain.

EDDIE: (*Turning on him*) Maybe the Wizard could give you a nice long rod!

JOBY: That was a good one, Eddie. You're really very clever tonight. You should get drunk and tell off your boss and make a complete fool of yourself in front of a nightclub full of people more often. It sharpens your sense of the literary.

EDDIE: Shut up! Will you just shut up?

JOBY: Okay. We can discuss all this on the train.

EDDIE: *What train?*

JOBY: Any train. Any train that comes through here, Eddie. Any train that you decide to board. That's where I hop on, too. We'll be traveling companions, Eddie, off into the night. Strangers on a train, or what-have-you. Just like something out of the *Saturday Evening Post.*

EDDIE: Yeah, that's us, Joby. Right outta the *Saturday Evening Post!*

JOBY: I'm ready to board.

EDDIE: Well, traveling companion, aren't you forgetting something? Your luggage? After a few days you'll look pretty messy in just that one pair of your tight faggot pants. (*Needling*) Won't you need something with a few more frills? Something perhaps a little *gayer?*

JOBY: (*He doesn't wound easily*) Oh, I travel light. If I need another pair of tight faggot pants I can always charm them off some weed-sucking stud in one of the whistle stops. There's always some small town Narcissus with a guitar or a trumpet or maybe just a shopworn baritone that'll come through.

EDDIE: You finished?

JOBY: I don't know, Eddie. *Am I finished?*

EDDIE: Just what is it you want, Joby, huh?

JOBY: (*Swallowing a little*) *You,* I think, Eddie. God knows why! Maybe I just want someone to look up at over a platter of pepperoni.

EDDIE: (*He's caught this act before*) All right, Irene Dunne, come off it. . .

JOBY: I don't know. There're a lot of things I'd like—to be able to fly, all pretty like one of those gulls we saw last summer, or to be able to. . .to swim the English Channel or make a home run or even be able to publish just one poem again. . .(*Suddenly*) Do you know what I'd like more than anything else in the world? *Really*. To be on a train going somewhere. *Anywhere!* Just to be able to hop on and ride through the night from here to God knows where. Where all the spickets pour brandy and all the barkeeps spout poetry. And, I guess, to have someone to drink that brandy with and sing those poems to. . .(*Pause*) You like brandy, Eddie? (*A longer pause*) I talk an awful lot. . .

EDDIE: (*Melting just a little*) Yeah, Joby, you talk an awful lot.

JOBY: There's such an awful lot to say.

EDDIE: There's not a damn thing to say, Joby. Not a damn thing. . .

JOBY: (*Brightening*) Then why don't we dance? Or race around the block? Or play hopscotch?

EDDIE: We're too old to play hopscotch. And you're too short-winded to cross the street, let alone run the block.

JOBY: What time does this train come in?

EDDIE: I told you I don't know.

JOBY: (*Desperately*) Where are you goin'? And, and what are you gonna do? I don't want you to go! You don't *have* to go! It's all so stupid. *I* could go to Harry.

EDDIE: Yeah, now that would be a real pretty picture.

JOBY: Are you gonna stay here all night?

EDDIE: Until a train comes. . .

JOBY: There may not be a train through here for hours.

EDDIE: Maybe not. . .

JOBY: What do you hope to gain by all this? Huh? Just what are you trying to *prove?*

EDDIE: I'm not trying to prove anything, Joby.

JOBY: You want a woman? Is that it? You want a woman. Pangs of guilt and remorse so now you're gonna reinstate your masculinity by humping some yellow-toothed slut?

EDDIE: Shut up! I've had enough. Now get out! Get out before I break your rotten—

JOBY: I'm waitin' for the goddam train!

(*As they are about to come to blows, the swinging door goes into motion and Linda Lou enters. She is an enormously fat, rouge-cheeked streetwalker, almost a caricature of obesity with long, circus-gold tresses. She appears as one just summoned from a deep sleep, dizzy and weighted down with two tattered suitcases. Obviously drunk, she moves unsteadily toward Eddie*)

LINDA LOU: Of all people to meet in a dump like this, two in the morning! (*She looks him over*) Eddie. Same Eddie. Same hips. Same chest. (*A glance at Joby*) Same entourage.

EDDIE: Hello, Linda.

LINDA LOU: Well, that's a fine how-do-you-do, I must say. But I'll forgive you! I'm in great spirits and I'm not even tanked up. Haven't touched a drop in days. Well, maybe a drink or two, but nothin' like before. Nothin'. (*She swirls around*) I look great, huh?

EDDIE: You, er. . .you look great.

JOBY: *Fat!*

EDDIE: (*To Joby*) Shut up! (*Then, to Linda Lou*) Yeah, you sure look great. . .

JOBY: . . .great with *child!*

LINDA LOU: (*Ignoring Joby*) Look at me, Eddie. Look at me. I'm gonna be a bride!

JOBY: Wedding bells in Transylvania. Congratulations to both you and the Count!

EDDIE: (*Astonished*) You're gonna be a bride. . .?

LINDA LOU: Close your mouth, Eddie, you make me nervous. Yeh, I'm gonna be a bride. Well, ain't you going to congratulate me, huh?

EDDIE: Linda Lou, I—I don't know what—

LINDA LOU: I know. I know. You don't believe me, huh? You don't believe it. No one does. Poor dumb Linda Lou. No one believes it! Well, *I* do. I—I had this vision.

EDDIE: (*Unable to find humor in this pitiful woman*) You had a vision?

LINDA LOU: Now don't laugh! Everybody always *laughs*. But it's gonna come true. Really. It really is!. . . I went to bed early tonight. I'd been out before. Out, huh. Late supper at the diner again. Didn't set well. Greasy. Had to wash it down somehow. All that grease. Started walkin' home, stumbled. My back hurt. Bursitis. Saw a doctor last week. He told me bursitis. Anyway, these boys come along. Four of 'em, teenage boys in an old Rambler and gave me a ride home. Laughed at the old stooped cow, they called me. They was so young. They could've been my sons, any one of 'em, they could've been my sons. *Today* was my birthday, Eddie. You know how old I was today? Guess how old I was today, Eddie. Forty. I was forty years old today.

EDDIE: Linda Lou, I think—

LINDA LOU: You realize what it's like to be forty years old? That's *old,* Eddie. That's plenty old. And it's even older when you're. . .

JOBY: Aha. The moment of truth.

EDDIE: Joby!

LINDA LOU: All right. All right. I know it. . .I'm not pretty. But I don't have to take him laughin' at me. I know it. I'm plain. And heavy. I—I got big bones. But, look, I'm still a *woman.* Eddie, Eddie, all my life I've never had a man. A *real* man. A man of my own. Oh, there've been the kids with pimples whose buddies teased 'em into it, and the sailors, and the Puerto Rican butchers, who go in and out at hourly intervals, but *never* a real man. And, I—I got a lot of. . .warmth in me. Well, well now, I'm gonna be Linda Lou, *the bride.*

EDDIE: Congratulations, Linda, but—

LINDA LOU: Oh, I know! I know! You *don't* believe me. Play along with her, you tell yourself. Play along and let the old hag have her pipe dream before they whisk her off to the side show! Well, I don't want your pity. It's not a pipe dream. It's gonna come true! There's a man waitin' for me in the next town! *How do I know?* You ask yourself how do I know? *God* told me! I was layin' there in bed tonight and I had this dream. God spoke to me in this dream. He said to me, Linda Lou, *there is a man waitin' for you in the next town!* (*Joby snickers; she turns on him*)

LINDA LOU: Laugh! You think it's funny? Laugh your silly ass off, but it's *true!* I'm not drunk. I may've been drinkin', but I'm not drunk. And I tell you, with all the power to believe that's in me, that there's a man *waitin'* for me in the next town. A man who's gonna marry me. Yeah, *me!* I'm gonna be a bride! As soon as that train comes in, I get on it. Off I go, and *I'll* be laughin'. Laughin', you hear me? Laughing at all you wise bastards that laughed at *me!* (*She has shouted herself hoarse, and is convulsed with a hacking cough as Eddie tries to steady her*)

EDDIE: Nobody's laughing, Linda. *I* never laughed. . .

LINDA LOU: (*Suddenly struck with self-pity*) You never got the joke, Eddie. *I'm a joke!* An old, up-the-stairs and on-the-far-right, stinkin' joke! That's what he said tonight. . .This kid. This skinny little kid with Saturday night on his breath called me the *human joke!* But *somebody* wants me. There's gotta be *someone.* I may be a little drunk but I know that much.

(*Nervous and panicky*) I gotta get outta here. I gotta find him! I gotta get outta here and find him quick, or—

EDDIE: (*Stopping her*) Linda Lou. Now calm down. You're drunk. You can't leave what you've got to—

LINDA LOU: What I've got? Eddie, what I've got is *old!* And I'm. . .not pretty. I don't wanna die this way. There's gotta be a God! There's just gotta be. Maybe in the next town . . .I'm through layin' in the corner with my legs in the air waitin' for the mangy dogs to come laughin'. . .

EDDIE: (*Shaking her*) Linda! Linda Lou—

LINDA LOU: (*Clutching him*) You're a man, Eddie. I watched you tonight at that club. I watched all those rouge-cheeked fairies flittin' aroun' you and I said to myself, there's a *man,* an honest-to-goodness man! Oh, I've heard all about Harry and the others, but still, you're a man, Eddie! And I wouldn't have to go to the next town to—(*She breaks off, weeping*)

JOBY: (*Erupting*) How touching! She wants *you.* Eddie, she wants you! Here's your *woman.* For you, Eddie! Aren't you proud? Aren't you happy and masculine and proud?

EDDIE: Shut up, Joby! Shut up!!

JOBY: There it is, Eddie. Your ticket to that trip you wanted to take. Here's what you've been sittin' aroun' all night waitin' for. A three-hundred-pound souse. (*In the distance can be heard the sound of an approaching train*) Oh, *you* won't laugh, will you, Eddie? It's a sure thing. Hop to it. She's begging. Begging for you, Eddie. For you! (*Eddie is like a caught animal; the train sound grows louder and louder*) And you, lady—you think you can claim him? You think your big bones and warted hands can manage him? Do you think you'll ever know him—the way I do? Those few strands of black hair between his shoulder blades—how many—ten? twelve? The little knot in the ridge of his right ear—how does it taste, huh? The burn in that long, rigid neck; the sweet sweat of his gut; that small, dented white rump—when it starts, where to hold on to? what to grasp? when to—

(*Eddie whirls on Joby and slugs him, sending him sprawling to the floor. He starts for him as the noise from the train becomes louder and louder until it is unbearable, and all are frozen motionless as their eyes travel in disbelief from stage left to stage right. The Sleeping Man awakens and stares blankly at the passing noise.*

All four faces reflect despair and loss. The noise of the train fades off, right, and for a long while, they all remain fixed. Finally, The Sleeping Man comes forward and breaks the silence)

THE SLEEPING MAN: I—wanted to go to Greenville. . .

JOBY: There goes the train.

THE SLEEPING MAN: But I wanted to go to Greenville. . . (*A pause; then, to Joby*) Another train come through tomorrow—?

JOBY: I don't know. . .

THE SLEEPING MAN: Maybe, I could catch it then. . .

JOBY: Yes, perhaps. Perhaps you can.

THE SLEEPING MAN: Yes, I'll try again. Tomorrow. I have to get there soon, y'know.

(*He goes off, right*)

LINDA LOU: It's late, Eddie. I'd better get goin'. I—I guess maybe I *have* been drinkin' a little too much tonight. It was the supper—all that grease. . .(*She crosses toward her suitcases; then, turns back to Eddie*) I *did* have a vision, Eddie. I really did have a vision. . .

EDDIE: (*Softly*) I'll call you tomorrow, Linda Lou.

LINDA LOU: No. . .no, you won't, Eddie. . .(*She picks up her suitcases and goes out through the swinging door*)

JOBY: (*Coming to his side*) Eddie. . .

EDDIE: (*Without raising his voice*) Will you get away from me? I don't want you to touch me again ever. Ever. . .

JOBY: (*Gently*) Eddie.

(*Eddie hides his face in his hands as Joby gently, methodically, strokes his shoulders. Sam enters, right, and silently begins sweeping*)

Curtain

Megan Terry

THE MAGIC REALISTS

For Ellen Stewart

Megan Terry

Born in Seattle, Washington, on July 22, 1932, Megan Terry received a Bachelor of Education degree from the University of Washington, then went on to advanced studies at the University of Alberta, Banff School of Fine Arts, and the Yale Drama School.

Before devoting her "prime time" to dramatic writing, Miss Terry taught elementary school and drama classes at the Cornish School of Allied Arts.

A recipient of several leading drama awards and a Rockefeller Grant in playwriting, Miss Terry first came to national prominence with her explosive tour de force, *Viet Rock,* in which she re-created "the ambience of the Vietnam war, and our feelings about it." Originally, the play was presented at *Cafe La Mama,* New York City, then was chosen by Robert Brustein for his first production at the Yale Drama School. In 1966, the play reappeared in Manhattan, at the Martinique Theatre, in a presentation directed by the authoress. The volitant drama also has been seen in such foreign territories as Norway, Sweden, Germany, Italy, Mexico, and Japan.

An active and principal proponent of the Off-Off-Broadway movement, Miss Terry is a charter member of Joseph Chaiken's *Open Theatre* and a director of one of its playmaking workshops. A number of her own plays (including *Keep Tightly Closed in a Cool Dry Place, Calm Down, Mother,* and *Comings and Goings*) originated at *The Open Theatre* where, according to the authoress, we *build* our actors and our shows—together."

Regarded as one of Off-Off-Broadway's most compelling and successful dramatists, Miss Terry continues: "At *The Open Theatre,* Mr. Chaiken is working to make a whole new vocabulary for the actor. A vocabulary that encompasses every possible kind of expression. We take the method and explode it."

Miss Terry also would be among the first to admit that the area of Off-Off-Broadway has taken hold of some explosive themes and set them into withering satirical attacks upon establishment-orthodoxy, bourgeois social graces and middle-class vegetation, as she does in *The Magic Realists,* originally presented by *The Open Theatre* at New York's prevailing coffeehouse theatre club, Ellen Stewart's *Cafe La Mama,* and now being published for the first time anywhere in this anthology.

Miss Terry's other works for the stage include: *Miss Copper Queen on a Set of Pills* (presented by the Edward Albee-Richard Barr-Clinton Wilder Playwrights Unit at the Cherry Lane Theatre, New York), *The People vs. Ranchman* (Firehouse Theatre, Minneapolis), and *The Key Is on the Bottom* (Mark Taper Forum, Los Angeles).

A collection of four of Miss Terry's plays—including *Viet Rock*—was published in 1967 and, early in 1968, her drama, *Home*—a comment on the effects of overpopulation on the world of the future—was televised by National Educational Television as the first commissioned play to be presented on *N. E. T. Playhouse.*

Characters

T. P. CHESTER, *An ultra-successful businessman with solar system-wide enterprises.*

DON, *A handsome teen-age outlaw.*

PERSON, *An actor or actress, who represents Chester's various children.*

DANA, *A beautiful woman.*

A JAPANESE AMERICAN, *A secret agent.*

AN AMERICAN INDIAN, *Another secret agent.*

Scene:

A private lake on an estate in New England. It is almost dusk. A large rock formation is at back. On stage are an inflated rubber raft, an innertube, and a weather-proof storage shed, very small and compact, situated near the fire.

T. P. Chester paces around the campfire. He is bald, neat, and dressed in a warm, loosely fitting suit.

We hear sounds of insects, small animals, water turning, ice melting, trees rustling—as spring approaches.

CHESTER: (*Records numbers in a ledger he carries. His concentration is enormous*) J&B up an eighth, A&P up three-quarters, V-D up fifteen. . .V-D up fifteen! (*He shakes his head and walks on*) No control. No control.

(*Person, one of Mr. Chester's youngest children, enters with a little hop and jump. She is dressed in the clothes of a pre-school girl. She spots Chester and smiles happily*)

CHESTER: Carry the minus, add the plus, divide by x, send up the ratio, the index shows—D&A down a quarter. . .

PERSON: (*Hops and tumbles to Chester*) Da DaDa Da DaDa Da. . .

CHESTER: D&A? D&A? (*Mumbles, stops*) I just recorded that.

PERSON: Da Da Da Da Da.

CHESTER: What is that sound? What connection? Familiar. . .

PERSON: (*Grabs at Chester*) Me me me me me. Dada Da Da. . .

CHESTER: All my children are morons.

PERSON: Da Da Da Da Da. . .

CHESTER: Go home, your mother wants you!

PERSON: No nonononono. . .

CHESTER: I get it, the negative stage.

PERSON: NO nonononono. . .

CHESTER: Father must work. Work, work, work. Father equals work.

PERSON: Nononono. . .

CHESTER: Go home immediately, Morgan Guarantee! Father has work to do before bedtime.* (*Names of local banks should be substituted for the children's names*)

PERSON: Memememe. . .

CHESTER: My God, the human baby! A few weeks after birth, any other animal can fend for itself. But *you!* A basket case till you're twenty-one.

PERSON: Da da da. No No No. . .

CHESTER: You're interfering with my concentration. My connections must be kept open. Circuits to monitor. Now! Back to the house. (*Person cowers, looks at him sadly*) I was never like that. I sprang full-blown from my father's wallet. (*Person sits, cries a bit. He ignores it*) Where was I? Oh, yes—BO up a ninth, LSD doubled, P.O.T. bounding—Big H at new high. . .

(*Person, seeing that Chester is lost again in his figures, crawls a bit, stands up, attempts to follow him and emulate his walk*)

CHESTER: F.B.I. bullish, C.I.A. clownish, Celestial Sanitation bearish, Rod and Rail down four, Rod and Rail up four. What am I here for. . .down twenty. (*Person follows Chester closely; counts on fingers and attempts to repeat numbers*) Price Index spells Boom. Boom, boom. Unprecedented, endlessly extended boom. All planning has come to fruition. Unprecedented boom! Triple boom, trillion boom, zillion boom.

PERSON: Boom, boom, boom. . .

CHESTER: Get back to the house or your mother'll come looking for you. And I'm not in the mood.

PERSON: Boom boom, Mama boom. . .

CHESTER: Boom, you!

(He swats Person two good swats to propel it back to the house. Person, too startled to cry, shakes its little fists and jumps out of sight)

CHESTER: Fourteen buckets of flesh. Fourteen mewling brats and not a business brain in a bucketful. Where did you go wrong, Chester? When you married a woman! *(Pokes at his fire. Begins to undress. Stirs the stew cooking on the fire)* I'm a good man. A thoughtful man. Responsible for empires. My efforts have made bounty for millions. When do *I* get mine? I need a replica. *(Removing his coat and shirt)* 78910 78910 78910. *(Calling, with deep concentration)* All connections? All connections? *(He concentrates; beats on his chest, coughs chokingly)* Wanted. Help wanted. Immediately! Bright young man. Aptitude for numbers. Wanted immediately, bright young man. Opportunity unlimited to right applicant. Sky's no longer the limit. Sky's. . .

(Don drops down from a nearby tree. He is about seventeen, wears dungarees, a dirty sweatshirt, faded and torn levi jacket and a seaman's cap)

DON: I'm hungry!

CHESTER: That's the first condition. *(He hands him a bowl of food)* Here, this'll romance you.

DON: *(Gulps food)* I'm still hungry.

CHESTER: Excellent. You'll be a top salesman in nothing flat. *(Whipping out a questionnaire)* Your application number is *one*. *(He stops, considers the number)* Been a *long time* since one. Sweet. *(He smiles sweetly at Don, as he writes)* One.

DON: One.

CHESTER: Last name, first?

DON: Don.

CHESTER: First name, second?

DON: Don.

CHESTER: Middle name, last?

DON: Don.

CHESTER: (*Writing*) One: Don Don Don. (*Rapidly going to the next question*) Are you single-married-divorced-separated-widowed-remarried?

DON: (*Smiles*) One.

CHESTER: Single. Whom shall I notify in case of emergency?

DON: Me.

(*Chester makes a checkmark and smiles glowingly. He walks around Don, measures him and marks his paper*)

CHESTER: Height? Weight? Health? (*He punches him in the stomach*) Superb! Hobbies?

DON: I'm hungry.

CHESTER: It's essential for success.

DON: (*Counting on his first finger*) One. (*Then, on his second finger*) Two. One. Two.

CHESTER: Aha! A problem solver. Dear Lord, thank you! He certainly has number aptitude. Now repeat after me: One, two, three. . .

DON: One, two, three.

CHESTER: That's it, you're getting it! Don't stop. Four, five, six, seven, eight, nine, ten.

DON: Four, five, six, seven, eight, nine, ten.

CHESTER: Magnificent! (*He tears up application and joyfully flings bits of paper into the air*) You're *hired!*

DON: *Me?* You want me?

CHESTER: You, yes, you. Where have you been? (*He washes dishes*)

DON: I'd like to've been here sooner—but I been sort of away from the action. You see, they kept feelin' like they have to put me in the cooler. And well, the last time, they stashed me there was on account a—(*Relating the story of his life; matter-of-factly*)—I killed this here whole family that wouldn't let me drive their Volkswagen bus. Shot the dog, too. Then I tried to drive. But I didn't know how to drive. So I shot the bus. They busted me—but I escaped. I been walkin' a lot. I just won't be locked up no more. Ever since I was a tiny fella, they had me locked up somewheres. Even my old Granddad tied me to the clothesline, or to the tree or porch railin', so's I couldn't get run over or anything. I thought maybe I'd be lucky when he kicked off, but they didn't know what to do with me, so they put me in these here places and every time I'd get a little older, they'd stick me in another place. But I got away. Been travelin'. Climb up and down trees—it takes longer that way, and very interesting. I know a lot about bugs and bees and birds now. Been studyin' 'em, first-hand. And I found this terrific woods here. Must be some ways from yer camp here? Know somethin'? You're the first guy I talked to since I sprung myself from the can. . .They fed us lots a food there. Terrible, but it was lots. I never had a mother. I was a skinny ugly mean little kid and no foster family'd take me; so here I am. Handsome and lovely at last, and too big to be adopted. I'm hungry.

CHESTER: (*As he hands him another bowl of food*) Not in this great country, you're not! My fellow American. My fellow. . .(*Carried away by what he's heard; gleefully scrubbing his dishes*) Control yourself, Chester. First take it up with the Board of Directors.

DON: (*Sitting on the bench*) You gonna wash 'em pots all night?

CHESTER: Must guard against hepatitis, lad. It can incapacitate your business.

DON: (*Casually*) I can't stand that scrapin' noise.

CHESTER: Fetch me more water then.

DON: No. I'm still hungry. That wild root stew didn't settle too good.

CHESTER: (*The visionary*) Remittance tomorrow. You will eat like a king, if you stay. (*Then, checking himself*) Control yourself, Chester, more tests must be passed.

DON: (*Jumping up*) *Now!* I wouldn't a stopped here if I'd knowed you was so stingy with the garbage you cook.

CHESTER: (*Hurt*) The Mohicans lived on that stew for centuries.

DON: Seconds, thirds, and fourths, I could eat!

CHESTER: Tighten the belt. Tough it out. Fellow American, tough it out! Now, like a good lad, run down and fetch me some more water.

DON: (*Indignantly*) No.

CHESTER: (*With a winning smile*) I'm going to clean my teeth before bedtime. And fellow American, I'm going to clean your teeth, too.

DON: (*Laughs, in spite of himself*) No.

CHESTER: (*With charm*) Do you want your salary tomorrow?

DON: Yeah. I'm hungry. Sleepy. . .(*He piles the rubber raft on top of the picnic table and prepares to settle down*)

CHESTER: (*Angrily*) Then I order you to fetch the water!

DON: Dry up or I'll kick yer ass in.

CHESTER: You're talking to your *boss!*

DON: (*Pulling air-mattress onto ground and flopping on it*) Up yours with a rusty. . .

CHESTER: (*Furiously*) Oh, stop that jail jargon!

DON: (*Pulling innertube over a pillow, as he mimics him*) Oh, stop now, you bad boy. Oh, stop!

CHESTER: (*Lapsing into a business-like tone*) I deeply appreciate your company, nevertheless. Dear Lord, I could teach him *everything* I know. It would cost a lot. A high hourly rate —would make a fatter weekly salary! Respectfully yours.

DON: (*Turning away*) I'm hungry. Sleepy.

CHESTER: (*Roaring, in a powerful voice of command*) Get me that water on the double—*and get it now!*

DON: (*Scrambles to his feet and rushes to the water*) I'm on my way!

CHESTER: As long as authority can still extract such positive response—all is not lost. Thank you again, dear Lord! (*He picks up his accounting equipment; writes in ledger*) Dressing in order to plan, $25. Eating in order to move and to defecate in order to keep planning, $50 per meal at three meals—$150. Drinking water in order to urinate, circulate blood, lubricate tissues in order to plan—$10. Four times drinking, four times urinating, $40. Giving orders to carry out planning, four hours at $500 per hour—$2,000. Sleeping at minimum four hours per night, maximum six, at minus $100 per hour is a possible minus $600. (*He refigures, speculates, shakes his head*) Masturbating in order to get to sleep, $5, times two is. . .Terrible! Must be cut down, if not done away with. Sharks don't sleep. Should have been a shark, should have planned more carefully. . .(*Don returns with a pail of water*) Pour it there, please. (*He indicates pan on fire grate*)

DON: Right.

(*The water makes clinking and plopping sounds as he transfers it from one pan to another*)

CHESTER: (*Continuing*) Planning in order to clean—one hour, $1000.

DON: You pay yourself how much to wash yer shorts?

CHESTER: Clear connections must have clean circuits. People underestimate their executive worth. (*Don collapses on the innertube and bounces. He makes mad, idiot sounds with his mouth*) I must ask you for one minute of silence while I total my night and day. (*Rapidly and ecstatically*) Total $2,625 to be paid as one full night and day salary to T. P. Chester, President of T. P. Chester, Chairman of the Board of Chester Industries and Subsidiary Chesters. (*He sinks back into a satisfied stupor, basking in his numbers, and sighs*) I've worked such a good day, such a clean, thorough day, one of my best planned. (*He looks fondly at Don*) And you, dear boy, are the reward at the bottom of the Cracker Jacks. What a future we have before us! I envy you. Yes, I envy all the things I'm going to teach you.

(*Person, now dressed in boy's clothes, enters listlessly and stops near Chester, who does not wish to be roused from his euphoria*)

PERSON: (*Bleakly*) Pa. . .

DON: (*Alarmed*) Fuzz!

PERSON: Pa. . .

DON: (*Diving toward the rock*) So long, T.P.!

CHESTER: Here! Don't be frightened.

DON: It's a fuzz!

CHESTER: Nonsense. It's only a tax deduction. One of my children.

DON: (*Turning*) Kids? You got time—?

CHESTER: A capital investment of time. Twenty minutes horizontally—presto!—$600 in pocket each year for eighteen years.

PERSON: Pa? Ma wants you.

CHESTER: Run along, Chemical Corn. . .

PERSON: Ma says it's time you should come to bed.

CHESTER: I'm working on my income tax.

PERSON: But, Pa—

CHESTER: Inform your mother that I won't be sleeping with her. (*Clapping his arm around Don*) The good Lord has seen fit to bless me with another deduction, free of time charges.

PERSON: But—

CHESTER: I'm plowing her under this year. Now, get yourself back to that house, Chemical Corn! (*Person turns mechanically and hastens off like a wind-up toy*)

CHESTER: Don, m'lad, you are under eighteen? (*Don nods*) Well, I'm going to show you the ropes.

DON: Much obliged, Mr. Chester. But I don't want no more ropes. Think I better push on.

CHESTER: Two weeks in advance—?

DON: That's a long time.

CHESTER: Stay a *week* then. I'll give you a crash course. You have the right aptitude for business, considering your record.

DON: It take *that* long to learn business?

CHESTER: Three days?

DON: I dunno, Mr. Chester. There's still lots of trees to climb. . .That forest there, it could go on forever.

CHESTER: *Three hours!* I'll make you a bonus baby.

DON: (*Brightening*) A bonus baby!

CHESTER: And if it all works out, there may even be stock options for you as a key employee.

DON: Why me? Outta all the other applicants?

CHESTER: Because I can earn more money by coaching you.

DON: Yeah?

CHESTER: You see, you're completely ignorant. Therefore, I get paid *more* for my planning.

DON: I'm hungry.

CHESTER: You'll have a Frontiersman's meal to embark you upon our Great Society! A meal—planned by the founding family firm of T. P. Chester, Inordinately.

DON: No more toots and berries—?

CHESTER: I'll order it from my house.

DON: I don't see no house.

CHESTER: There, there beyond those stone walls, see my wilderness house? The Chester family seat—built by T. P. Chester the first, before the Revolutionary War. This land was granted to the original T. P. Chester, by King Charles II. All the American Chesters were born and buried on this homely plot, this beloved humble ground, and that is the secret of our success—*low overhead!*

DON: Listen, Mr. Chester. If I stay the night, which is very, very dangerous and uncool, you're gonna have to order me one helluva hero sandwich. In fact, let's you and me march up to yer house and raid yer low-taxed icebox.

CHESTER: No!

DON: Why not?

CHESTER: My water's boiling. (*He peels off his jacket and shirt*)

DON: You scared a yer wife?

CHESTER: I must wash my underthings while I still have water. (*He shucks his undershirt and drops it into the boiling pot. He goes to his little compact storage unit and extracts an imported robe, puts it on, then slips out of his trousers*)

DON: C'mon, she can't be *that* bad. You had a kid by 'er.

CHESTER: For the Bureau of Internal Revenue.

DON: The which of what?

CHESTER: You don't seem to realize that I'm constantly conducting business. You think I've been talking exclusively to you? Not at all! I'm constantly buying and selling the world over. That's why I find it disorienting to go inside the walls of my wife's house. . .er, my house. I know the transaction of every piece from here to Calcutta. Emotional walls destroy contact. It's true that in the past, once a year. . .(*He slips his shorts off under his robe and drops them into the boiling water*). . .I've had to relinquish my business contacts for one night, and one night only—luckily, being extremely virile. You can't imagine the concentration and work involved in getting re-established upon my return! (*He removes his socks and drops them into the water*)

DON: (*Rapidly, as if he had spent his years behind bars figuring the perfect combination*) A four-decker, peanut butter, bacon, lettuce, tomato, mayonnaise, ketchup, jam, sardine, pickle and relish, salami, pastrami, hamburger. And sprinkle the outside a the bun with cinnamon and sugar.

CHESTER: (*Stirring his clothes, pitifully, and almost retching at the thought of Don's idea of food*) What do you want to drink?

DON: (*Settling himself comfortably in the deck chair*) A double chocolate coffee malted, six pack a coke, box of hot-buttered popcorn, pack a gum, and, and, and a box of marshmallows. The fire's perfect fer roasting.

CHESTER: Cigarettes? Liquor?

DON: Don't smoke. But some cognac maybe, if it ain't too much trouble.

CHESTER: Thy will be done. (*He extracts a red signal light from the pocket of his robe, and blinks signals toward the house. After a moment*) They're not giving me a return signal.

DON: I'm goin' up there.

CHESTER: Wait, I'll have to use Phase Two. (*He extracts a signal flare, the type used at sea, and lights it*) I hope this doesn't bring them *all* down here.

DON: All who?

CHESTER: My children.

DON: How many ya got?

CHESTER: Fourteen.

(*Don looks Chester up and down and whistles. Person, now in female night attire, enters, pushing a canopied tea caddy. A red cross is painted on the side*)

PERSON: Evening, Pa.

CHESTER: (*Hastening to cart and whipping off lid of food warmer*) Let's rush the sandwich to this lad.

PERSON: Oh, is that what it is?

CHESTER: Food, Don!

DON: Man. . .(*He melts together with the food*)

PERSON: (*Curiously*) What's that, Pa?

CHESTER: A sandwich.

PERSON: (*Pointing at Don*) No. *That—?*

CHESTER: Ah! My new junior business partner.

PERSON: (*Beckoning*) Pa. . .(*Chester advances, but does not touch Person*)

PERSON: (*Whispering*) I think you're being tooken in, Pa. . .that's a T-V, J.D.

CHESTER: Don't talk dirty, Federal Reserve!

PERSON: I just can't communicate with you, Pa! But never mind, Ma is waiting.

CHESTER: I'm in conference. Will be. . .(*Consulting watch*). . .for exactly one year.

PERSON: Ma don't have that sweet, long-suffering feminine grin on her mouth anymore. She's got fangs growing down like this. (*Person illustrates with its teeth*)

CHESTER: (*Scribbling out a check*) Here, uh—take your mother my regards. (*He hands Person the check*)

PERSON: She wants *you*.

CHESTER: Later. I'm working.

PERSON: She says *tonight,* Pa.

(*Person whips a tommy gun out of a leg holster*)

CHESTER: What is that?

PERSON: Gun, Pa, come on.

CHESTER: I don't believe it.

PERSON: I've something I wanted to say to you a long time, Pa. . .

(*Person opens fire. Don leaps between the gun and Chester*)

DON: (*Shouting*) Hit the dirt! (*The bullets bounce off his chest. He bravely wrenches the gun from Person's grasp*) Little kids like you shouldn't play with these here!

CHESTER: Lad, you'll get a pension for this!

DON: Aw. It was nothin'.

PERSON: Ma's going to be mad at me.

CHESTER: This ought to make up for it.

(He scribbles out another check and hands it to her)

PERSON: *(Eating the check)* Thanks, Pa.

(Person exits. As Don bites into his sandwich, there is a loud crunching of twigs behind the rocks)

CHESTER: I want you to enjoy your food, but try to chew with your mouth closed—it interferes with my reception.

(Don bites again. There is a louder crunch. Chester glares at him. Don looks apologetically at Chester, then quizzically at the sandwich. He starts to bite into it again, but before he makes contact there is another loud crunching through the underbrush. We see—but Don and Chester do not—Two Men in trench coats carrying something, then disappear behind the rock)

CHESTER: Really, even if you are a J.D.—whatever that is?—you're going too far.

DON: But, T. P.—

CHESTER: The very least you can do is. . .

(There is a loud crash directly behind them)

DON: See, I didn't even bite that time.

(We hear a string of terrible curses, in a low male voice, from the direction of the crunching. Don and Chester exchange anxious looks. Then, Don dives under the picnic table and pulls the raft over himself)

CHESTER: No, she couldn't be. . .?

DON: Shut up! *It's the fuzz!!*

CHESTER: *(Still and quivering, he almost tastes the air trying to determine the direction of the sound)* If that's my wife, I shall buy a diving bell and live under the lake! *(There is another crash, then voices)*

1ST MAN: Here's a good place to dump her.

2ND MAN: Yeah, this hollow will do.

1ST MAN: I smell smoke.

2ND MAN: Picnickers. *Quiet!*

1ST MAN: *Let's get out of here! (There is a loud thump, as if a body had been tossed onto the ground. Then more sounds*

—gradually fading off into the distance—as the two men go crashing and cursing through the underbrush)

CHESTER: It wasn't the quality of my wife's voice, but the choice of words was familiar.

DON: (*Scrambling out and crouching toward the rock*) I'll take a look-see.

CHESTER: Careful! It may be a trap.

(*Don disappears behind the rock. Chester follows, very gingerly, at a great distance. A moment later, Don emerges, carrying the limp form of a lithe Negro girl. Her hair is short and cut to show off the shape of her head. One of her nylon stockings is knotted around her neck. The other is half off and floating in the air. Her skirt is torn, and her white long-sleeved blouse is stained with her own blood*)

CHESTER: (*Casually inspecting her body*) Is it one of mine?

(*Don deposits the girl on the raft and hastens to the tea caddy. He returns with a small first aid kit and the bottle of brandy*)

DON: I never seen a grown woman up close. (*He kneels down; examines her throat and head*) Hey! This here woman's been strangled.

CHESTER: We mustn't touch the body.

DON: She's still warm! There's only one thing could work.

CHESTER: I'll signal the police.

DON: (*Leaping up*) Then I'll have to go!

CHESTER: But. . .

DON: And I'll take her with me.

(*Chester throws up his hands. Don looks into the girl's mouth to make sure there are no obstructions, then he places his mouth on hers and breathes in, waits, and breathes in again*)

CHESTER: (*Taken aback*) What kind of a depraved fiend are you? Is *that* what a J.D. is?

(*Don angrily waves Chester away. He continues his work. He pauses; there is a horrible rasping sound from the girl's throat. Her eyelids flutter, one arm drops down, and then tries to pull itself back upon her body. Don stares at her slowly moving form, transfixed at the sight of his power. Dana, the girl, opens her eyes wide, closes them quickly, then opens them again. Her body writhes, her chest buckles. She struggles to turn on her stomach, coughing and choking. Her eyes roll back as she grabs her head in her hands*)

DANA: Crushed! (*She beats violently with her fists*) Let go a me! I'll mess you good. (*Don bends closer to her, attempts to soothe her with his hands*) What I do to you, flour face?! Take your hands off me!

DON: I just found you.

DANA: Let go! You don't get a second chance to kill me. You done good the first time.

DON: Now, now lady, calm yourself. I found you out there in a hole.

DANA: (*Sits up suddenly and notices Chester*) Who's that?

DON: He owns this place.

DANA: What place is this?

DON: We thought you was dead.

DANA: I'm not sure I ain't!

CHESTER: They're all alike. You see, you should have left her in peace.

DANA: You and that fat ofay, get out a my sight! I'll mix you in your own mess. Nobody can kill me and get away with it.

DON: (*Pouring out some brandy*) You don't know where you are yet.

DANA: Who are you to tell anyone? (*Don tries to pour brandy into her mouth. She snatches it out of his hand and belts it down. It sets her coughing again*) I may be dead, but I *ain't* helpless! Give me another jolt. My feets cold.

CHESTER: (*Has been considering her from every angle all the while*) By the way, how old are you?

DANA: (*To Don*) How far are we from town?

DON: Far enough.

CHESTER: (*To Dana*) Are you currently employed?

DANA: No.

CHESTER: You're hired!

DANA: *For what?*

DON: Maybe she don't want to work?

CHESTER: (*Preoccupied; rapidly figuring*) *Another* deduction. She can come under "head of household support". . .

DON: (*To Dana*) You got your breath yet, darling?

DANA: We still here? Another blast, bread-white. My eyes is beginning to clear, yeah, that's better. And you are gettin' better looking. You ain't he. No, you ain't the one wanted to part me from my shoulders. No, you too young and pretty to do a thing like that. Give me some sugar, baby.

(*Chester continues to calculate*)

DON: We had some marshmallows ordered, but they didn't arrive.

DANA: I mean a kiss, son. You ain't mad at me?

DON: I ain't mad at you. No, ma'am, I ain't a bit mad.

DANA: Well, come on then and I'll show you what *real* sugar tastes like.

DON: Why thank you, ma'am. (*He starts to embrace her*)

CHESTER: (*Wringing out his underthings and hanging them on a little line that he has strung between the picnic table and deck chair*) Hand me her blouse. I'll do it up for morning. I believe it has blood stains. (*Don starts to unbutton her blouse*)

DANA: I'm so tired, honey. . .I'm beat down to the balls of my feet. This is a good bed. How come your hands is so gentle and kind? How come. . .this is a good bed. . .You're swingin'—y'know that?—right between my eyes! What name you go by, cat? I'm Dana.

DON: (*Awkwardly pulls off her torn blouse*) Don.

DANA: Hey, hey. . .Don, Don, Don, Don, do hold my hand, Don. . .hang onto me a minute, somethin' is falling. . . (*She closes her eyes*)

CHESTER: Has she expired again?

DON: Just passed out. I'll watch her while she takes a little snooze.

CHESTER: Resurrection's always exhausting.

DON: (*Tosses the blouse to Chester*) Here.

CHESTER: (*Rinses blouse and hangs it on the little line*) Well, much as I hate to, I suppose I must get some sleep. There's so much I have to teach you tomorrow, and you've only allowed me *three hours* in which to do it. (*He settles himself in the chaise beach chair, pulls a brightly colored blanket up over his legs, and gets himself arranged for the night*) You warm enough, my boy?

DON: Tonight, even my eyes feel warm. . .

CHESTER: Mustn't take cold. . .pneumonia weather now . . .don't want your head thickened up.

(*Don moves closer to Dana. He pulls his inner tube up to her, so he can rest his head on it while he gazes at her*)

DON: Say, T.P., your woman as pretty as Dana?

CHESTER: Keep your mind on your business future, lad. There's plenty of time for women.

DON: I know all I need to know, now.

CHESTER: (*Becoming jealous*) But she's penniless. Only recently back from the dead. I'll wager she's never worked in an office in her entire life.

DON: And she ain't going to, neither.

CHESTER: (*Sitting upright*) Look, you! You're working for *me* now. I want you full of energy for morning. You're not to lay a hand on her.

DON: (*Hurt and indignant*) I wouldn't think a touchin' her. . .unless she wanted me to. (*He falls asleep*)

CHESTER: Goodnight, my boy. (*He takes out his ledger, opens it*) Sixteen times $600 is $9,600. That's better. Nothing like an increase in *deductions* to settle the nerves! (*He pretends to doze, then checks to see if Dana and Don are asleep. When he makes "connection," however, Dana watches him out of the corner of one eye. Suddenly, he sits straight up in his chair and concentrates fiercely*) Click, click, click, click, click, click. 7891078910 78910. AT&T, AT&T, AT&T, ConED, ConED. AT&T, AT&T. Seven Up, Seven Up, Seven Up, Seven Up. Alberto VO5, Alberto VO5. Come in please, come in please. Seven Up, this is Yankee Worsted! Yankee Worsted. Come in,

Seven Up. Come in, Seven Up. Come into Yankee. (*He feels the connective juices pouring into his brain. He relaxes a bit, his face lights up*) Ahhhhhhhhhhh Yes! That's it. That's it! You're coming in loud and clear. Roger. . .Rockefeller-Ford-G.E. . .Buy, buy dark side of moon—industrial redevelopment futures. Buy buy. Corner satellite market. Take over NASA Service Station Chain. Sneak into Venus Real Estate Trusts. Never mind the mist! We'll blow it off. Florida soon be overrun. Future winter resort for entire planet: Venus. Ensure population explosion. Yes, yes. Agreed!
Sell, sell. Sell all holdings fraudulent Mars Canals. Fraud! Astronomical trickery. Non-existent! Last pictures from Mariner rocket prove canals do not exist. Dump all holdings. Dump all holdings! Seven Up, are you there—? Repeat: dump all holdings!
Click, click, click, 7891078910 click, click, AT&T, AT&T. Rockefeller-Ford-G.E., Rockefeller-Ford-G.E., Rockefeller-Ford-G.E. . . .Click, click, click, Rockefeller-Ford-G.E.—Rockefeller-Ford-G.E. . . .(*He nods his head, stares straight ahead. Suddenly, he relaxes and falls sound asleep*)

DANA: (*Awakens. Checks to see that Chester and Don are asleep. Carefully, she gets up and crosses to Chester. She pulls a tiny camera out of her bra. She bends over Chester's ledger and films the pages. We hear the whirring noise of the camera motor. She nods and smacks her lips in satisfaction at what she sees*)

DON: (*Moans in his sleep*)

CHESTER: (*Gives an answering bleat*)

DANA: (*Alarmed, she hops back to Don*)

(*Everyone goes sound asleep. For a moment, we hear only deep-sleep breathing and the sounds of spring on the way*)

DREAM SEQUENCE

DON: (*His dream takes over and he lives it. He is the LONE WOLF chief of the forest. He jumps up, sniffs the air. Leaps on top of picnic table and howls to the others to join him*)

Owwwwwww Ow Ow Ow Ow Ow Oooooooooooooooooooooo-ooooooooooooo! Owwwwwww Ow Ow Ow Ow Ow Oooooooooo-ooooooooooooooooooooooooo!

DANA: (*Cat-like, she awakens, peers around cautiously. She sees LONE WOLF, her mate, and answers him*) Meowwwwwww-wwww Mewoooooooooo Mewoooooo Roowwwwwwwww Rooo-wwwwww Meowwwwwwwwwww Mewoooooooooo Mewoooooo Rowwwwwwwwww Meow!

CHESTER: (*Opens and closes his eyes; hunches his shoulders like a baby owl*) ooooooooooo ooooooot oooot hoot hoot hoot Hoot ooooooooot oooooooooooot ooooooooooo hoot hoot hoot.

DANA: (*Like an angry mother calling to her baby, she goes after Chester and claws him into the life raft*) Ro-wwwwwww rowwww rowwwww.

DON: (*Leaps to life raft; sniffs and licks Dana*) RRRRRRRmmmmmmmmmmmrrrrmmmmmm rrrmmmmmm-rrrrmmmmrmmmmmmm

DANA: (*Purrs and, as she purrs, keeps pushing Chester away from her*) RRRRRRRmmmmmmmmmm rrrrrmmmmm-mmm rrrrrmmmmmmmmmmmmmm

CHESTER: (*Crying like a baby owl*) Umhooooooo um-hoooooo umhoooooooooooooooooooo umhoooooooo hoot

DON: (*Growls and gives him a cuff*)

CHESTER: (*Ineffectually cuffs back at Don*) Wuuf hoot. Wuf hoot.

DON AND DANA: (*Growl, laugh, roll around; cuff and laugh at baby Chester*)

CHESTER: (*Laughs too*)

DON AND DANA: (*Summon him to them. They pet and soothe him. Then they start to eat him with robust glee*)

CHESTER: (*As they dine on his arms and legs, his dream takes over. He laughs and begins to move; gets to his feet and bounces up and down. He is a red rubber ball*)

DON AND DANA: (*Bounce Chester back and forth. They dribble him; they fight over him. This makes him gurgle*)

CHESTER: (*He becomes a ball with wings. He crashes and turns into a wheelbarrow*)

DON AND DANA: *(Heap goods on him and wheel him to the life raft. They hitch him to the life raft. He pulls it with them on it, snorting and pawing at the ground. The life raft breaks down)*

CHESTER: *(Throws himself on the picnic table and is a canoe)*

DON AND DANA: *(Climb onto the canoe and paddle and look; paddle and look)*

CHESTER: *(He shoots the rapids. He has a difficult time keeping his nose above water; nearly chokes and drowns)*

DON AND DANA: *(Leap ashore and drag in their canoe. They pour the water out of it, then build a fire, and everyone gets dry)*

DANA: *(Her dream takes over. She begins to grieve. Tears start to trickle down her face)*

CHESTER: *(Coughs and moans)*

DANA: *(Bends close and soothes his forehead)*

DON: *(Wipes tears from Dana's face)*

CHESTER: *(A convulsion and then death)*

DANA: *(Laments)*

DON: *(Heaps wood on the fire)*

DANA: *(Her lament grows)*

DON: *(Begins to mumble incantations and throws more wood on the fire)*

DANA: *(Bangs her head against the ground)*

DON: *(Chants prayers, and heaps more wood on the fire)*

DANA: *(Calls in animal tones to the spirit of Chester)*

DON: *(With a ritual gesture and a whoop, he pulls Chester into the fire. He heaps more wood onto the fire. He hands a stick of wood to Dana)*

DANA: *(Starts to toss the wood onto the fire, then jumps into the fire, too)*

DON: *(Pulls her out of the fire and beats out the flames)*

DANA: *(Moans in pain and grief)*

DON: *(Whoops and shouts to revive her)*

DANA: *(She embraces him)*

DON: *(He yells, triumphantly)*

(They all sink back to their former sleeping positions.

They each begin to emerge from their deep dreams and restlessly thrash and roll around, as they start to awaken)

DON: (*Shudders, moans; then shouts*) Please stop killing them bugs! Please, please, please!

DANA: (*Cuddling and rocking him*) There. . .there, little cat. . .there there. . .tell Dana, Momma, all about it. . .there there, shooby doop shooby doop. . .ba. . .ba. . .ba. . .be-bop little cat. . .What's the matter that you howling in the night time when you got old Dana to hold you tight like—?

DON: (*Pitifully*) Look at all those squashed bugs, them poor, poor little things. . .please stop him. . .(*He opens his eyes and looks around, startled. He doesn't know where he is at first*)

CHESTER: (*Has awakened and is alert*) What is it, lad?

DANA: There, there, I sing you a sleepy song. . .(*She begins a crazy, wild nonsense sound*)

CHESTER: You're both having nightmares?

DANA: Go back to sleep, T.P. I'll handle this.

CHESTER: That's just what I'm afraid of. Listen to me, Don. (*He comes to the other side of Don, and fervently tries to engage him*) I have some facts for you, boy. Dollars and cents facts make sweeter sounds than nightmare songs. Facts, son, and soybean futures. I can show you how *I* did it. Do you know how I built *my* empire, lad? With only my allowance. That's all. My father sent me out on my own. I had to make good the way all we Chesters have. Only ten thousand a week allowance and my God-given brains—but thank God, I was born into this God-given land of God-given opportunity to make a Chester-earned fortune. And I'm going to start *you* out the same way, lad. But you'll have a plus, you'll have the benefit of *my know-how and business-intuition. Money,* that's the force, boy. Money, that's creation, boy. . .Tell you what, I'm going to triple your salary.

DON: (*Seeing his dream again*) Make him stop it! Stop it!

CHESTER: See here, I feel it's more than fair. You've not even proved yourself. I'm betting on *potential.*

DANA: Go back to bed, T.P.! You're upsetting my little cat here.

CHESTER: (*To Dana*) Look you, my enterprises support enough men and families to populate the whole emerging nation of Africa!

DANA: Tell it to the Africans.

CHESTER: This is *my* corporation, and *he* is *my* employee! *His* interests are *my* interests.

DANA: Get to bed, bad news. I'm tired and so is my baby.

CHESTER: Uppity, insolent. . .

DANA: Get to thy bed, T.P., or I'll. . .

CHESTER: You'll what?

DON: (*Coming fully awake*) Oh, Mothercat, you are so warm and soft and. . .

DANA: (*Petting his head*) There there, itsy baby, baby. . .

DON: He always comes to me in the nighttime. Just before he died, he'd sit on his front porch and kill bugs in the sun. Then he died, and they made me ward a the court.

DANA: Don't you worry, no more, no more. Dana's got you now. Where was that, little cat?

DON: Out West. They locked me up, cause there was no one to take me. They sent me from one place to another whenever my age changed. I didn't kill the bugs. Granddad did it. He did it. I love bugs. I love bugs!

DANA: You *are* a love bug—a little ole love bug, safe in Dana's rug a bug. How did you get way out here, little love bug?

DON: I ran away.

DANA: (*In a professional tone*) I see. (*Reverting to her jazz style*) Shooby doop, good cat, clever bug.

DON: You won't tell anyone, will you?

DANA: What you think I am?

DON: Well, I left sort of a mess at the jail. I had to blast through solid rock. Strangle three guards. Kill all my cell mates, 'cause they were gonna tell on me.

DANA: What a "gig." How long you been escaped?

DON: I don't know, but I'm hungry.

CHESTER: Don, I've decided you're to sleep in my chair. You'll rest more easily.

DON: (*Innocently*) Thank you, T.P.

DANA: (*Holding onto Don*) Stay in my arms, little cat.

CHESTER: What are you trying to do? This bonus baby's in training. *I'm* going to teach him *everything* I know.

DANA: That's what we're concerned about. . .

CHESTER: *We?* We? Who—?

DANA: I been watching this outdoor cabin in the sky for years, T.P. We got every rock and blade bugged.

CHESTER: You're delirious from your strangling!

DANA: We know your activities from hell to breakfast. There are *laws* against you, T.P.!

CHESTER: Nonsense! You're on the sauce, you're in the pot, you're LSDeeing. Why, the interconnections I've created will not be interfered with by the courts for decades. *Generations!* It'll take that long to unravel how I've done it before you even can *pass* a law against me!

DON: Dana, honey, sing to me again.

DANA: In a little bitty, little cat.

DON: Now. I want a song *now.*

DANA: My bitty cat. Come to mama do.

DON: (*He snuggles closer*) Yeah. . .

DANA: (*Rocking Don*) Just watch your step, T.P.

CHESTER: Don't you dare threaten me! I've planned perfectly—for everything.

DANA: Everything but disaster.

DON: Sing to me.

DANA: (*Singing, but directing it at Chester*)
"Whatcha gonna do when the boom goes boom?
Whatcha gonna do when the boom goes boom
Whatcha gonna do when the boom goes boom
When prices down zoom zoom
Whatcha gonna do when the boom goes boom?
Boom. Boom. Boom."

CHESTER: (*Singing*) "Buy, buy, buy, buy, buy, buy, buy. I'll buy, buy, buy, buy." (*Then, angry with himself for having sung*) I'll buy and sell short, and I'll buy again. I can stabilize any market. No more busts in our economy. It's a great country, and it's all planned! I don't mind a slight recession, nobody can panic me. A little slant perhaps, a mere tip, but no more bust.

DANA: Everything but disaster, T.P. . . .

DON: Sing me some more, Sweet Dana.

DANA: Get to your barricade, T.P.

CHESTER: My grandfather said, give 'em an inch and they'll take five miles. Listen you! You can't have my *assistant,* too! I gave you a job, what more do you want?

DANA: I ain't about to spend my life licking your stamps, paleface.

CHESTER: Coward! Afraid of me! Luring him away with warm breasts and sweet songs. A coward's way out if ever there was one.

DANA: Don, baby—come here and revive me again, honey.

DON: Okay. (*He stretches her out*) Oh, man! (*He goes through the same reviving methods that he used earlier. It terminates in a lovely kiss*)

CHESTER: I must ask you to end that! Interferes with my concentration.

DON: Don't fight it, T.P. Come here and see how sweet she is.

CHESTER: No!

DANA: Chicken shit.

CHESTER: No Chester has ever been called that!

(*Don laughs like a child*)

DANA: Chickie, chickie, chickie, come and get some sugar. Come and get some sugar. Come and get some noodlies, come and get some lickums, come and get some um-ums. . .come on, fat thing, sugie, sugie, sugie. . .(*She clucks at him. Drawn against his will, Chester approaches her inexorably and pushes and pulls his way to her mouth*)

DANA: Closer, bread-white.

CHESTER: I'm not afraid of you!

DANA: Why should you be, now really, why should you be? I'm a pretty gal of local color.

CHESTER: I suppose one could say you were likeable looking.

DANA: I'm lovely, T.P. Come here, give me your hand.

CHESTER: My hand?

DANA: That's one of the things you feel with, ain't it?

CHESTER: (*Puts out his hand; it trembles*) You did say you were under eighteen?

DANA: Let go all the way, white Daddy. Give. Put it under. Right under there. Now. Ain't that soft? Ain't that nice to press into? What ya say we try for two?

CHESTER: (*A short nervous laugh*) I'm married.

DANA: Just makes it *more* fun.

CHESTER: Where's Don?

DANA: Come here Don Don, baby cat, and show old T.P. what you got.

DON: (*Crawls onto the raft with Dana*) Come on, T.P. You never felt anything so soft or sweet in your whole entire life. Touch Dana once and you'll never, never want to stop.

CHESTER: (*His voice grows a bit husky*) I suppose I could enter it under employee relations—?

DANA: That's it, that's it, T.P. Now you're swinging, Just a little bit closer—closer—it don't hurt, T.P. Let's let the sugar spread all the way—mmmmmmmmmmm. . .Let's turn that mouth of yours on. 'Bout time you learned it could make *other* shapes and sounds. Give it to me, T.P., and I'll show you what your mouth is for. (*As they kiss, she bites him and shoots a horrible tasting liquid into his mouth*)

CHESTER: (*Draws himself away; sputtering and stamping on it*) Saliva! Gad! How it burns.

DANA: Acid kisses for acid tongues. (*Turning back to Don and rocking him*) Now. Tell your Momma sugar, all about it, baby. I won't let big Daddy hurt thee.

DON: After I shot all the kids on my block, they put me away. But I didn't like it there. It was too clean. I'm hungry. I couldn't learn nothin'. First thing I did when I escaped to the woods was pick my ears and lick my fingers. Did that for months, while I climbed up and down trees studying the life of the beetles and the birds and the ants. I'm hungry!

DANA: (*Kissing him*) Then have some more sugar, little cat.

CHESTER: (*Wrenching Don out of Dana's arms*) See here. You're on a business administration course, young man. You can nature-love on your time off. You've got a contract with *me!*

DON: Yes, sir.

DANA: (*Wistfully*) I wanted to be a singer, but I had to join the F.B.I.

DON: (*Rushing to hide under the rubber raft*) I knew this was too good to be true!

DANA: But the F.B.I. canned me.

CHESTER: Strange. I was under the impression it was a lifetime job?

DANA: After the witch hunt, the undercover agents in the F.B.I. outnumbered the real Communists in the party. They had to let me go.

CHESTER: I should think you could have a new career in the KKK—?

DANA: *You* got the figure for it, T.P.

CHESTER: What pleasure does it give you to taunt me? I've done nothing but try to make you comfortable.

DANA: Don't try *too* hard, ofay! Come here, Don, and I'll hold you till you go back to sleep.

DON: (*Starts to snuggle down again*) Yes, ma'am.

CHESTER: (*Dragging Don away*) Come with me, my boy!

DANA: *I* can care for him.

CHESTER: I know what's best for my junior partner. I want him rested, refreshed, ready to go in the morning.

DANA: You mean—?

CHESTER: Yes, I mean I'm going to teach him everything I know! I'm getting on, my children are morons, and I refuse to have planned in vain. My best skills, knowledge, and connections must and *will* live after me. *In him!*

DANA: So, you mean you're gonna turn that sweet little cat, that dear-white-little-escaped-convict-cat, into a businessman?

DON: (*To Dana*) Mr. Chester says he'll teach me all about planning to plan. I'm an ignorant kid and Mr. Chester here's gonna give me a big chance to learn. I only gotta stick around *three hours* tomorrow. Then we can start a new life.

CHESTER: Come with me, Don.

DANA: Go with *me,* Don. We'll leave right now. We don't need money. I'll hustle for you.

DON: That's real kind a you, Dana, honey. But I been kept by the state all my life.

DANA: You don't know what you're getting into! Leave with me now!

CHESTER: Calm yourself, young woman, or I'll have you expelled from my property. The service entrance is in the rear.

DANA: THAT DID IT!! (*She blows a tiny whistle attached to her bracelet*)

DON: (*Holding his ears*) Dana, baby, stop with the whistle!

(*At that moment, the two men in trench coats, whom we saw earlier, dash out from behind the rock and pin the arms of both our boys. One of the men is Japanese; the other, an American Indian. Dana pulls a folding wallet out of her bra and flashes it before the eyes of Chester and Don*)

DANA: (*Now speaks in ultra-cultured tones*) It is my duty to warn you gentlemen that anything you say will be used against you.

CHESTER: What does this mean?!

DANA: Lorna Dana Hansen of the C.A.I.A., F.T.D., O.P.A., and Q.T. You boys can consider yourselves pinched!

CHESTER: Don, son, do *something!*

DON: (*Helplessly*) I can't, T.P. I'm in love with her.

CHESTER: (*Turning to Dana*) But you're a nice young girl. Only a minute ago, you wanted to take care of him. . .he brought you back to life, and. . .you. . .

DANA: I wasn't dead, T.P.

CHESTER: May I ask please, what is the charge?

DANA: We tapped your wires. The invisible ones, T.P.

CHESTER: It isn't possible! (*He wrenches himself free from the man and flings his ledger into the fire*) Wiretapping isn't admissible! This can't happen. I've planned for everything —*everything!*

DANA: *Everything but disaster, T.P.!* You're charged with

being a one-man inter-planetary cartel. And I have microfilmed everything you just burned!

CHESTER: Oh, my God. . .!

DANA: (*To Don*) And you, dear boy, I hereby arrest you for kidnapping yourself across state lines. Take 'em away, boys!

THE MEN: Right, Chief!

DON: Oh, Dana. . .will I ever hear your voice again—?

DANA: Yes, love, in the courtroom.

CHESTER: I will not budge from this land! You can't put me in jail! I can't go behind walls—you'll ruin my decades of work—my carefully conceived connections—my—*My God!* My wife can visit me in jail! NO! You can't do this. I forbid you.

DANA: Remove the prisoners, men.

(*The Men, in a single movement, convert Chester to a horizontal state*)

CHESTER: I'll have your jobs for this. . .your homes. . . your wives. . .no, no, *keep* your wives!. . .your children. . .your future. Even see that you never vote again!

DANA: (*Flashing her gun at Don*) On the double, bread-white! I have a "gig" to play in The Milky Way by noon tomorrow.

(*Person, dressed as a girl, suddenly appears. It carries a sub-machine gun. It stalks right up behind Dana, without being detected, and slams the barrel of the gun into Dana's back*)

PERSON: You, hey you! Drop it!

DANA: (*Dropping her gun*) May I ask, who's got me covered—?

CHESTER: (*Joyously*) Dime Savings of Brooklyn!

PERSON: Hi, Pa.

CHESTER: Thank you, D.B.

PERSON: I been waiting for this chance, Pa.

(*Dana tries to flip the gun out of Person's hand, but Don grabs her*)

PERSON: I had to *prove* myself to you, Pa!

CHESTER: (*Climbing out of the arms of the men in trench coats*) You don't know how *much* you've saved me, child!

PERSON: (*Pointedly*) Yes, I do, Pa.

DANA: Don, baby cat, let's jump the kid together. I can get you into the C.A.I.A. with me.

DON: Nothing doing. I'll never trust in the dead again!

DANA: It's a good job. Unlimited funds, and you don't even have to write reports.

PERSON: *Now* will you let me, Pa?

CHESTER: Anything, D.B. Anything!

PERSON: I want to sleep out here all night with you.

CHESTER: Granted.

PERSON: And I want to wash my clothes outside, just like you.

CHESTER: I'll fetch the water for you, child.

PERSON: I want them. . .(*Indicating the two men in trench coats*). . .to carry my guns. . .

CHESTER: Of course. . .

PERSON: And I want her. . .(*Indicating Dana*). . .to teach me to sing shooby doop songs.

CHESTER: But she, my sweet, wants to arrest me for the Government.

PERSON: Tell them if she does, I'll turn over all your gold bricks in them Swiss banks to the Chinese Reds.

DANA: That's treason!

PERSON: I'd do *anything* to save my Dad.

CHESTER: (*To Person*) And I'm going to give you *love,* all the father love I've longed to give a worthy child all these years.

PERSON: Don't want love, Pa.

CHESTER: (*Hurt, but pulls himself together*) Name it and it's yours.

PERSON: I want to train him. . .(*Indicating Don*). . .to understand me.

CHESTER: Agreed. But let me give you something substantial.

PERSON: All right, Pa. I want 80% of your stocks and bonds, 60% of your real estate holdings. 50% of all current action. . .(*The lights begin to dim*). . .All bank accounts to be in both our names. Title to this house and land, your recipe for wild root stew. . .And all the small change you got right now in your bathrobe pocket.

CHESTER: (*Overcome with happiness*) A true Chester! (*He holds out his arms*) Dime Savings of Brooklyn, come into my arms. . .

(*The lights have almost faded by now. Person hastens to Chester's arms. They whirl in an embrace. The submachine gun gets crushed between them and fires throughout their embrace, killing Don, Dana, and the two men in trench coats. Person speaks the final words like the Scarecrow in The Wizard of Oz*)

PERSON: Fawther—Fawther—

(*Music up, punctuated by sounds from the gun. Lights completely down*)

Curtain

Sherry Kafka

THE MAN WHO LOVED GOD

Sherry Kafka

Sherry Kafka was born in Jonesboro, Arkansas, in 1937. Her father was a minister and, as she recalls, "when I was growing up, we constantly were moving from place to place." Among them: small towns in Arkansas, Louisiana, and Texas.

Miss Kafka studied drama under Paul Baker at Baylor University (Texas) and received a B.A. in dramatic arts from the State University of Iowa, where *The Man Who Loved God* initially was produced in 1963.

The Man Who Loved God represents Miss Kafka's third play and her first to be published. However, she is no stranger to print, for her novel, *Hannah Jackson,* published in 1966, brought forth many accolades from the literary critics in the nation's press. Currently working on a second novel, she has stated in a note to this editor: "I will write anything. Plays, poems, essays, short stories, novels. And usually do. Thus, I find it quite difficult to settle myself into a single niche."

Additionally, Miss Kafka serves as a consultant to *Unlimited Potential,* an experimental program for the public schools of Texas "aimed at developing creativity as a basis for learning, especially with disadvantaged children." She also officiates as the director of the children's program at the William Edrington Scott Theatre of the Fort Worth Art Center and was a consultant for the "Theme Development Department of Hemis Fair, 1968," the international exposition recently held in San Antonio, Texas, where she resides "in a green house surrounded by trees, two lively daughters and an assortment of equally lively pets."

Characters

THE READER
BERNARD KOVAC
RAY STAUFFER
BENNIE WATERS
JIM KRUGER
LEM SELPH
DAVE CROUSE
DAVID KOVAC
LISA KOVAC
MARY KOVAC
EXAMINERS

The play happens in and above a small southern town; in the 1950's.

The setting is divided into three units: a home, a store, a church. Above and behind these areas: a pulpit which commands a view of each unit. A winding staircase leads up to the pulpit.

The set pieces should all be of the starkest, barest, simplest arrangements possible.

The Reader enters, climbs the winding stairs to the pulpit. He places a large book that he is carrying on the pulpit, then arranges the lamp for reading.

Simultaneously, Bernard Kovac enters from the rear of the auditorium. He is about forty-five, dressed in a double-breasted suit, unbuttoned, a wide tie of the '40's. He carries a dusty, worn briefcase. As he comes down the center aisle, the Examiners begin to file in and unobtrusively seat themselves to one side of the stage. Kovac stops and watches them. The Reader finishes his preparations. A bell sounds three times. He begins to read from his book.

READER: The First Book of the Preacher, of the Man Alone, of the Man Powerful, of the Man Impotent, of the Man

Wise, of the Man Foolish, of the Man Hopeful, of the Man Despairing, of the Man Loving, of the Man Hating. He that hath ears, let him hear. The First Book of the Preacher, of the Man alone. . .(*As he finishes, he gazes out into the auditorium. After a moment, he calls:*) Bernard Kovac—?

KOVAC: (*Wearily*) I'm here. (*He slowly continues down the aisle, climbs the steps to the stage and crosses to the foot of the pulpit*) It was a long journey. . .

READER: All journeys are long. (*Indicating a plain wooden bench, stage left*) There. Opposite the Examiners.

(*Kovac crosses to the bench and sits. The bell sounds again. The Reader returns to his book*)

READER: The First Book of the Preacher. In the Beginning was God.

KOVAC: No. In the beginning was the Word. The word, the task, the path. In the beginning there was longing and darkness. That is all.

READER: Nonsense. There were people.

KOVAC: I can only remember the dark and the need. It is difficult to remember beginnings. . .(*Indicating Examiners*) But I can tell them about the *ending*. In the end there was only myself.

READER: There was no ending.

KOVAC: Yes. Yes, there was! There *was* an ending. I acted. I had an ending. You cannot deny me that!

READER: There is nothing in the book about it.

KOVAC: There is nothing to be said about it. It simply came. It was neither comic nor tragic, yet it was both. It was neither caused nor begun, it happened. It was neither reasoned nor imagined, it was willed. But I had an ending! (*The lights dim on The Reader, as Kovac rises and addresses the Examiners*) I am the Preacher. And I *did* have an ending. In the end, there was a man and silence. And the silence was wrapped about me like a piercing scream. Out of that silence, I could not, would not, speak. Because the ending was willed. In the end, there is the "I." The "I" and silence. . .

(*There is a burst of raucous male laughter emanating from the darkened area down right. The lights gradually come up, revealing a tableau in the hardware store. The men are posed in the casual, lounging attitudes that one might expect in a small southern country store. They are an assorted group of diverse ages and sizes: Lem Selph, Dave Crouse, Ray Stauffer, Bennie Waters, and Jim Kruger, who is behind the counter. The latter is about twenty-seven, a veteran of the Korean War. He walks with a limp*)

STAUFFER: So I says to Ben, "Now look here, boy. You know your place even if that Preacher don't."

WATERS: What'd he say to that?

STAUFFER: Hell, man, *nothing!* I got them niggers down at the gin trained real good. (*Laughter. Then, to Waters*) What you mean, what'd he say? I don't take no sass off 'em darkies.

KRUGER: (*Pacing nervously as he goes about his work with exaggerated energy and purpose*) Look here, did y'all want anything? Or did you just come in here to loaf? 'Cause I got work to do.

SELPH: Easy, boy. We ain't aimin' to get in your way.

CROUSE: What's the matter, Jim? You been on a high horse all morning.

KRUGER: I'm just tired, that's all. Tired of hearing about that funeral and that Preacher.

SELPH: You'd better move out of this town, then; 'cause you can bet your wooden leg that you're goin' to hear more.

WATERS: Won't be many sorry to see *that* Preacher go!

KRUGER: He ain't done anything yet.

SELPH: I'm willin' to bet five dollars he goes down to that nigger church and preaches that darkie's funeral.

KRUGER: The boy's got to be buried. And you know how big a store niggers set by havin' a preacher do the funeralizing—?

WATERS: Don't make no difference.

KRUGER: They ain't got no preacher. . .

WATERS: Still, that nigger don't have to be buried by a white man. You think every nigger what smashes himself up in a car oughta get a funeral from a white preacher? Well, I'm all for stoppin' the practice, 'fore it gets started.

SELPH: There won't be no stopping it. I want to see what happens.

CROUSE: If he goes through with it, he'll be handed his walkin' papers soon enough.

STAUFFER: Yeah, we don't need no nigger-lovers preachin' to us!

KRUGER: Ever think you might have a hard time gettin' rid of him if he *don't* preach that funeral? Lots of folks 'round here like him. Besides, I never heard nothin' against him, except this nigger business.

STAUFFER: Hell, man, that's enough.

CROUSE: Everything depends on what he does now. . .

SELPH: That fool ain't got any more sense. . .

KRUGER: I hope to hell he does it!

WATERS: Gentlemen, listen to that!

KRUGER: Yes, I hope to hell he goes down there with 'em darkies and buries that boy with the biggest, floweriest sermon he can find out of the Book! Yeah! And then I hope you shove him out of this town, so he'll never again have to get up in that church on Sunday and look out at you sons-of-bitches and call you *God's people!* I want him out of here. And know why? 'Cause he's crazy, that's why! Any man who'd come into this town and build a church and get up there on Sunday and talk about God is bound to be crazy! Yeah. . .I want him out of here, so I don't have to look at him and feel sorry for him walkin' 'round here crazy and not even knowin' it.

CROUSE: We didn't think you liked nobody, Jim—?

KRUGER: I pity him, that's all.

SELPH: Well, if he preaches that nigger funeral, you're goin' to have plenty reason for pity. . .

(*The lights fade on the store and come up on The Reader and Kovac*)

READER: You knew those people—?

KOVAC: Yes. I knew them all. At one time I trusted in them, even loved them. I wasn't very far along the path then. I thought it was broader than it is.

READER: In the beginning, then, there *were* people?

KOVAC: More people than I could ever remember. . .

READER: Perhaps you will recognize some of the others. . .

(*The lights fade and come up on a room in the Kovac*

home. Again, the set should be stylized with just a few pieces: a table and three non-matching chairs. David, about twenty, is looking out the window. It is obvious that he is worried and under tension. Lisa, fifteen, is curled up in a chair, reading)

DAVID: (*Moving away from the window*) Lisa, put down that book! This is the third time I've asked you. . .

LISA: (*Abstractedly*) What, David?

DAVID: Shouldn't mother be home by now?

LISA: Guess she had to work a little later than usual. Or else stopped by the store.

(David crosses back to the window. Lisa continues to read)

DAVID: (*After a moment; his back toward her*) Lisa? You heard anything yet? About Paul's funeral—?

LISA: (*Not looking up from her reading*) No. . .

DAVID: (*Turns*) Little Lisa! Always with her silly little nose in a book. . .

LISA: (*As before*). . .And, furthermore, I don't see that there's anything to be said about it.

DAVID: You going to hide behind the covers of a book forever—?

(Mary enters, carrying a package of groceries. Though an attractive woman, she is beginning to show the strain of defeat and bitterness. She puts the package down and stands for a moment, as though drawing strength from being inside the house)

MARY: I thought this day would never end.

DAVID: So did I.

MARY: (*Crosses to wall switch and turns on overhead light*) Again, Lisa! Reading without a proper light. (*Turning to David*) Something unusual happen today?—

DAVID: Might say that it was "interesting and enlightening."

MARY: Oh—?

DAVID: My boss came by my desk. Chatted with me. Said that I was a first-rate teller—with strong possibilities—and that he liked having me in the bank.

MARY: My! Old Mr. Gregory is getting mellow.

DAVID: Then, he went on: "This talk about your father going down the river to preach a darkie's funeral, David. That's a lot of nonsense, ain't it?"

MARY: (*Quietly*) I see. . .

DAVID: Know what I replied? "Sure is, Mr. Gregory. Just a heaping lot of nonsense!"

LISA: (*Looks up from her book*) It's not a lot of nonsense, David! Paul was his friend.

MARY: Why did you tell Mr. Gregory that?

DAVID: Because I hoped it to be true. . .

LISA: Did it ever occur to you that it wouldn't be right. . .?

DAVID: (*Interrupting her*) *Right?* Just what *is* right? You think it's "right" that we've spent our lives constantly running from Dad's failures, his mistakes—? Take your nose out of your book and look around you! This place is the *bottom!* If he gets kicked out of this church, there isn't going to *be* another one! I may not know about "right," but I sure as hell can read the handwriting on the wall!

LISA: He doesn't know what he's talking about. Better set him straight, Mother. (*She resumes reading*)

MARY: (*To David*) We'll make out. We always have.

DAVID: This time, it isn't going to be *we.*

MARY: I'm afraid I don't. . .—?

DAVID: It's simple, Mother! This time, I'm *not* having any part of Dad's fight. I'm tired of packing up and running from place to place, grubbing out a living any way we can. No, I've had enough of it. . .

MARY: Perhaps it isn't easy, for any of us, but we must do what your father thinks is best.

DAVID: Best—? For whom? No, from now on, I must do what *I* think is best! I want to belong *somewhere,* Mother. Be able to stay in a town, where I can hold up my head. . .walk about. . .able to look everyone clear in the eye. . .without fear . . .without embarrassment. . .(*A second*) And I shall never have this, if I go on following after Dad.

MARY: Your father wants that for you, too, David. Every man wants to serve his family. (*A slight pause*) Though, perhaps, your father wants most of all to serve God. . .

DAVID: (*Reflectively*) When Mr. Gregory came over to my desk today, I felt just like I did when I was a kid. Remember when I came home. . .that first day at school. . .beaten and bruised? Some boy said he'd bet I'd grow up to be a preacher, just like my Dad—? Maybe it shouldn't have been the kind of remark you fight over. But it was. For he meant it as an insult and I understood it as such. And so did all the other kids. . . .I still can hear them. . .laughing and jeering. . .(*Then, in a change of tone*) It's been like that. . .through the years. . .over and over. . .And I'm sick and tired of being ashamed. I've got to reach out for more than *shame* in this world and if he preaches that funeral, he and I will go our separate ways!

LISA: You're not being fair about this, and you know it, David!

MARY: Lisa, please—will you take the groceries into the kitchen?

(*Lisa reluctantly puts her book down, rises, and picks up the package*)

DAVID: (*To Lisa*) Look, Missy, there's no such thing as being fair. That's one of those hard facts you're going to have to learn. This "truth and right" that Dad keeps pursuing—battling over—well, they just don't exist! The *only* truths are those facts of life a man has to recognize, in order to live in this world. Like the glaring down-to-earth fact that black and white don't mix in this town.

LISA: If that's the kind of fact you've got to accept in order to live in this "little acre of southern loveliness," then I want to leave! (*She goes off, to the kitchen*)

MARY: (*After a moment*) I love you, David. Yet, I must realize that you're no longer a boy. And I must not interfere. This is something between you and your father. (*Another moment*) Whatever his decision, though, I will go with him. . .

(*The lights fade and come up on The Reader and Kovac*)

READER: (*To Kovac*) Do you still find it painful?

KOVAC: I shall never think of them without my soul dividing within me. If only I could have put out my hand to them, just once. . .

(*He rises and slowly moves toward the area*)

READER: Perhaps the time has come for you to. . .

KOVAC: Yes. . .(*After a moment*) It might be best to begin with that same evening. All day I had been walking in the country, asking myself—with each step—should I preach that sermon? Should I? The sun was low in the sky, when I returned home. I had made five dollars that day, selling Bibles. . .

(*The lights gradually come up on a tableau of the Kovac family, at the table, awaiting his arrival for the evening meal. He halts, just outside the area*)

KOVAC: As I reached the house, I could see them through the window. I remember it clearly. I paused there, looking at them, and prayed.

READER: What did you say in your prayer?

KOVAC: "Oh, God, show me a way to love You and them as well."

READER: Is that all?

KOVAC: Then I entered the house.

(*He steps into the lighted area*)

LISA: About time, Dad! We thought you'd gotten lost or deserted us.

KOVAC: No, no. I just seemed to lose track of the time. (*He crosses to Mary; kisses her*) I hope all went well with you today.

MARY: A bit tiring, as usual.

KOVAC: And you, son? Have a good day? (*David remains silent, as he crosses to Lisa and kisses her*) Did you manage to put your book down long enough to practice the piano?

LISA: Two hours, Dad!

KOVAC: Good. For you may be asked to play tomorrow, at the funeral services. I'm not certain if they have anyone at their church.

DAVID: (*Shoving his chair back*) You're going to go through with it, then—?

KOVAC: Yes, David. It's the only right thing to do. And it is the wish of God.

DAVID: (*Rising; facing him*) Don't give me any talk about "right," Dad! This may shock you, but I'm plain just not interested! All I care about is what my boss sees, what this town sees. . .feels about us! You've been doing things God's way for years—and where—*where* has it gotten us?

KOVAC: God's ways are mysterious, David.

DAVID: They're non-existent! There is only *man's* way. That's all!

KOVAC: I'm aware of how all of you have suffered because of my actions. And you may have to suffer again—because of this. I know that and I dread it. Yet, I must not allow it to restrain God's hand. . .

DAVID: I'm going to ask you something I've never asked before, Dad, and probably never will again. Won't you think of your family first? *Just this one time—?* Help us—? Because if you don't, then we'll have to help ourselves. We can't afford to have you shatter our lives, over and over. If you go out to that colored church tomorrow, I don't want to see you again. Ever! Because you know whose path you will be following—? Not God's! But Bernard Kovac's! And it leads straight to hell for all of us!

KOVAC: Paul loved me, David. How could I let him down?

DAVID: (*Quietly, deliberately*) I have loved you, too. How can you let *me* down?

(*He goes out*)

KOVAC: David!

MARY: No. Let him go. . .

LISA: He didn't really mean all that, Dad. He's just worried about his job.

MARY: I told you to stay out of this, Lisa!

LISA: (*Indignantly*) Well, excuse me for living! What's gotten into everybody around here? You're all so touchy.

MARY: Why don't you go to your room and finish reading your book?

LISA: When are you going to stop treating me like a child, Mother?

MARY: When you stop behaving like one.

KOVAC: Please. Must we snap at each other? Surely, it won't help us.

LISA: (*Rising*) I'm going to the church, to practice the piano. I want to be prepared—for tomorrow.

(*She starts*)

KOVAC: Lisa—? (*She stops, turns*) I just wanted to say—thank you.

(*Lisa rushes out*)

MARY: (*After a second*) You are determined, then—?

KOVAC: (*Sits at table*) If I turned my back on this, I never could enter the pulpit and preach about God again.

MARY: So you'll turn your back on your son instead?

KOVAC: Mary, when I was fifteen I made a vow to love and serve God. It was in the twilight under a lilac tree. All day I had been plowing in the fields, watching the plow cut into the ground and turn the earth back in two even rows of brown. All day it had seemed to me that the plow was cutting into me, laying me open in two parts. One part of me kept saying, you are all there is, Bernard. Love and serve yourself. And the other kept saying, you are nothing. Love and serve God. Then at last the evening came. And under that lilac bush I knelt and said, God, I will serve You. I will love You. And I will not compromise. I will speak truth. I will follow Your way. I will bend my ear only to the sound of Your voice.

MARY: And has he spoken so clearly?

KOVAC: He has never spoken at all.

MARY: A man can't live without compromise, Bernard. Don't you know that? You've tried all these years and you've always failed. Even the church doesn't want a man who can't compromise. You can't be perfect!

KOVAC: I have no choice. I am an imperfect being living in an imperfect world. God himself admits that. But then He instructs man to be perfect. And if he would love God, a man has no choice.

MARY: Do you consider it more "perfect" to preach this funeral than to retain your own son's love? All David wants is just that one sign, that one deed, to prove that you love him, love us, more than anything else! Is that sermon a more "perfect" action than giving him this one assurance—?

KOVAC: I don't know. Perhaps I shall never know. I can only choose what seems to be the right way, then pray that I have chosen correctly.

MARY: No, Bernard, you have never compromised, have you? But *we* have. We've given up a good deal—because we love you. Like any man, your way *has* been paved with compromises. Only in your case, it's always been the compromises of others!

(*She rises*)

KOVAC: What about you, Mary—? If I. . .?

MARY: (*Pause*) I will still follow you. . .whatever you do.

KOVAC: I shall have to leave this church and this town. You are aware of that?

MARY: Yes. (*A slight pause*) But I cannot promise that it will be forever. Each day, I tire more quickly. And like David, I shall want the security of things I can know and understand. I won't be able to follow you, *endlessly,* in pursuit of a God who has never looked upon *our* suffering!

(*She goes out. For a moment, Bernard sits with head bowed; then, he speaks quietly*)

KOVAC: Oh God, if You would only comfort me! If You would only give me some light, some knowledge, some understanding. I have placed my feet upon a path that I thought would lead me to You and I have stumbled along it, never knowing from moment to moment where it would take me, or even if it were the right path. With each step I have gazed steadfastly before me, pushing away any hands that would grasp me, ignoring any call while my heart cried out and my body trembled with the effort of climbing such a path alone. With every step I have asked, Is this the way of God, and I've heard only the rushing of the wind. Is it the way of God to love other men and lose the love of your family? Is it the way of God to build a church and to stand before people and praise the Holy Name?

Is it the way of God to see only one duty and one path in every human action? My God, my God, if You did have to ask of man the impossible, why did You not prepare a comfort for him?

(Lisa enters during the last line or two of the above speech. She stands gazing at her father for a second, then finally breaks the silence)

LISA: You better check the piano when you're over at the church, Daddy. That stupid pedal is sticking again.

KOVAC: I'll take a look at it.

LISA: *(A pause)* I'm glad you're going to do it tomorrow. . .

KOVAC: Why?

LISA: You know how Paul felt about you? Even wanted to be a preacher. . .

KOVAC: He was just a young boy. He might have changed his mind.

LISA: But when he got in that car to come and see you, he *hadn't* changed his mind. And when his family asked you. . . I knew you wouldn't ever let him be buried without anything, without a single word. If you did, it wouldn't mean anything.

KOVAC: What. . .?

LISA: His belief.

KOVAC: Does our belief *have* to mean something, Lisa?

LISA: Yes. I think so. Don't you?

KOVAC: I don't know. I don't know. . .

(The area darkens as the lights come up on empty pulpit. Kovac slowly ascends to pulpit and reads from the Bible)

KOVAC: *(Reading)* Then I proclaimed a fast there, at the river of Ahava, that we might afflict ourselves before our God, to seek of him a right way for us, and for our little ones, and for all our substance. (Ezra 8:21) *(He closes Bible and looks out at the invisible funeral crowd)* I have come here in sorrow to join you in this remembrance of Paul, our friend, our beloved. I pray that his soul is now with the God that he loved and sought so earnestly. For him the struggle is ended. May we, the bereaved, draw comfort from that fact. No longer must Paul afflict himself before God to find the right way for his life is accomplished. And may we, the living, the remaining, have the courage to see a right way where no way exists. May we have the faith to pick a path of stone out of the swirling of mist. Amen. Amen.

(*Lights out immediately on pulpit and up on the Reader, alone*)

READER: That is the end of the beginning. Are there any questions? (*He waits a moment, then:*) Book One of the Preacher, of the Man Alone, of the Man Powerful. . .

(*The lights dim as his voice fades away into the darkness. The bell sounds three times. The lights come up again. The Reader is in the pulpit; Kovac is seated on the bench*)

READER: (*To Kovac*) Shall we continue?

KOVAC: Once time is set in motion, none of us can stop it.

(*The Reader opens another large book and begins to read*)

READER: The Second Book of the Preacher. The Second Book of the Man Alone. And it is written, Be ye therefore perfect, even as your Father which is in heaven is perfect. And it is written, For there is not a just man upon earth that doeth good, and sinneth not. He that hath ears, let him hear. The Second Book of the Preacher.

KOVAC: Why isn't it written that man knows *only* after knowing can no longer help him? Why is it not told him that the only understanding is in completion?

READER: It is not necessary to tell man this. He lives it. (*He turns to the Examiners, then to Kovac*) Shall we begin with silence?

KOVAC: No. With laughter. (*The same laughter as in the first scene, but from a different area of the stage*) Theirs. . .(*He gestures toward the area*). . .and my own.

(*He joins the laughter as it swells again and the lights come up on a new tableau. This tableau is the same as the first, with the set changed. The people are in the same clothes, same positions, but are now in the stark, simple interior of a church with the same stylization and representational quality of the other set pieces. But something about the set should convey the agonizing, reaching simplicity of the Gothic*)

STAUFFER: . . .So when the boys at the gin asked off to

go to the funeral, I says, "Yessir, boys, I'll let you off 'cause I bet this is the first time you ever had a white man preaching in your church." Then I says, "And I can tell you one more thing. It's goin' to be the *last!*" (*Laughter, except from Jim Kruger*)

SELPH: Guess we'll be a little bit of a surprise to the Preacher. I don't figure he was plannin' on seein' us so soon.

WATERS: (*Nervously*) Told you, we shoulda stopped it 'fore it began.

STAUFFER: Hell! And missed all the fun? Where's your sense a humor, Bennie? Hidin' in your crotch—?

(*Laughter*)

KRUGER: (*To Stauffer; angrily*) And where's your sense of *decency?* This is a church you're in.

CROUSE: The boy's right. Let's just tone it down a bit. The church is the church, regardless of *why* we're in it.

WATERS: I just hope he takes our kind advice, without any back talk.

CROUSE: Hard to say what that fool bastard will do. Reckon he feels pretty close to this church. Built it almost singlehanded.

SELPH: A church ain't a building, Dave. It's people. That's the whole damn trouble. The Preacher done forgot that the church is *people.*

KRUGER: Maybe not. Maybe he just thought the darkies were people, too. That boy used to help him clean this church—do odd chores—and not always for payment either. Yeah, made him seem like a person to the Preacher, regardless of how you feel about it!

SELPH: Listen, boy. You know who brought that Preacher to this town? *I* did! One day, he turned up at my farm, peddlin' Bibles. We got to talkin' and he said that he was a Preacher, but he didn't have no church. Said it was important that he have a way of praising God, so he was out sellin' Bibles—so he'd still be able to talk about God to people. Well, I told him about this little congregation here, about us not havin' no church or Preacher. . .(*Emphatically*) *I'm* the one who brought him here. Now *I'm* the one who's sayin' he's gotta go!

WATERS: People in this town, hell, never are gonna get over what transpired today. And havin' that man here only hurts the church!

CROUSE: (*To Kruger*) They're right, Jim. We worked hard to get this church goin'. Now we're doin' pretty good. Got a building, people comin' every week. We can't afford to let this fellow kill it.

KRUGER: If he hadn't done most of the work, what would you have, eh? Nothing! So, I say: you owe him a chance to speak!

STAUFFER: (*Slowly, deliberately*) There ain't nothing he could say that'd change anything.

KRUGER: That may be true. But we treat him right. Understand—? And he gets his fair chance to defend himself.

SELPH: Oh, we'll treat him right, boy. Just as long as he acts right. . .

(*The area darkens, as the lights come up on The Reader and Kovac*)

KOVAC: (*To Reader*) I hope you noticed that building. It took me six months to build that church.

READER: Six months. A measure of human time.

KOVAC: Yes, a measure. A counting of repetitions. Breathe in, breathe out. An accumulation of struggles, a spending of life, a gradual dying. Time—a measure of man's death.

(*From the home area comes the sound of a suitcase being placed on the floor, followed by nervous pacing. The lights gradually come up, revealing David's tense figure*)

READER: I believe someone is waiting for you.

KOVAC: Waiting. Impatient with time.

(*The lights dim on Kovac and The Reader. Breathlessly, Mary enters the home area. She notices David and stops. They gaze at each other, silently, for a moment. Then David breaks the silence*)

DAVID: Know something, Mother? All the time I was waiting here, all the time I was packing, I kept saying to myself: at the last minute, he changed his mind. . .

MARY: You don't really have to go, David.

DAVID: . . .When I got home and there was nobody here, I told myself all sorts of stories. They've gone to the store. They've gone visiting. Somewhere. Because I wanted to believe in the end he *wouldn't* go through with it.

MARY: He felt that he had to.

DAVID: I know, Mother. Whether he wanted to or not. . . Well, now I feel *I* must leave, whether I want to or not!

(*Kovac and Lisa come in as David picks up the suitcase*)

LISA: (*Hastening to his side*) David!

DAVID: (*Gently*) Missy, I know you're going to turn out well. Though, I'm sure you'll always be a lousy bookworm!

KOVAC: Son. . .

DAVID: I—I'd better get on, if I'm going to make that six-twenty-five. . .

KOVAC: (*His voice is filled with pleading and love*) Please don't leave us. . .

DAVID: (*Sad, kind; yet firm*) You don't really need me. You've got God. (*Moving away*) And if I'm to have any kind of life at all. . .

LISA: David, sometimes you can be the most stubborn human on earth! (*She embraces him, weeping*)

DAVID: (*Softly*) And you, dear Missy, sometimes can be the softest. . .

(*He is touched, confused. He doesn't know whether to put down his suitcase and put his arms about his sister or quickly leave. Kovac, noting David's confusion, goes to Lisa and gently takes her away*)

DAVID: Well, I—I guess there's little left so say. . .

MARY: (*Restraining her emotions*) Except, forgive us. . .

KOVAC: (*To David*) Perhaps if you waited for morning—slept on it—you'd view things differently—?

DAVID: No, Dad. You chose your path, now I must choose mine. Unfortunately, they're not the same. . .(*He moves slowly toward Mary*) Mother. . .(*Unable to continue, he turns to Kovac*) Goodbye, Dad. Take care of yourself. (*He hurries out. There is a moment of silence, except for Lisa's weeping*)

KOVAC: I believe I'll go over to the church for awhile.

MARY: Now?

KOVAC: Yes.

MARY: Why?

KOVAC: It's the customary place for me to go, isn't it? When I was building it, you said that I wasn't building a church at all, but a place of refuge.

MARY: When do you think the men will ask us to leave—?

KOVAC: Possibly in the morning.

LISA: Will they come here?

MARY: I do wish you'd use your handkerchief, Lisa.

KOVAC: (*To Lisa*) No, dear. To the church.

LISA: I want to be there. To hear what they say.

MARY: (*With a trace of bitterness*) Your father can handle it. He's had this kind of experience before!

KOVAC: (*After a moment*) You're right, Mary. I've never been a congregation-pleaser.

(*He goes out*)

MARY: (*Apprehensively*) Lisa? Did you notice the cars—?

LISA: Which cars?

MARY: Lem Selph's. Mr. Stauffer's. Parked behind the church—?

LISA: Then, they're not going to wait till. . .?

MARY: I'm afraid not.

LISA: (*Makes a move to start*) I'll go after Dad and warn him!

MARY: No, Lisa. He knows. That's why he's gone over.

LISA: They won't harm him, will they?

MARY: Sometimes they're business-like and orderly. At others, they can be cruel and nasty.

LISA: We can't let him face them alone, Mother!

MARY: They're his congregation, not ours.

LISA: Still. . .

(*She dashes out*)

MARY: (*Abstractedly*) No. . .no. . .there's no stopping any one of you, is there? (*No longer able to control her emotions, she bursts into tears*) David!

(*The lights fade on the area and come up on the church,*

as Kovac enters. The men swing around and, for a moment, they silently stare at each other—the hunters and the hunted)

SELPH: Evening, Preacher. We been waitin' for you.

KOVAC: Yes, I see that.

STAUFFER: We have a little business to talk over. . .

KOVAC: Well, I'm here now.

SELPH: How long you been here, Preacher?

KOVAC: Almost two years.

SELPH: Guess that's a record for you, ain't it? Stayin' in a church two years—?

KOVAC: I've never thought along those lines.

SELPH: From what I hear, you never could keep a church any longer'n that.

KRUGER: For God's sake, stop all this beating round the bush!

CROUSE: Easy, boy. Easy.

KOVAC: Kruger's right. Say what you came here to say, Selph.

SELPH: (*Facing Kovac*) We have a way of life around here, Preacher, that we think is right. And we don't intend to have nobody muddy the water. Nobody. For no reason. (*A slight pause*) You see, Preacher, my Bible tells me that the nigger is not as good as the white man. It tells me that his color is a mark of punishment from God. And we don't intend to have no mixin' with niggers.

CROUSE: We think it best you pack up your belongin's and. . .

KOVAC: It all seems so simple to you, doesn't it? A man breaks one of your little rules and you send him on his way.

SELPH: It's not our rule. It's God's.

KOVAC: (*Aroused*) God! What do you know about *God?* Just what do *any* of you know about God?!

STAUFER: Man, you'd better watch what you're saying!

KOVAC: Let me tell you a few things about this God you're dealing with. He speaks one thing out of his mouth while his hands do another. He blesses man with the same breath that curses him. He puts a glass mountain in front of man and says to him, scale it. Then to make sure that man understands the size of the task before him, he takes away his legs. Don't talk to me about God's rules, Selph. Even his name is a blasphemy in your mouth!

(*Lisa enters, and stands unnoticed at the rear of the church*)

SELPH: We came here peaceably. Now we're goin' to tell you. You're gonna be outta here by midnight. You and your family. We don't want nothin' left behind. Understand—?

KOVAC: Oh, no, Selph. You can deny me this pulpit. You can keep me from praising God in this building—which *I* built. But you cannot deny me this town!

KRUGER: Right! You can't force him to leave town.

SELPH: Shut up, boy. This is between me and the Preacher. The Preacher seems to've gotten the Kingdom of Heaven mixed up with the Kingdom of Earth. Now, you may know all about the rules of God, Preacher, but *I* know about the rules of this town. And I say you're leavin' here. That's all you need to know. The fact that *I* say it. That *I* speak for the people here. It's your kind that stirs up trouble and you're leavin'. Period.

STAUFFER: You're helpless here, Preacher, 'cause we can do anything we like with you.

SELPH: The Preacher is a servant, ain't he? A servant of God, of the church, of the people—? Well, servant, we're tellin' you plain, we don't want the likes of you anymore. The sight of you alone makes us vomit! Yessir, by tonight midnight. . . You hear us, Preacher?

KOVAC: (*Quietly*) I hear you. . .

(*Lisa suddenly comes forward*)

LISA: No, Dad, no! You *didn't* hear them! Only the sound of their filthy voices, not their words!

KOVAC: Lisa!

LISA: Tell them, tell them—you're staying! This is your church! And if God wants you to. . .

SELPH: Get outta here, girl, this ain't none of your business!

LISA: (*To Selph*) You're not going to tell me what is or isn't my business, you old mealy-mouthed hypocrite!

STAUFFER: (*Grabs hold of Lisa's arm; roughly and angrily*) Come on, kid! Get the hell on home where you belong.

LISA: Don't you touch me! (*She slaps Stauffer hard across the face. The sound seems to echo through the church*)

STAUFFER: Why, you little bitch! Someone's gonna have to teach you some manners and. . .(*He grabs hold of her again and begins to drag her away, screaming uncontrollably*)

KRUGER: Let her go, Stauffer!

STAUFFER: Like hell, I will! Tamin' a wildcat's always been one of my specialties. . .!

(*Mary appears at the rear of the church*)

KOVAC: (*Going after Stauffer; furiously*) Let go of that child! (*He manages to pull the struggling Lisa away from Stauffer's grasp; then, he strikes a blow at Stauffer, knocking him to the floor*)

SELPH: (*Ominously*) You done it now, Preacher!

(*Mary has come forward and Lisa, upon seeing her, rushes to her arms*)

STAUFFER: (*As he raises himself up from the floor*) I'm goin' to teach you somethin' about the flesh, Preacher. Just like I always wanted to. . .

(*The men begin to circle in toward Kovac, backing up Stauffer. Their eyes are hard and menacing. Kovac stands crouching, waiting, looking from one to the other as they slowly move in, encircling him*)

STAUFFER: Yessir, you're goin' to be taught somethin' ain't in your sacred Bible.

(*Kruger, who has remained apart from the others, suddenly pushes the menacing circle apart, breaking the tension*)

KRUGER: Damn you! Damn all of you—!

MARY: (*With mounting fury*) You're animals, animals! Every one of you! (*Turning sharply to Kovac*) You, too! All of you. Go on! Destroy each other, I don't care! But not here, not in this church—!

KRUGER: (*To Mary*) Better take the girl home.

MARY: Yes! And I will take my family—and whatever little we possess—away from this revolting town tonight! Now all of you! Get out of this building! There's nothing more you can do here—or to us!

KRUGER: Mrs. Kovac, I'm really sorry about all this. . .

MARY: Get out!

(*Slowly, the men start to leave. Mary watches—her face, a hard, cold mask of contempt. She is stronger than they are. Kovac stands silently, at the foot of the pulpit. Lisa remains downstage, alone*)

KOVAC: (*After a moment; crosses to Lisa*) Let me take you home.

LISA: (*Her back to him*) I'm all right now. I—I don't need any help.

KOVAC: Things aren't as bad as they sometimes seem. Tomorrow—tomorrow, everything will be. . .

LISA: (*Reflectively*) It's funny, Dad. I always believed that evil and good were two separate things. That good was strong and could protect us. (*Turning to him*) Why didn't you tell me sooner—?

KOVAC: I didn't know how, Lisa. I just didn't know how. . .

LISA: (*Slowly moves upstage*) I'll start packing, Mother.

KOVAC: Lisa! I'll walk along with you.

LISA: No. I'd rather go alone. . .

(*She leaves*)

MARY: And now both of our children know the truth.

KOVAC: What is this truth they know, Mary?

MARY: The truth is that your God, Bernard, is not worth the pain! He has asked more than a human can pay. I've lived for years, hoping that someday you'd realize that! I've waited—oh, how I've waited!—for that day when you'd turn to me and say, "You are enough, Mary. You and the children and our measure of time on this earth. That is all I have and all I need."

. . .It's your only chance, Bernard! Because even if you pay with your life, you will never satisfy the God that you seek!

KOVAC: (*Quietly*) The children are gone now.

MARY: And so is most of your life! Stumbled away on a path that led us nowhere, except to despair.

KOVAC: And yours, Mary—?

MARY: Yes, my life, too! Tossed away wrongly hoping that you might turn to me for the comfort and love that your precious God has denied you.

KOVAC: Is it too late?

MARY: (*Pause*) Not if you renounce God.

KOVAC: Renounce God, Mary?

MARY: I'm too tired to *compete* with Him any longer!

KOVAC: What would we do? Where would we go?

MARY: Somewhere. Anywhere. What does it matter? The world is wide, flexible. People can mold it to fit their needs. But only if they can bear to be wrong, to have flaws, to live in imperfection. . .

KOVAC: I made a choice when I was a boy, Mary.

MARY: To make the wrong choice, and have to choose again—that is part of being *human!*

KOVAC: I have been choosing each second of my life, never certain whether I was right or wrong, but always having to act as though I were right. That has been my curse. To know that it was all meaningless, yet having to act as though it *had* meaning.

MARY: Then—none of the things you've suffered for, that we *all* suffered for, have had *any* meaning for you?

KOVAC: Only in the struggle, in the suffering. God has not given me enough knowledge to separate all the right from all the wrong. If I am to love him, to serve him, then I must choose the most difficult. Only my struggle had meaning, Mary. The pain, the tears. . .

MARY: Is this what your God requires of you?

KOVAC: I'm not sure. But it's all I have to give.

MARY: (*Turns away from him*) Our time here is almost up. . .

KOVAC: Yes—soon it shall be midnight.

MARY: Will you go with me?

KOVAC: Let me remain here alone for awhile.

MARY: If you're not back by twelve, we shall have to leave without you.

(*She starts to go*)

KOVAC: Mary—? (*She stops, turns*) I—I wanted so much to love you better.

MARY: (*Quietly*) Yes. I know.

(*She leaves*)

(*Kovac stands looking around the empty church for a moment. Then he moves up behind the pulpit and opens the big Bible resting upon it. The only light comes from over the pulpit and seems to illuminate his face until it is in stark lines and planes, impersonalized into a mask. The simple, yearning lines of the structure seem to be gaunt and straining, the entire picture one of starkness and pain*)

KOVAC: My God! My God! If only once I could have heard your voice! But now, and now only, do I know that You have never seen nor known of my pain, that You have turned your back upon me. And I have suffered each pain in order to cast them as jewels before eyes that are blind. What shall I do now? Shall I go with Mary into the world and embrace it? Shall I love myself and my humanness? Or shall I destroy my imperfect being in the perfection of silence? Oh, my God, if I could only believe that You would see my sacrifice, then how gladly would I lay down my life! If I could believe that my soul would fly to You, how gladly would I quit my body! But I know that even though I die for love of You, You may never know of it or care. Beyond death I see no hope of heaven, only the dark nothingness stretching away beyond the space of thought. For, regardless of what I do, You shall never know that I, Bernard Kovac, existed, that I sought You all my days. This, then, is the final horror. That at the end of the path there is a void. A void and silence. Even if one speaks, there is nobody to hear. And all that has been sacrificed has disappeared with the smoke of the offering.

(*He bows his head for a moment. When he raises it again,*

there is a transformation. The pain and despair have been subtly replaced by the beginning of glory and triumph)

KOVAC: Yet, still I raise my voice to You, O God! Knowing full well that I will not be heard, I cry Hosanna. Knowing that the sacrifices of my human longings, my loves, even of my life have been meaningless, I will give to You the only thing I have left. I can choose to love You. And I can choose to sacrifice the power of being to You, as the supreme example of my love, knowing that You will not look upon my pain. Yet this is all I know of love. . .to suffer, to struggle, to renounce.

(*He takes a match and lights a page of the Bible. The flame glows quickly and his face is grotesquely illumined by the flickering of the fire on the pulpit*)

KOVAC: (*Crying out, triumphantly*) Blessed is the name of the Almighty God. Glory to His name!

(*The light flames up and blinds the audience. The gaunt outline of the structure shines through the red momentarily, then blackness. Out of the darkness, the bell sounds three times. The lights come up, dimly, on The Reader, The Examiners, and the empty bench*)

READER: There is nothing more. At the end, there was the "I" and silence. After the "I" is gone, only the silence is left. Thus, it shall be written in the book, that the man Bernard Kovac, did live. (*He writes, then firmly closes the book*) There is nothing more to be said.

(*The stage darkens, with the exception of a solitary spot shining upon the empty bench*)

Curtain

The Editor

STANLEY RICHARDS is a man of wide and varied experience in the world of the theatre. He has written 25 plays, among them *Through a Glass Darkly, Tunnel of Love, August Heat, O Distant Land, Sun Deck,* and *Marriage Is for Single People,* the latter to be made into a film by Columbia Pictures. He is the editor of the recently published *Best Short Plays of the World Theatre: 1958–1967*. Twelve of his short plays have appeared in the prize annuals *The Best One-Act Plays* and *The Best Short Plays,* and he holds the record for live television productions of a single play, *Mr. Bell's Creation*. This play has been produced on the networks (both here and abroad) eight times with such stars as Peter Falk, Janet Blair, Veronica Lake, Virginia Vincent, and Romney Brent.

Mr. Richards' latest play, *Journey to Bahia,* adapted from the prize-winning Brazilian play and film, *O Pagador de Promessas,* had its world premiere at The Berkshire Playhouse under the direction of Joan White. Later, it was produced in Washington under the auspices of the Brazilian Ambassador and the Brazilian American Cultural Institute, and recently published in book form.

His plays have been translated for production and publication abroad into Portuguese, Afrikaans, Dutch, Tagalog, French, German, Spanish and Italian.

In addition, he has been the New York theatre critic for *Player's Magazine,* and a frequent contributor to *Writer's Digest, Theatre Arts, Playbill, Writer's Yearbook, The Theatre, Actor's Equity Magazine,* and *The Dramatists' Guild Quarterly*.

As "American Theater Specialist," Mr. Richards has been awarded three successive grants by the United States Department of State's International Cultural Exchange Program, and in this capacity has lectured, taught playwriting, and directed in a number of Latin American countries, notably Brazil and Chile.

For more than ten years, he conducted the Western Ontario Playwriting Seminar in London, Ontario, co-sponsored by the University of Western Ontario and the Department of Education of Ontario. In 1966, Mr. Richards was appointed Visiting Professor of Drama of the University of Guelph, Ontario.